THE GAELIC NOTES
IN THE BOOK OF DEER

THE OSBORN BERGIN MEMORIAL LECTURE 1970

The Gaelic Notes in the Book of Deer

KENNETH JACKSON

Professor of Celtic in the University of Edinburgh

CAMBRIDGE

at the University Press

1972

CAMBRIDGE UNIVERSITY PRESS
Cambridge, New York, Melbourne, Madrid, Cape Town, Singapore, São Paulo

Cambridge University Press
The Edinburgh Building, Cambridge CB2 8RU, UK

Published in the United States of America by Cambridge University Press, New York

www.cambridge.org
Information on this title: www.cambridge.org/9780521082648

© Cambridge University Press 1972

First published 1972
This digitally printed version 2008

A catalogue record for this publication is available from the British Library

Library of Congress Catalogue Card Number: 78–161293

ISBN 978-0-521-08264-8 hardback
ISBN 978-0-521-07675-3 paperback

CONTENTS

PREFACE

The manuscript called the Book of Deer, with the notes on grants of land to the monastery of Deer written into it in the Gaelic spoken in Buchan towards the middle of the twelfth century, has been known ever since it was 're-discovered' in 1860, as is described below. The Gaelic notes have been edited, with or without facsimiles, translated, and discussed a number of times, so that one might suppose that any further treatment was unnecessary. But no completely satisfactory edition, or translation, exists as yet, as appears from the comments in this Preface, and some of the conclusions which have been drawn by previous authors about the social system and the principles of land-holding and land-granting, taxation, etc., in the north-east of what was still Celtic Scotland in the twelfth century, and about the date, genuineness, and language of these 'charters', need re-assessment. These documents are, after all, unique, and of unique interest to the study of the language and history of mediaeval Celtic Scotland, Scotland before the process of Normanisation which began there early in the twelfth century under Alexander I and David I had had more than the most superficial effect in the north. The language is the Gaelic used by the upper classes of northern Scotland of that period, and it is instructive to see that it is virtually indistinguishable from contemporary Irish, as will be shown in detail in this book. When we realise that there are literally no other documents extant in the Gaelic of Scotland for almost three hundred years after these in the Book of Deer were written, we can understand their great interest and importance. The social system and principles of land-tenure, though having certain similarities to those of the feudal Norman world, are again remarkably dissimilar in other respects; and since, in some cases, there is no exact parallel in corresponding Irish custom, one must ask oneself whether there are any traces here of the Pictish system which had been the established one in north-eastern Scotland (including Buchan) until Pictland was conquered and absorbed by the Gaelic civilisation from the west some three hundred years before. Then too, the personal and place-names which are found here throw much interesting light on early Celtic nomenclature in Scotland, and are specially valuable since some of the people mentioned are known to history elsewhere, and some of the place-names can still be identified on the modern map. These documents, preserved by an extraordinary chance, thus deserve and need a fresh treatment.

This is the more so, since almost all the previous ones they have had are hidden away in what are, from the layman's point of view, more or less obscure periodicals, or as unimportant items in books chiefly devoted to other subjects, and themselves long out of print. There is only one case of a whole book given to the manuscript and its contents, and this, published just over a hundred years ago and of course now unobtainable, is badly in need of revision. Such revision is needed especially in respect of the linguistic commentary which the texts have received, much of which has been unsatisfactory. The present work has another purpose also. These Gaelic texts are of considerable importance to the student, and the author for one has for many years used them in teaching Celtic classes at Edinburgh University; but since no edition whatever exists which is intended for students other than Watson's in his *Rosg Gàidhlig*, now out of print (and this with very little annotation, etc.), it is desirable that they should be available again for this reason also, and in a form adapted to the student's needs in class work.

A bibliography, then, of previous publications of and studies on the Gaelic notes in the Book of Deer is as follows:

(1) Cosmo Innes, *Scotland in the Middle Ages* (Edinburgh, 1860), pp. 321–5. This is a postscript to the book, saying that since Innes wrote, this MS had been discovered, though he had not himself seen it; and giving a translation of the legend of the foundation of Deer [= no. 1] and of one or two other sentences.

Preface

The names are in some cases misread, and the translations inaccurate. It seems that this had been sent him by Henry Bradshaw (see below), though the source of the translation is not stated, but he mentions that Bradshaw had undertaken to publish the texts (which he never did).

(2) A translation in the *Saturday Review* for 8 December 1860, pp. 734f., with commentary and the Latin text of no. VII (David I's charter), but not the Gaelic texts. This is unsigned, but is evidently the work of Whitley Stokes, as is to be inferred from the footnote on p. 106 of no. (7) below.

(3) Joseph Robertson, *Illustrations of the Topography and Antiquities of the Shires of Aberdeen and Banff*, IV, 545–50 (Aberdeen, the Spalding Club, vol. XXXII, 1862). Reprint of the translation from (2), 'with a few verbal alterations', and the text of no. VII.

(4) Whitley Stokes, *Goidilica*,[1] *or Notes on the Gaelic Manuscripts Preserved at Turin, etc.* (Calcutta, 1866), pp. 47–63. Introduction, texts (including no. VII), translations, linguistic discussion, and glossarial index. Cf. (7) below.

(5) Cosmo Innes, *Facsimiles of the National Manuscripts of Scotland*, I (Southampton, 1867), nos. 1 and 18. Discussion, texts (including no. VII), translations, and facsimiles. The facsimiles are the best yet published, but the readings and translations are sometimes incorrect.

(6) J. Stuart, *The Book of Deer* (Edinburgh, the Spalding Club, 1869); clxix plus 95 pages, and 22 plates. Discussion of the entire MS, with edition of the whole of the Latin Gospel texts as well as of the Gaelic notes (and also no. VII), the latter with translation, and facsimiles of all the illuminated pages, all the Gaelic texts, and some of the Gospels. Long historical introduction. The Gaelic notes, and translations, are on pp. 91–5; they are essentially Stokes', with a few minor modifications particularly in the texts, not always for the better.

(7) Whitley Stokes, *Goidelica; Old and Early Middle Irish Glosses, Prose, and Verse* (London, 1872), pp. 106–21. This

[1] *Sic.*

ix

Preface

is a reprint of (4) with a couple of trifling changes; and the correction of *arardchellaib* in no. VI to *arahardchellaib*, the insertion of some words in no. VII omitted in (4), and the italicisation of the contractions in no. VII not thus distinguished in (4).

(8) Alexander Macbain, 'The Book of Deer', *Transactions of the Gaelic Society of Inverness*, XI (1885), 137–66. Introduction, texts and literal translations, notes historical and linguistic, and glossary-index. A number of improvements on Stokes' texts (e.g. all contractions are italicised) and translations, but also some deteriorations,[1] and a few misprints. On the whole, this was the best treatment up to that time.

(9) J. Strachan, in an article 'The Study of Scottish Gaelic', *Transactions of the Gaelic Society of Inverness*, XIX (1893), 13ff., edits and discusses the language of part of no. I, pp. 15–20.

(10) T. O. Russell, 'The Book of Dier', in *Celtia*, I (March 1901), 43f. Texts based on Stokes with a number of curious extra errors (some perhaps misprints), and inaccurate translations.

(11) A. Lawrie, *Early Scottish Charters prior to 1153* (Glasgow, 1905), nos. 1, 95, 97, 107, 223, and pp. 219ff., 337f., 346ff., 424ff. Translations (sometimes incorrect, with misreadings of some of the names), and notes.

(12) J. F. Tocher (editor), *The Book of Buchan* (Peterhead, the Buchan Club, 1910), pp. 106–14. Text and translations from (6); facsimile of fo. 3*a*; some commentary.

(13) W. J. Watson, *Rosg Gàidhlig* (2nd ed., Glasgow, 1929), pp. 184–92 and 249–51; texts (including no. VII), translations into Scottish Gaelic, a few notes, and facsimiles of fos. 3*a* and 3*b*. The texts were the best so far, but include some errors none the less.

(14) A. O. Anderson, *Early Sources of Scottish History, A.D. 500 to 1286*, II (Edinburgh, 1922), 174–83. Fresh translations, with valuable historical notes. A few mistranslations, and the treatment of a number of the names is still unsatisfactory.

(15) R. S. Kemp, 'The Book of Deer', in *Transactions of the*

---

[1] E.g. his 'between mountain and field' in no. V.

Preface

Scottish Ecclesiological Society, VIII (1925), 164ff. Discussion, but no texts or translations.

(16) J. Cameron, *Celtic Law* (London, 1937), pp. 199–211 and 229–42. General description, historical discussion, texts (omitting no. VII), translations into Scottish Gaelic (Watson's) and English, and notes. The text is Stokes'.

(17) Donald Mackay, 'New Light on the Book of Deer', in *Scottish Gaelic Studies*, V (1938), 50. A brief note on an early reference to the MS; see p. 8 below.

(18) J. Fraser, 'The Gaelic *Notitiae* in the Book of Deer', *Scottish Gaelic Studies*, V (1938), 51–66. Texts from photostats of the originals, translations, and some valuable notes, chiefly textual and linguistic. The translations are the best yet published and in the main so are the texts; but there are several curious misreadings (possibly misprints in most cases), chiefly where no-one has misread the MS before.[1]

(19) K. Jackson, 'Some Remarks on the Gaelic *Notitiae* in the Book of Deer', *Ériu*, XVI (1952; Bergin memorial volume), 86–98. Notes on the spelling, language, and date.

My thanks are due in the first place to the Faculty of Celtic Studies of University College, Dublin, for inviting me to give the Second Osborn Bergin Memorial Lecture, delivered on 10 March 1970, of which lecture this book is an expansion. Then to several friends and colleagues who have very kindly allowed me to trouble them with questions about early Scottish history, names, etc.: Professors Geoffrey Barrow and Gordon Donaldson, Messrs. John Dunbar of the Royal Commission for the Ancient Monuments of Scotland, Ian Fraser of the School of Scottish Studies, Neil R. Ker, F.B.A., A. T. Lucas, Director of the National Museum of Ireland, the Rev. W. Matheson of the Department of Celtic at Edinburgh University, the Right Rev. Mgr. D. McRoberts, Dr Hermann Pálsson of the Department of Icelandic of Edinburgh University, and Dr A. B. Taylor. I am particularly indebted to Professors Barrow and

[1] For a list of these see *Ériu*, XVI, 86, footnote.

Preface

Donaldson for the trouble they very kindly took to help; Professor Barrow at a time when, as Dean of the Faculty of Arts at his University, he was under great pressure of administrative work. Finally, I wish to thank the committee of the Carnegie Trust for the Universities of Scotland for a generous grant in aid of publication.

K.J.

Edinburgh
March 1971

ABBREVIATIONS

AI   S. Mac Airt, *The Annals of Inisfallen* (Dublin, 1951).

AU   W. M. Hennessy, *The Annals of Ulster* (Dublin, 1887). Down to the end of 1013 the year-dates are wrongly antedated by one year (e.g. '950' is really 951), and the figures given in this book are the corrected ones.

BD   J. Stuart, *The Book of Deer* (see Preface, no. 6).

CGH   M. A. O'Brien, *Corpus Genealogiarum Hiberniae*, I (Dublin, 1962).

CL   J. Cameron, *Celtic Law* (see Preface, no. 16).

Contribb. K. Meyer, *Contributions to Irish Lexicography* (Halle, 1906; issued in parts in Stokes and Meyer, *Archiv für Celtische Lexicographie*).

CPNS   W. J. Watson, *The History of the Celtic Place-Names of Scotland* (Edinburgh, 1926).

CPS   W. F. Skene, *Chronicles of the Picts and Scots* (Edinburgh, 1867).

EC   A. Lawrie, *Early Scottish Charters* (Glasgow, 1905).

EIHM   T. F. O'Rahilly, *Early Irish History and Mythology* (Dublin, 1946).

ES   H. M. Chadwick, *Early Scotland* (Cambridge, 1949).

ESSH   A. O. Anderson, *Early Sources of Scottish History* (see Preface, no. 14).

'Félire'   W. Stokes, *The Martyrology of Oengus*

Abbreviations

	the Culdee (Henry Bradshaw Society, vol. XXIX; London, 1905).
GG	J. H. Todd, *The War of the Gaedhil with the Gaill* (London, 1867).
Gr. O. Ir.	R. Thurneysen, *A Grammar of Old Irish* (Dublin, 1946).
ITAAB	J. Robertson, *Illustrations of the Topography and Antiquities of the Shires of Aberdeen and Banff*, 4 vols. (Aberdeen, the Spalding Club, XVII, 1847; XXIX, 1857; XXXII, 1862; XXXVII, 1869 [= vol. I]).
LHEB	K. Jackson, *Language and History in Early Britain* (Edinburgh, 1953).
Lib. Cart. St. And.	*Liber Cartarum Prioratus Sancti Andree* (Edinburgh, the Bannatyne Club, 1841).
Lib. Eccl. Scon.	*Liber Ecclesiae de Scon* (Edinburgh, the Bannatyne Club, 1843).
M. Ir.	Middle Irish.
NLC	G. Mac Niocaill, *Notitiae as Leabhar Cheanannais, 1033–1161* (Dublin, 1961) [The charters in the Book of Kells].
NPE	E. Björkman, 'Nordische Personennamen in England', *Stud. z. Englischen Phil.*, XXXVII (Halle, 1910).
OG	E. Hogan, *Onomasticon Goedelicum* (Dublin, 1910).
O. Ir.	Old Irish.
PBA	*The Proceedings of the British Academy.*
PCPN	O. von Feilitzen, 'The Pre-Conquest Personal Names of Domesday Book', *Nomina Germanica, Arkiv för Germansk Namnforskning*, III (Uppsala, 1937).
PNA	W. M. Alexander, *The Place-Names of Aberdeenshire* (Aberdeen, the Spalding Club, 1952).
PP	F. T. Wainwright and others, *The Problem of the Picts* (Edinburgh, 1955).

Abbreviations

RC	*Revue Celtique*
Reg. Dunferm.	*Registrum de Dunfermelyn* (Edinburgh, the Bannatyne Club, 1842).
Reg. Episc. Aber.	Cosmo Innes, *Registrum Episcopatus Aberdonensis*, 2 vols. (Aberdeen, the Spalding Club, vols. XIII–XIV; 1845).
Reg. Episc. Brechin.	*Registrum Episcopatus Brechinensis* (Edinburgh, the Bannatyne Club, 1856).
Reg. Episc. Morav.	*Registrum Episcopatus Moraviensis* (Edinburgh, the Bannatyne Club, 1837).
Reg. Mag. Sig.	J. M. Thomson, *The Register of the Great Seal of Scotland* (Edinburgh, 1912ff.).
Reg. Reg. Scott.	G. W. S. Barrow, *Regesta Regum Scottorum*, I (Edinburgh, 1960); II (Edinburgh, forthcoming).[1]
RIA *Conts.*	The Royal Irish Academy's *Contributions to a Dictionary of the Irish Language* (Dublin, 1939ff.).
RIA *Dict.*	The Royal Irish Academy's *Dictionary of the Irish Language* (Dublin, 1913ff.).
Sc. G.	Scottish Gaelic
Sc. G. St.	*Scottish Gaelic Studies.*
SEHI	J. F. Kenney, *The Sources for the Early History of Ireland*, I (New York, 1929).
SHR	*The Scottish Historical Review.*
SPLY	G. F. Jensen, *Scandinavian Personal Names in Lincolnshire and Yorkshire* (Copenhagen, 1968).
TGSI	*The Transactions of the Gaelic Society of Inverness.*
Thes. Pal.	W. Stokes and J. Strachan, *Thesaurus Palaeohibernicus* (Cambridge, 1901).
TPhS	*The Transactions of the Philological Society.*
VC	A. O. and M. O. Anderson, *Adomnan's Life of Columba* (Edinburgh, 1961).
ZCP	*Zeitschrift für Celtische Philologie.*

[1] I am indebted to Professor Barrow for sending me page-references to this as yet unpublished volume.

INTRODUCTION

I. THE MONASTERY OF DEER

The Cistercian abbey of Deer was founded by William Comyn, earl of Buchan, in 1219, on the site about half a mile west of the village of Old Deer in north-east Aberdeenshire where its ruins still stand, in a beautiful situation among trees on a sunny, southern-facing slope beside the South Ugie Water. With the overthrow of the Comyns by Bruce, the local lordship passed to the Keiths, in the person of Sir Robert de Keith, Marischal of Scotland, and remained with them throughout the history of the monastery. One of the family, Robert Keith, son of William Keith the fourth Earl Marischal, was Commendator of the abbey when, in 1587, after the Reformation, all its lands, dues, and properties were resigned into the hands of James VI and made by him into a temporal lordship called the Lordship of Altrie, in favour of the said Robert Keith for life, and afterwards to his nephew George Keith, the then Earl Marischal, and to his heirs. The royal grant by which this lordship was set up is extant in the Register of the Great Seal,[1] and includes a very complete list of the lands formerly belonging to the abbey and now to the Keiths. A slightly older list is to be found in the decree of 1574 for the teinds of Deer, Peterhead, and Foveran due to the Earl Marischal:[2] and a later one, in a contract of 1638 between the Earl Marischal and the king.[3] From these it is possible to extract a very clear picture of what lands in Buchan had belonged to the Cistercian abbey – almost all of them in the present parishes of Old and New Deer, plus a few in the parishes of Longside, St Fergus, Peterhead, Ellon, and Foveran, though some of these more scattered estates are known to have come to the abbey as the result of grants subsequent to 1219.

But the Cistercian monastery was not the one to which the

[1] *Reg. Mag. Sig.*, v, 445, no. 1309. [2] *ITAAB*, II, 431.
[3] *Op. cit.*, p. 439.

Introduction

Book of Deer and its Gaelic charters originally belonged and to which the latter refer. This must have been an older, 'Celtic', one of which the Cistercian was by way of being a re-foundation under Norman auspices. There is almost no evidence for the existence of such a monastery outside the Book of Deer itself, but unless we are prepared to believe that the Gaelic 'charters' it contains are a forgery (a point taken up below, see pp. 97ff.) we are bound to accept that it did exist. There is now no recognisable trace of its buildings, or any visible identification of its site. It is hardly to be looked for in the area of the Cistercian abbey, since such re-foundations were normally made on fresh sites. It is commonly believed that the Celtic monastery was situated on the headland forming a peninsula partly surrounded by the South Ugie Water in the village of Old Deer, on which the parish church now stands;[1] but however intrinsically probable this may be, no actual remains of it have been recognised. Some of the lands which are mentioned in the Gaelic charters as belonging to this monastery are later found in the possession of the Cistercian abbey and still later of the Keiths, so that in trying to identify the hitherto unidentified names in the charters it is reasonable – but alas, virtually entirely unprofitable – to look for them in the general region which belonged to the later abbey; mainly the parishes of Old and New Deer.

Apart from the question of the lands and other grants deeded to it, and the legal proceedings it undertook to defend its rights, the little that is known about the Celtic monastery is soon told. The first Gaelic entry in the Book of Deer is the legend of its foundation; see the translation on p. 33.[2] This is of a type familiar in the history of Celtic monastic literature, where it is standard procedure that the Celtic saint to whom the monastery or church is dedicated, who is reputed to have been its actual founder in the flesh, meets with the local lord, who may or may not be a heathen, and, by the performance of a miracle, per-

---

[1] So e.g. Stuart, *BD*, p. x, and W. Douglas Simpson, *The Abbey of Deer* (pamphlet in the Ministry of Works' series *Ancient Monuments and Historic Buildings*; Edinburgh, H.M. Stationery Office, 1952).

[2] And the text on pp. 19 and 30.

suades him to make a grant of land for the purpose. Commonly, the lord behaves in some aggressive manner to the saint, who miraculously humbles him; or, as in the present case, the saint cures him or some member of his family from a dangerous sickness, and in gratitude for this is given the land he asks for. By inventing these 'foundation legends' the early monks, before the days of legal charters, provided their monastery at once with a remote 'historical' origin and a 'title deed'.

In the case of Deer two saints are involved, St Columba and St Drostán, and the subsequent 'charters' make their grants to both of them by name – which is simply a way of saying 'to the monastery of Deer'.[1] The mention of St Columba merely means that in the twelfth century the monks believed that their foundation went back to the time of the Gaelic Columban church in northern Scotland; either to that of the original Columban sway over the churches of N. Pictland between about 563 when St Columba came as missionary to the Northern Picts and 710 when Neiton king of the Picts went over to the Roman church, or after 848, when Pictland was absorbed by the Gaelic Scots and the Columban church was re-introduced there. The monks of Deer clearly asserted the former, and made one of their founders the saint in person, as is natural, but the latter might just as well have been the case, if it were not for the possible references to a monastery already at Deer in 623 and 679, on which see below. In view of these early references, if we accept that Deer is meant, it cannot be said to be impossible that St Columba himself did indeed come to Deer and take part in its foundation. In this connection it is interesting to note that two of the grants, one in no. III and one in no. VI, the first dated 1131–2 and the second presumably from some time between

---

[1] In fact there is no explicit statement anywhere in the MS that these grants are made to the monastery of Deer, the only approximation being the phrase just mentioned, which could apply in theory to any of the churches dedicated to Drostán. Nevertheless, it would be an excess of scepticism to doubt it, as is shown by three considerations: (1) it is explicitly called 'Deer' in no. I; (2) the monks are 'the clergy of Deer' in no. VII; and (3) the identifiable place-names are all lands held by the later abbey.

then and the late 1140s, both add 'the apostle Peter' to the names of Columba and Drostán. This is probably an aspect of the Norman influence in Buchan which was already beginning to show itself in other ways, as we shall see. In view of these late dates, it is not very likely to be an aspect of the Pictish veneration of St Peter which followed the conversion of King Neiton to the Roman observance in 710, which was to some extent countered by the Gaelicisation of the church in Pictland after 848.

As to Drostán, here again we know extremely little. *Drostán* is a known Pictish name,[1] as is natural in a character hailing from Buchan at this time. The foundation legend makes him son of a certain Coscrach (a Gaelic name), unknown, and disciple of St Columba. The two come to Aberdour, on the north coast of Buchan about 12 miles north-north-west of Old Deer, where the Pictish mormaer[2] grants them land for a monastery, and afterwards to Deer, with the same result. Fordoun makes him son of 'Fynewennis' daughter of 'Griffin' son of Aedán mac Gabráin, king of Dál Riada,[3] which would put his *floruit* in the second half of the seventh century, and would appear to make him a Gael rather than a Pict, but of course Fordoun's authority is worth very little, and he was in any case biassed in favour of the royal, Dalriadic Scottish, line. So, too, the Breviary of Aberdeen, giving the tradition about him as it was current in Aberdeen (and doubtless at Deer) in 1509, makes him 'of the royal race of the Scots', nephew of St Columba and given to him in Ireland to be educated;[4] he afterwards 'took the religious habit' at 'Dalquongale',[5] and when the abbot of that monastery died he was himself elected abbot in his place. Later he became a hermit in Glenesk, where he built a church; and finally he died and was buried at Aberdour, in a stone tomb where miracu-

---

[1] See *EIHM*, p. 367; *PP*, pp. 140, 145; Mrs Bromwich, *Trioedd Ynys Prydein* (Cardiff, 1961), pp. 329ff.

[2] On the meaning of this word see pp. 102ff.

[3] John of Fordoun, *Chronica Gentis Scotorum* (ed. W. F. Skene, Edinburgh, 1871–2), III, 31.   [4] Cf. the fact that Deer calls him Columba's disciple.

[5] Cf. St Drostanus of Dál Congaile, *OG*, p. 332.

lous cures were still worked.[1] His day was 14 December. It is curious that the Breviary has nothing to say about Deer.[2]

A number of Scottish churches, chiefly concentrated in the north-east, with outliers further afield, are or were dedicated to St Drostán. In addition to Deer and Old Aberdour (where 'St Drostán's Well' is still to be seen) there is Skirdurstan, 'St Drostán's Parish,' now part of Aberlour on the Spey above Craigellachie; Alvie also on the Spey, above Aviemore, and St Drostán's chapel near Dunachton still further up between Alvie and Kingussie; Rothiemay in Banffshire near Huntly; Insch in Aberdeenshire ('the church of St Drostán of Inchemabani' in 1230); 'Droustie's well' and 'Droustie's meadow' near Lochlee, in upper Glenesk, which represent Drostán's 'hermitage' of the Aberdeen Breviary; and Edzell not very far from the mouth of the Esk. More remotely, there is Ard Trostain on Loch Earn; 'the church of Mo-Dhrust' at Markinch in Fife; Urquhart in Inverness-shire, which is Urchardan Mo-Chrostain (= Mo-Dhrostáin) in Gaelic, and Croit Mo-Chrostain in Glen Urquhart where his relics were kept; also in Caithness the dedications at Westfield in Hallkirk parish, Brabster, and Canisbay.[3] According to Robertson (*ITAAB*, II, 373), an Aberdeen almanac of the year 1703 mentions 'Dustan [*sic*] Fair at Deer' on St Drostán's day, 14 December. This distribution of dedications and other commemorations shows that the 'cult' of Drostán was concentrated in the north-eastern triangle within a curving line drawn roughly from Montrose to Kingussie and thence to the head of the Beauly Firth. This distribution is, of course, consistent with a popularity of the saint during the period of Pictish independence at any time prior to 848, nor are the 'outliers' at Markinch, and, if early enough, on Loch Earn and in Caithness, inconsistent with it. But such attempts

---

[1] *Breviary of Aberdeen* (Bannatyne Club, 1854), II, 3, fo. xix.
[2] According to the Annals of Ulster a Drostán *dairtaighe* ('of the oratory') died at Ardbraccan in Co. Meath in 719. Ardbraccan was one of the monasteries of the Columban church in Ireland, but it would be rash to identify this with our Drostán.
[3] See Watson, *CPNS*, p. 318; *BD*, pp. ivff.; Macbain, *TGSI*, XI, 150.

to equate the cult of saints with the countries of independent Celtic nations are wholly misconceived, when we are dealing with the international Celtic church; and there is in fact no reason at all why a cult of a saint belonging at first properly to Aberdeenshire and its environs should not have spread widely outside this in eastern Scotland over a period of many centuries after the time of Kenneth Mac Alpine, even into the later Middle Ages.

The leaders of the late unlamented 'Pictomaniac' school of the first half of this century were of course not slow to seize on Drostán, claiming him as a pure Pict, older than the time of Columba (the date *c.* 520 is mentioned) and uncontaminated by that ambitious schemer's influence, but wrongly forced into the Columban pattern by the later apologists of his church. The 'evidence' on which this claim was based was, however, quite imaginary, and is now of no more than academic interest; for the proof of this the curious may consult J. A. Duke, *The Columban Church* (Oxford, 1932), p. 38 and Appendix v; cf. Watson, *CPNS*, p. 317.

The possible early references to the Celtic monastery of Deer mentioned above occur in the Annals of Ulster under the years 623 and 679. As T. F. O'Rahilly pointed out,[1] the name of the monastery of 'Ner' which is seen in the entry *quies Uinei abbatis Neir*, 'the death of Vineus Abbot of Ner', in 623, and in *dormitatio Nectain Neir*, 'the death of Nechtan of Ner', in 679, might really be a deformation of *Dér*, 'Deer', arising from the common instances where the name stood in the 'locative' after the preposition 'in'; that is, *i nDér*, pronounced *i Nér*. He refers also to the line in the Old Irish 'Félire of Oengus the Culdee', composed *c.* 800, *Nechtán nár de Albae*, 'modest Nechtán from Scotland',[2] and suggests that we should read *Nechtan Néir de Albae*, 'Nechtan of Deer, from Scotland'. If this interpretation is correct, as it may be, we have evidence that a Celtic monastery, with abbots, existed at Deer at least as early as 623. If so, the possibility that it may indeed have been founded by a dis-

---

[1] *EIHM*, p. 373n.   [2] W. Stokes, 'Félire', p. 34.

ciple of St Columba, if not by the saint himself, becomes more than a mere guess, and the idea that it belonged to the period of Pictish independence becomes a fact. In that case the Drostán who died at Ardbraccan in 719 could certainly not have been its founder.

However that may be, it is quite likely that by the twelfth century it had undergone the fate of so many early Celtic ecclesiastical foundations in Scotland, having ceased to be a true monastery and becoming rather a small 'college' of 'secular clerks'. A study by I. B. Cowan[1] suggests that such 'monasteries', and specifically that of Deer, were by now bodies of secular clerics living a communal life, who served a considerable area as priests before the time when regular and numerous parish churches had been established in the region, analogous to the Anglo-Saxon 'minster' churches; such churches gradually declining in status thereafter and finally themselves assuming the position of a normal parish church. The reference in King David's charter (= no. VII) to the *clerici de Der* suggests at any rate that the 'monastery' had not become simply a lay corporation, as so often happened by this time. The wish on the part of William Comyn to found a new and genuinely monastic abbey at Deer would arise partly from this, although of course also as a consequence of the introduction of the Cistercian Order to Scotland under Norman influence.

2. THE MANUSCRIPT, AND THE HANDS
OF THE GAELIC NOTES

The manuscript known as the Book of Deer is so-called because of the references to the 'monastery' contained in the interpolated Gaelic entries and the charter of David I. Apart from these, there is nothing at all to connect it with Deer. It is MS no. I.i.6.32 in the Cambridge University Library, a small octavo of 43 folios, which has been recently repaired and handsomely re-bound. The history of how it got there and how it was

---

[1] *SHR*, XL, 43ff.

Introduction

'discovered' a century and a half later is as follows. It was acquired by the University in 1715, when George I presented it with the library of the late John Moore, bishop of Ely. Mr Donald Mackay drew attention[1] to an entry in Evelyn's Diary for 10 March 1695, to the effect that Dr Gale, who was High Master of St Paul's School from 1672 to 1697, and had a considerable number of MSS, had shown him one 'of some parts of the New Test. in vulg: Lect: that had belonged to a Monastery in the north of Scotland, which he esteemed to be above 800 years old: some considerable various readings observable as in I. John:, & Genealogies of St. Luke'. Mackay has little doubt that this was the Book of Deer, presumably then belonging to Gale, and certainly the coincidence is striking.[2] From 1715 to 1860 the manuscript lay unnoticed in the University Library until it was discovered by Henry Bradshaw, the Librarian, who drew the attention of Cosmo Innes and Whitley Stokes to it, with the results summarised above in the preface.

Apart from the interpolated Gaelic notes and charter of David I, almost the whole of the MS is written in one single hand, apparently of the ninth century. The chief text which it contains is the whole of the Gospel of St John, but this is preceded by parts (the beginnings) of those of Matthew, Mark, and Luke. Following it, seemingly in the same hand, is the Apostles' Creed, and the MS ends with the well-known scribal colophon in Old Irish: *For chubus caich duini i mbia arrath in lebrán collí ara tardda a bendacht for anmain in truagain ro-d scríbai;*[3] that is, 'May it be on the conscience of everyone with whom[4] the

---

[1] *Sc. G. St.*, v, 50. I quote the Diary in the edition of E. S. de Beer (Oxford, 1959), p. 993, which differs somewhat from that used by Mr Mackay.

[2] He suggests that a study of the catalogue of Gale's books in Bernard's *Catalogus* might throw some light on the earlier history of the Book; but I have failed to find traces of any such thing in it (*Catalogus*, II, i, 185ff.).

[3] For this verbal ending, probably not older than the ninth century, cf. *Gr. O. Ir.*, pp. 419f.; and *Thes. Pal.*, II, xxx.

[4] Lit. 'in whose presence', O. Ir. *arrad*; cf. *Thes. Pal.* II, 257. Attempts to take this as *a rath* 'its grace', or 'its property', are unsatisfactory with regard both to sense and to prepositional idiom. I am grateful to Professor Binchy for a note on the legal meaning of *rath*, and on the passage in general.

8

splendid little book shall be, that he should give his blessing on the soul of the poor wretch who has written it.' Between the fragments of St Mark's Gospel and that of St Luke, a later hand[1] has inserted the concluding part of an Office for the Visitation of the Sick. It is edited and discussed by F. E. Warren,[2] who notes similarities of character to the Visitations in the early Irish MSS of the Gospels called the Book of Dimma and the Book of Moling (all three belong to the Ephesine family of Offices). He advances the close coincidences with the Mozarabic and Gallican Missals, and the marked deviations from the Roman liturgy, as evidence that the liturgy of the Columban church in Scotland belonged to the Ephesine and not the Petrine family. This Deer text too contains a brief passage in Old Irish. After the words *Libera nos Domine a malo; Domine Christe Ihesu custodi nos semper in omni opere bona fons et auctor omnium bonorum; Deus evacua nos vitiis et reple nos virtutibus bonis; per te Christe Ihesu*, there is the rubric *Hi sund du-beir*[3] *sacorfaic dáu*, 'Here he gives him the sacrament.' The hands of the MS are neat and clear, but the illuminated pages are of the most grotesque and barbarous crudeness. There is nothing to show where it was written, whether in Ireland or Scotland, whether at Deer itself or somewhere else within the Gaelic Christian world. By a detailed comparison of variant readings from the Old Latin Bible, the Vulgate, and several Irish Gospels, Stuart showed[4] that the text is the 'Irish' one so-called, basically the Vulgate but with occasional readings from older versions; but that it was copied into this MS in an outrageously careless and

---

[1] So Stokes, Stuart, and Fraser (Fraser 'eleventh century', which is probably rather too late). According to *Thes. Pal.*, II, xxx, the Gospels, the Office, and the colophon are all in one single hand certainly as old as the ninth century; but for 'the Office' read unquestionably 'the Creed'.

[2] *The Liturgy and Ritual of the Celtic Church* (Oxford, 1881), pp. 163ff.

[3] MS *dub-*. This is rendered by Stokes and others as 'thou givest', as if *du-bir* (though they read *dubeir*), which interpretation may be due to the *das ei eucharistam* of the Book of Dimma; and in *Thes. Pal.*, II, xxx, as 'is given', reading *duberr*. But the most natural expansion is *du-beir* 'he gives', which fits the context perfectly well. However, *du-bir* is quite possible.

[4] *BD*, pp. xxviiiff.

Introduction

corrupt manner, with numerous omissions, transpositions, repetitions, interpolations, capricious spellings, and violations of grammar. Some of the errors suggest carelessness rather than ignorance.

To describe the contents briefly in greater detail, they are as follows:

Fo. 1*a* is blank. Fo. 1*b* is a full-page illustration of four human figures, perhaps the Evangelists, two of them carrying what appear to be 'house-shaped' reliquaries comparable to the Monymusk reliquary, within a decorative frame.[1]

Fos. 2*a* to the upper half of 3*a* contains the beginning of the Gospel of St Matthew, Chapter I (the first page within a decorative frame with an elaborate initial),[2] down to the end of verse 17, treated as a prologue (*Finit prologus, item incipit nunc evangelium secundum Mattheum*).

Fos. 3*a* lower half to 4*a* was left blank, and it is here that the Gaelic notes nos. I, II, III, and IV were subsequently written.[3] The reason why this large gap had been left, and for drawing the picture of St Matthew on fo. 4*b* instead of 3*b*, is presumably the hole in the vellum at the bottom of 3*a* and 3*b*, which would have spoiled the look of it.

Fo. 4*b*, a full-page illumination of St Matthew,[4] seated and carrying a sword, with two small figures behind him, probably angels; the whole within a decorative frame. In the top margin the end of Gaelic no. II appears in a large hand; and in the left hand and bottom margins, no. V.

Fos. 5*a*–15*a*, Matthew I. 18 to 7. 23; headed on fo. 5*a* *Christi autem generatio*, the whole page within a decorated frame and with an elaborate initial. In the right hand and bottom margins the Gaelic entry no. VI is interpolated.[5]

Fos. 15*b*–16*a* are blank, and 16*b* is a full-page illustration of St Mark, carrying a reliquary, and within the same type of

---

[1] See *BD*, plate I. One would have expected the 'portraits' of the Evangelists in Deer to hold book-satchels or boxes containing their Gospels, as in some other Celtic illuminated MSS, but it seems clear that these are reliquaries of the kind mentioned.   [2] See *BD*, plate II.
[3] See *BD*, plates III, IV, V.   [4] *BD*, plate VI.   [5] *BD*, plate VII.

frame as before.[1] Fos. 17a–27b are the Gospel of St Mark as far as the middle of verse 35 of Chapter 5; 17a is within a frame of interlacing work, with an elaborate initial.[2]

Fo. 28a is blank; on fo. 28b–the top half of fo. 29a is the part of the Office for the Visitation of the Sick referred to above;[3] the bottom half of 29a is blank.

Fo. 29b is a full-page illumination of St Luke,[4] with the same type of reliquary and within the same sort of border; and fos. 30a as far as the upper third of 40a has the Gospel of St Luke, beginning within a decorative frame and with elaborate initial,[5] down to the middle of verse 2 of Chapter 4.

The bottom two-thirds of fo. 40a was left blank, and here the charter of David I, entry no. VII, was subsequently interpolated.[6]

Fos. 40b and 41a are blank, and then on fo. 41b comes the illuminated page of St John,[7] with the usual reliquary, surrounded by six smaller figures, perhaps angels, all within a decorative border. Facing this, on fo. 42a, his Gospel begins, with a more elaborate border and decorative initial,[8] and continues thereafter until the complete Gospel ends on fo. 84b. The lower half of 84b is a drawing of two figures with reliquaries within a double frame.[9]

On fo. 85a is the Apostles' Creed, and at the foot, the scribal colophon.[10] Fo. 85b is an illuminated page of four figures in a frame between the arms of a cross,[11] and fo. 86a another four figures, the lower two with reliquaries, in a quite elaborate framework.[12] The MS ends with fo. 86b, which is blank.

Five separate hands can be distinguished in the writing of the notes connected with the lands of Deer. The only serious discussion of this question is Fraser's, with which however I can-

[1] *BD*, plate VIII. [2] *BD*, plate IX.
[3] *BD*, plates X, XI. [4] *BD*, plate XII.
[5] *BD*, plate XIII. [6] *BD*, plate XIV.
[7] *BD*, plate XV. [8] *BD*, plate XVI.
[9] *BD*, plate XVII. [10] *BD*, plate XVIII.
[11] *BD*, plate XIX. [12] *BD*, plate XX.

not agree in certain particulars.[1] The situation appears to be this:

Hand A wrote first, on the first available blank space after the outside page 1*a* (which he naturally left empty), beginning with the bottom half of fo. 3*a*. Here and on fos. 3*b* and the top half of 4*a* he wrote the items I and II, ending in the top margin of fo. 4*b*. The writing commences relatively small, but near the top of fo. 4*a* it grows larger, rather variably, appearing at first sight to do so suddenly at *Cainnech* in the sixth line, but on closer examination this is seen to be a more gradual process. A evidently continued originally to the bottom of fo. 4*a*, before the whole lower half of this page was erased (see below), and ended across the top margin of 4*b* with the closing formula *7 bennact*, etc., 'And the blessing of the Lord on every mormaer and on every toísech who shall comply with it, and to their descendants after them.' These words are in letters even larger than those towards the end of the part of II on fo. 4*a*, but the hand appears to be the same. Fraser thought it different from all the other hands (*Sc. G. St.*, V, 56), but this was perhaps partly because he believed it to be an 'elaboration' of the last clause of V. This is unlikely, however; first, because if a further scribe did wish to do this there is plenty of room at the bottom immediately after V, and secondly because it is really a variety of the closing formula already given at the end of V, and therefore unnecessary. It seems that A commenced by determining to write small and neatly, and gradually began to sprawl more and more on fo. 4*a*, perhaps finding he had rather more room than he had thought his material would take; and ended at the top of 4*b* with really large lettering.[2] There seems to be no palaeographical reason why this hand need be any older than the

---

[1] I would now withdraw some of the remarks in *Ériu*, XVI, 87; e.g., though there appear to be no traces of erased letters on the lower half of fo. 4*a*, there is no question but that it is a palimpsest; see below.

[2] The author of this book, whose handwriting is very bad, often begins something which he wants to look neat (such as formal letters) in a small, careful hand, which however gets larger and less careful as he warms to the task. Hand A would seem to have been constituted likewise.

middle of the twelfth century, but in any event it must be later than 1058, since the Mal-Snechta mentioned in it as making a grant, obviously as mormaer of Moray, is the one who succeeded to this title in that year.

Hand B is quite similar to A, but not the same.[1] He followed on A, writing almost the whole of the present note v in the next obvious available space, down the rather wide left-hand margin of 4*b*, beside the illustration of St Matthew and across the bottom margin below it, as far as ...*etar sliab 7 achad*. If he had not used this margin, or that on the next page, he would have had to jump to the blank fo. 15*b*, unnecessarily far away. But writing where he did, he was able to make his note immediately follow the preceding one, and had also the advantage that the decorative character of the illumination draws attention to it.

Hand C. This man then followed directly on B, beginning to write note vi at the top of the right-hand margin of fo. 5*a*[2] beside the decorative border which contains verses 18–21 of Matthew 1, and continuing and ending across the bottom margin. His ink is paler and browner than that of the others, and the writing is comparatively rather spidery. But C also made two important additions, in the same ink, to what A and B had written. First, half-way down fo. 4*a* at the point where A *now* ends he erased the last third of the twelfth line. Here A had probably written, in his large hand, *o tosach go derad*, not quite filling the line, and had then continued at the start of the next line with a fresh document (as it were, '11*b*', now erased). But it was important to C, for reasons which will be discussed presently, to make an addition at the end of the previous, still extant, section ('11*a*'), so he erased enough of its last line to enable him to squeeze it in by writing small. He carried this as far back as the middle of *tosach*, and having done so, re-wrote, considerably smaller, the final *-ach* of that word and then added the words which now

---

[1] Fraser: 'of the same general character', *Sc. G. St.*, v, 58. I would put it more closely than that.

[2] He might have begun across the top margin, but this was already partly occupied by the scribal note *in nomine Sancte Trinitatis*, now bisected by a binder.

follow, as far as the edge of the page. Even so he had not given himself adequate room, and was obliged to add the last three words in the margin immediately above the preceding ones there, with a line drawn round them to show that they belong to what stands just below. In making this addition, C automatically added to the *t* of *tosach*, visibly in the same pale brown ink, the lenition-mark which he often used but which A hardly ever did. Secondly, C also appended two extra lines at the end of B's note v, across the bottom margin where he had plenty of room, apparently without erasing anything.

Hand D. This is of a somewhat different type from the others. It is rather less formal, and sometimes makes use of a contraction mark for *m*, and for the vowel of *mac* and *meic*, different from the normal ones used by the others, and similar to two of the suspensions used by E. Moreover, at one point, in *ferleginn* in the tenth line of III, we have the continental *g*, not the Hiberno-Saxon one. It seems that the scribe knew and was influenced by the continental hand.

What D did first was to erase very thoroughly what A had written in the lower half of fo. 4*a*, damaging the parchment in the process. As may be seen by holding it up to the light, it is exceedingly thin here, and there are numerous minute holes and some larger ones right through it, notably that between the *e* and *a* of (Mec)-Bead in the seventh line of III. The roughened character of the parchment has caused the ink to blur slightly, but D skilfully dodged the larger holes so that they come between the words or lines, except in the case of -Bead, where he came up unavoidably against a rather large one. In the space thus cleared, D then entered notes III and IV; but in writing IV he found he had not left himself enough room (he could not continue on to the next page without further erasures, as all this was also already occupied), and so he inserted part of it in the blank half-line at the end of III, as Irish scribes often did, and added the last three words of the note underneath the end of the last whole line of IV, with a line drawn round them to connect them directly to the preceding. It would clearly not be worth his while to go to the trouble of erasing the closing formula of II at the top of fo. 4*b* for such a small advantage.

It has been suggested above that what D erased was a continuation of II, and this is a necessary assumption if the closing formula at the top of fo. 4*b* was written by A. But further, it is most improbable that it was something that had been there before A wrote at all, since no-one would start making a half-page entry at the *bottom* of a page, at this point, where there were already one half, one whole, and one half page blank before it. Besides, if there had been something already there, A would have begun to feel cramped as he reached the top of 4*a*, and would not gradually start to sprawl in the way he did. It could be argued, of course, that what D rubbed out was not something written by A, but by somebody else subsequent to A, who *had* stopped at the middle of the page, but apart from the point about the closing formula on 4*b*, this must be regarded as a less likely assumption than the other, on the principle of Occam's razor. It is clear further that D was writing not only after A but also after B, since the fact that he had to squeeze IV into fo. 4*a* in the way he did shows that 4*b* was already fully occupied. The fact that C was cramped in making his interpolation at the end of the present II (= 'II*a*') on fo. 4*a* does not necessarily imply that he was writing after D had done his work, since what cramped him would be the now vanished 'II*b*', and there is little doubt that D was later not merely than A but also than C. Moreover, C is subsequent to B, not only because he follows directly after him but also because he has added two lines at the bottom of B's note v. The conclusion is therefore that the above four hands wrote in the order A (= I and II, including his original 'II*b*' and the top of fo. 4*b* but excluding C's addition at the end of 'II*a*'); B (= v, except for its last two lines); C (= VI, and the additions at the ends of 'II*a*' and v); and D (= III and IV, written after the erasure of 'II*b*').

Hand E. This scribe could have written his entry VII, the Latin charter of David I, on the next sizeable blank in the MS, fo. 15*b*, or on the following 16*a*, or on fo. 28*a* or the lower half of 29*a*. For some reason, however, he preferred to put it at the beginning of the *last* empty space in the MS (other than the final page), the lower two-thirds of fo. 40*a*. This hand is of a quite different character from the others, being a 'continental' one, as appears clearly in for instance the *f, g, r, s*, and some of the contractions and suspensions, but with evident Hiberno-Saxon influence, such as is seen in the *t*. The scribe was probably one originally trained in the Hiberno-Saxon hand but having learned the continental one, which he used here as appropriate to a Norman-Latin royal charter.

The conclusion about the date or dates of the writing of all these entries depends largely on non-palaeographical factors, which are dealt with below, pp. 89ff., but from the purely palaeographical point of view hands A and B are obviously contemporaries and may belong to the later eleventh or earlier twelfth centuries; C would probably be rather lateish in that period, and D certainly so (in any event this scribe was writing not earlier than 1131); and E is evidently late in it. There is nothing against taking all five hands as more or less contemporary, differing in type and scribal background rather than much in date.

THE TEXTS AND TRANSLATIONS

Considering how short and how clearly written the Gaelic entries, nos. I–VI, and the Latin charter, no. VII, really are it is surprising how many misreadings and misinterpretations have appeared in the various editions listed above in the Preface. This may be due in part to what appears to be the fact, that not one of the editors examined the manuscript itself; that some used the unsatisfactory facsimiles published by Innes and Stuart; and that others merely copied their predecessors' texts. Stokes must have worked from a transcript sent him by Bradshaw, and even Fraser used photographs, though he acknowledges the help of Mr N. Ker, then of Magdalene, in 'a careful examination of certain parts of the MS'. This being so, it has seemed desirable to print here a 'diplomatic' edition of the texts, arranged as they stand in the MS (whether marginal or otherwise), with all the contraction marks, etc., reproduced unexpanded, followed by palaeographical notes; and after that an 'edited' text (partly for the use of students), a translation, and a full commentary, both general and linguistic. Further linguistic notes will be found in the discussion of the language and spelling, pp. 125ff., and in the Glossarial Index.

It should be mentioned that all the texts except the Latin of no. VII are liberally sprinkled with what appear to be acute accents, such as are normally used to indicate long vowels or diphthongs in Irish and Scottish Gaelic MSS. This cannot be their purpose here, however, since many of them are written over short vowels, and others even over consonants.[1] Actually, their function is evidently to indicate that the language is vernacular, not Latin – that is to say, they are used very much as we use italics. The same is true of the Irish words in Latin contexts in the notulae in the Book of Armagh;[2] and the Andersons

---

[1] Fraser thought the implication was that the scribes did not understand the language they were copying; but he cannot have been aware of the facts mentioned below.   [2] See L. Bieler in *Scriptorium*, VIII, 90f.

point out that short, roughly horizontal, over-dashes are used in the same way in the Schaffhausen manuscript of Adamnán's Life of St Columba.[1] The late eighth-century fragments of Muirchú's Life of St Patrick also mark Irish names in the Latin with rows of accents;[2] and the Old Welsh words in some Latin MSS glossed in Old Welsh are similarly distinguished, as well as the Old Welsh names in Asser's Life of King Alfred. Since the position of the accents in Deer is wholly meaningless, I have followed the example of some editors in omitting them altogether (in the 'edited' texts I have, however, marked long vowels with the acute accent in accordance with the usual editorial practice).

[1] *VC*, p. 169.
[2] See L. Bieler in the *Proceedings of the Royal Irish Academy*, LIX, C (1959), 182.

The texts and translations

[I]

[Fo. 3a] Colùcille 7 drostan m̄c cosgreg adalta
tangator ahi marroalseg dia doib go
nic abbordobọr 7bede cruthnec robomor
mær buẻan araginn 7 esse rothidnaig doib
5 īgaᵗraig sain īsaere gobraith omormaer
7othosec. tangator asaathle sen īcathraig
ele 7doraten ricolùcille ṣ iarfallan doraᵇ
de 7dorodlôg arīmormær.i.bede gondas
tabrad do 7nitharat 7rogab m̄c do galar
10 iarnere naglerec 7robomarẹb act madbec
iarsen dochuid īmoᵣ dattac naglerec gondendẹs
[Fo. 3b] ernacde les īm̄c gondisad slante do 7dorat
īedbaᵗt doib uacloic ītiprat gonice chloic pette
m̄c garnait doronsat īnernacde 7 tanic
15 slante do; iarsen dorat collùcille dodros
tan īchadraig sen 7rosbenact 7foracaib ībre
ther gebe tisad ris nabad blienec buadacc gat
tan dåra drostan arscarthain fri collùcille
rolaboir colùcille bedear anim ohunn imacc;

[II]

20 Comgeall m̄c eda dorat uaorti nice furene
docolùcille 7do drostan. Moridac m̄c morcunn
dorat pett m̄c garnait 7achad toche temni.
7bahe robomormair7robothosec. Matain
m̄c caerill dorat cuit mormoir īalᵗi 7culii m̄c
25 batin dorat cuit toiseg. Domnall m̄c giric
7malbrigte m̄c chathail dorat pett īmulenn.
dodrostan. Cathal m̄cmorcunt dorat achad
naglerec do drostan. Domnall m̄c ruadri 7
malcolù m̄c culeon doratsat bidbin do dia 7do
30 drostan. Malcoloù m̄c cinatha dorat cuit
riig ibbidbin 7īpett m̄c gobroig 7da dabeg

19   2-2

uactair rosabard. Malcolū m̄c moilbrigte
dorat īdelerc. Malsnecte m̄c luloig dorat
[Fo. 4*a*] pett malduib do drostan; Dŏnall m̄c meic
35 dubbacin robaith nahule ĕbarta rodros
tan arthabart ahule do. robaith cathal
arachoir ĉetna acuitid t̄oisig 7dorat
prǫnn chet cecnolloce 7ceccasc do dia
7do drostan. Cainnech m̄c meic dobarcon
40 7cathal doratsat̄ alt̄in alla uethe
na cā sse gonice ī beith edarda alt̄in;
dorat domnall 7cathal etdanin
do dia 7do drostan. Robaith cainnec
7dŏnall 7cathal nahule edbarta ri   culait̄i brat̄a
45 dia 7ri drostan ot̄osaĉ goderad issǫre omor. 7ot̄eseĉ

[Continued at the top of fo. 4*b*]

[III]

Gartnait mc̄ cannech 7ete īgengillemichel
doratsat petmec cobrig ricosecrad eclaṣ
crist 7petir abstoil 7docolūcille 7dodrostā
ser onahulib dolodib conanascad docormc̄
50 escob dunicallenn.īnocmad bliadī.rigi.dā
testib; istis.nectan.escob ab̄b̄.7leot ab brecini
7maledōni mc̄ mc̄b ead.7algune mc̄ arcill.7ruad
ri mormar marr 7matadī brit̄em.7gillecrist
mc̄ cormaic.7malpetir mc̄ dōnaill.7dō ongart
55 ferlegīn turbruad.7gillecolaī mc̄ muredig.7dub
ni mc̄ malcolaī ÷ docrist 7docolīcilli 7dodrostā

[IV]

Dorat gartnait7īgengillemicǫl ball dōin ipet ipuir
Teste.gillecallinesacart.7feradac mc̄ malbricī.7mal
girc mc̄ tralin

[Continuation of 11]

[Fo. 4b] 7 bennact īchŏded ar cecmormar 7ar
cectosech chomallfas 7dansl daneis

[v]

Donchad m̄c mec
bead mec hidid
dorat acchad
65 madchor docr
ac3dodrostan 7
docholuim cille
īsore gobrad ma
lechi 7comgell 7
70 gille c̄r m̄c fīgun
īnaienas ītest3.7
malcoluim m̄c
molini. Cormac
m̄c cennedig do
75 rat gonige sca
li merlec. Com
gell m̄c caenna
ig taesec clan
de canan do
80 rat do c̄r 7
dodrostan 7
docholuim cille
gonige īgort
he mor iggīn
85 īfris isnesu daldin alenn odubuci golurchari etarslib 7achad
issaeri othesseach cubrath 7abennact arcachen chomallfas
araes cubrath 7amallact arcacen ticfa ris;

[vi]

[Fo. 5a]   Robaid colban
                                            in mormer
                                            buchan 7e   90

21

ua īgen gar
nait a ben
phusta
7donnačac
m̄c şthig tœ   95
sech clenni
morgainn
nahuliedba
rta ri dia7
ridrostan   100
7 ria colum
cilli 7ripe
tar apstal
onahulib
dolaidib ar   105
chuit cetri
dabach do
nithissad
ꝗardmand
aidib alban   110
cucotčenn
7arȧrdčel
laib. tes.his
broccin 7cor
m̄c abb tur   115
bruaid 7
morgunn
m̄c donnch

id 7 gilli petair m̄c donnčaid 7 malæchin 7 da m̄c matni.
7mathe buchan huli naiaidnaisse in helain; –   120

[VII]

[Fo. 40a] Dauid.rex scotto꒦ oīb p̄bis hoīb s̃s̃.salutes.
Sciatis qđ clerici.deder.s̄t ꝙeti 7 īmunes
aboī laicorũ officio.7exactione īdebita
sič īlibro eorum scribtū est. 7diratio

22

nauert̄ ap̄. banb. 7iurauert̄ ap̄.abb̄dōͤn. quapp̄ firmit̄ p̄cipio.utnullus eis.aut eoꝝ catellis.aliquam īiuriam īferre p̄sumat. T. gōꝝ.ep̄o. deduncallden. T. andrea ep̄o. decāt. T. samsone ep̄o.d^{e}br̄e. T. doncado comite.defib.7 malmori.dat hotla. 7ggillebrite.comite.deng̃.7ġgil lecõded.mc̄ æd.7brocī.7cormac.det̃brud. 7adã. mc̄ ferdomnac. 7gillendrias.mc̄. matni. ap̄.abb̄deon.

The texts and translations

3. The *i* subscript to the second *o*, which is perfectly clear, was missed by Fraser. The reading *cruthnec* is certainly right, and Fraser's *cruithnec* wrong.

4 and 8. The *æ* is the digraph, not *ae*.

10. The word *mareb* has cancellation-points above and below the *e*. On this see p. 135.

11. The second *e* in *gondendes* has a small subscript *a*, as in *issere* in l. 45, so that *ae* is to be read; definitely not *ea*, *pace* Innes (no. (5)), nor *ei*, *pace* Fraser.

13. The *doib* is written in the left margin, with a reference-mark to this point in the line.

17. Fraser *buadaec*; the *cc* is perfectly clear.

22. It is not absolutely certain, but virtually so, that the reading is *temni* not *temin*.

24. *Culii* was misread by Innes (no. (5) in the Preface above) as *Culn*, and this was copied by Macbain (no. (8)) and misled Anderson (no. (14)). Macbain took it for the name *Cuilén* which occurs in l. 29. See the Notes on II, 5.

32. *Moilbrigte* was misread by Stokes as *moilbrigtæ*.

37. Fraser's *chor* is mistaken; there is no question but that *choir* is the reading.

40–1. At the end of l. 40, after *uethe*, five letters (or perhaps four arranged in two twos with a gap between) seem to have been written and then rubbed out; they are extremely faint and are not now legible. At the beginning of l. 41 the scribe bungled what he had first written, and he erased this too, as far as and including the letter before the *e* before *gonice*, rubbing two holes right through the parchment as he did so; the first between the present *na* and the *c* and the second after the present *ca*m.[1] He then had another try. He wrote *na* successfully before the first hole, and *ca*m, with the contraction-mark for *m* over the *a*,

---

[1] Both these holes have been mended with repairer's tissue since the first time the present writer saw the MS. This makes parts of the *a* of *ca*, and of the letter now following the second hole, look blurred in a photograph, but this is deceptive.

after it between the two holes. He then had to repeat what he had originally written and then erased where the second hole now is, squeezing it in between that hole and the *e* which he had previously written and had *not* erased. The whole problem turns on what it was he had first written here, and what he now tried to write. The hole in question was taken, doubtfully, by Stokes as an *o*, hence his reading '*camone*(?)', copied by subsequent editors. But this will not do; the thing is an elliptical hole rubbed through the parchment, and there is nothing at all to justify an *o*, as Fraser saw. Moreover, there are clear traces below the hole of what was previously written and evidently not wholly rubbed out – the remains of two long 'tails' like those of *f*, *p*, *r*, or *s*, coming well down below the level of the line, as far as such tails do normally extend. These could belong to no other letters of the Irish alphabet. But there is no room here for *ff*, *pp*, or *rr*, because of the space required for the second parts of these letters; whereas there is just room for *ss*. In re-writing what he had previously erased the scribe, on coming to this point, had another try. Between the hole and the *e* which he had left untouched he squeezed in another letter or letters on the rubbed parchment surface. Everyone has read this as an *n*, and its upper part does indeed look like an *n*. But its two uprights come down below the line as far as would those of *f*, *p*, *r*, or *s* – as far, in fact, as those previously half erased; it is really impossible that it should be an *n*, and it is like no other *n* anywhere in the notes in Deer. On the other hand it could be taken as *ss*, clumsily written because of the lack of room. There is only one difficulty here, that the second stroke of the second *s* seems to be lacking (hence, partly, no doubt the reading as *n*). But it is not completely lacking, there *is* a slight curved mark joining it to the following *e*, and the fact that it is no bigger is explained on the assumption that the scribe did not want to mutilate the *e* by extending this part of the previous letter across it. The most probable solution of what the scribe was trying to write would therefore appear to be *na camsse*,[1] though

---

[1] For a suggested interpretation see the Notes, II, 17.

this cannot be regarded as at all certain; and it would seem, therefore, that the mistake which he had made (whatever it was) which impelled him to erase all the beginning of this line did not include the 'ss' originally written where the hole now is, since he appears to have repeated it. But if all this is so, one would then wonder what letter or letters had originally stood where the second 'ss' was written, and was now not represented at all, and whether this does not upset the whole reconstruction. The answer is that the second *s* of the original 'ss', if its second stroke was slightly on the large side, would have stood so close to the *e* that there was really no room before the *e* for another *ss* at all, and that when the scribe wrote *ss* again he had to write the first part of the first *s* over that stroke where it protruded to the right beyond the hole, and to squeeze the second *s* so tightly in that he left himself hardly any room at all for the second stroke of it. Apart from the difficulties just mentioned, there is one other. The remains of the 'tails' below the hole are crossed by a trace of a short horizontal line extending each side of them, the whole looking like a hand-'printed' capital H. And what is even odder, in re-writing after the hole, the scribe seems to have tried to repeat this, but in the form of a squiggly line joining the two 'tails' at their very bottoms. What these things can mean is a mystery, and of course it casts further doubt on the reading as *ss* (or as *n*, equally – or any other letter or letters).

44–5. On the words in smaller type see p. 13. On the subscript *a* in *sere*, missed by Fraser, see Textual Note to l. 11. In *othesech* Fraser prints the first *h* as if it were a letter; it is really the lenition mark. Innes' *thasech* is inexplicable; perhaps a misprint.

51. *Maledomni* was misread by Innes as *Maledoni*, by Stuart as *Maledouni*, by Stokes and Cameron as *Maledonn*, by Macbain as *Maledonni*, and by Lawrie as *Maledoun*. See the Notes on the Texts below.

52. In *bead* there is a hole in the parchment between the *e* and the *a*, due to the erasure described on p. 14. The scribe came to the hole with his *e* and then continued with the *a* immediately

after it; it is clear that nothing which he himself wrote has been erased here, but the work of his predecessor. The hole has been mended with repairer's tissue, which rather obscures the facts in a photostat.

56. The words after the ÷ are the continuation of l. 57.

57. The *nait* in *Gartnait* is now covered with a piece of repairer's tissue to mend a hole between this line and the line above; but it was perfectly clear before this repair was made, and the hole itself does not get in the way of any of the letters. There is a small subscript *a* under the second *e* of *gillemicel* which has not been noticed by previous editors.

In *ipuir* the *u* is rather like an open-topped *a*, and has been so read by some editors, but it is certainly a *u*, as read by Fraser, and is quite unlike the *a*'s in the hand which wrote III and IV.

58. The mark over the *a* in *Feradac* is not an *i* (hence Innes' *Feraidac*) but is accidental.

70. There is a small dot over the *g* of *gille* which could be interpreted as a lenition-point, the late substitute for the older suprascript *h* indicating lenition (cf. note on l. 131); but this would be very anachronistic with a *g*, and it is more probably accidental.

83–4. On the reading *gorthe* see the Notes to v, 7. Fraser's *ggin* is incorrect, since there is a contraction mark for *n* over the *i*.

85. There is virtually no doubt about the reading *fris* (compare the *ri* of *lurchari* in the same line), which is due to Fraser. He queried this, and added 'the *i* of *fris* extends below the line almost as far as the *f* and *s*' (*Sc. G. St.*, v, 57). This curious statement is quite mistaken; perhaps he meant to say the first stroke of the letter he now (correctly) read as *r*. The *i* reaches down only to the line-level, only so far as does the second stroke of the letter now read as *r*; hence the older reading *fius*.

In *dubuci* the first *u* is certainly right; it is not *a*. Innes' *lurchori* is unquestionably wrong.

86. According to Fraser, *op. cit.*, p. 57, the *-as* of *chomallfas* has 'disappeared in the binding'. His photostat may have made

this appear to be so, but in fact these letters are wholly visible, and were so even before the present re-binding.

87. Fraser has missed the lenition mark over the second *c* of *cac*.

88. According to Fraser the left-hand stroke of the *n* of *Colban* is 'visible', at the end of the line; previous editors had missed this. It is exceedingly faint, but I think this is right. The second minim has become worn off with the corner of the page.

89. There is a small mark under the *e* of *mormer* which might be interpreted as a subscript *a*, but a careful re-examination of the MS now convinces me that this is probably not the case; withdraw therefore the remark in *Ériu*, XVI, 86, n. 1, l. 12.

91. There is no sign of any *t* after *gar*, nor is there room for it.

94. The first *ac* is ligatured.

95. In *tœ* the *œ* is the digraph, not *oe*.

97. The reading is certainly *morgainn*, not *morguinn* with Fraser.

105. Innes' *dobaidib* is wrong.

114. The reading *broccin* is quite certain; the *brocein* read by some, including Innes, Stokes,[1] and Lawrie, is wrong. There is no need to bracket the *r* of Cormac, as Fraser does. There is a triangular piece cut or broken off the edge of the page here and in the next two lines, but the first part of the *r* is quite clearly visible.

115. The same remark exactly applies to the *r* of *tur* and to its cause.

119. The *ni* of *matni* might be *in*, but the other is more probable, and is supported by the clearer *matni* in l. 134.

120. The first *n* of *in helain* is not a contraction mark, *pace* Fraser, but a letter.

121. Lawrie peculiarly reads *salute[m]* here. *Salutem* is of course normal in this phrase, but there is no doubt at all about *salutes* in l. 121.

128. The abbreviation for *Gregorio* is unclear and indeterminate; the second letter is apparently *o* with a stroke above it,

---

[1] In his translation in the *Saturday Review* he gives *Broccin*; in his text, commentary, and index in the edition of 1866 he has *brocin* and in the translation *Broccin*, all of which is repeated exactly in the 1872 edition except for *brocein* now in the text.

and the last is something like the abbreviation for *rum* in l. 127. However, it occurs elsewhere used of this man in twelfth-century documents. Innes' *Gormac* is impossible.

131. The deletion-point above the first *g* of *ggil* is evidently intended as such, and not as the late substitute for the mark for lenition-*h*, which would be an anachronism (cf. note on l. 70); read therefore *Gille-Comded*.

The texts and translations

Long vowels are here marked with the acute accent, which has no relation to the accents written in the MS; see p. 17. Expanded contractions are not italicised (unless there is reasonable doubt as to exactly how they should be expanded), since the diplomatic texts make this unnecessary. The numerous spelling 'mistakes' and other peculiarities discussed below on pp. 125ff. are not corrected or normalised, except in one or two places where missing letters are restored, for the sake of clarity: this is done in square brackets.

I

Colum Cille 7 Drostán mac Cosgreg a dalta tángator a hÍ mar ro [f]alseg Dia doib gonic' Abbordoboir, 7 Bede cruthnec robo mormær Buchan ar a ginn; 7 ess é ro thidnaig doib in gathraig-sain in saere go bráith ó mormaer 7 ó thosec.
5 Tángator as a athle-sen in cathraig ele, 7 do-raten ri Colum Cille sí, iar fa llán do rath Dé. Acus do-rodloeg ar in mormær .i. Bede go-ndas tabrad dó, 7 ní tharat. Acus ro gab mac dó galar, iar n-ére na glérec, 7 robo marb act mad bec. Iar sen do-chuid in mor*maer* d' attac na glérec go
10 ndéndaes ernacde lesin mac go ndísad slánte dó; 7 do-rat i n-edbairt doib ua Cloic in Tiprat gonice Chloic Pette Mec-Garnait. Do-rónsat in n-ernacde, 7 tánic slánte dó. Iar sen do-rat Collum Cille do Drostán in chadraig-sen, 7 ro-s benact, 7 fo-rácaib i[n] mbréther, ge bé tísad ris, ná
15 bad blienec buadacc. Tángat*or* déara Drostán ar scarthain fri Collum Cille. Ro laboir Colum Cille, 'Be[d] Déar [a] anim ó [s]hunn imacc.'

II

Comgeall mac Éda do-rat ua Orti 'nice Fúréne do Colum Cille 7 do Drostán. Moridac mac Morcunn do-rat Pett Mec-Garnait 7 achad Toche Temni; 7 ba h-é robo mormaír 7 robo thosec. Matain mac Caerill do-rat cuit mormoír
5 i n-Alt*er*i, 7 Cú Líi mac Batín do-rat cuit toíseg. Domnall mac Giric 7 Mal-Brigte mac Chathail do-rat Pett in Mulenn

do Drostán. Cathal mac Morcunt do-rat Achad na Glérec
do Drostán. Domnall mac Ruadrí 7 Mal-Colum mac Culéon
do-ratsat Bidbin do Dia 7 do Drostán. Mal-Coloum mac
10 Cinatha do-rat cuit ríig i bBidbin 7 in Pett Mec-Gobroig,
7 dá dabeg uactair Ros abard. Mal-Colum mac Moíl-Brigte
do-rat ind Elerc. Mal-Snecte mac Luloig do-rat Pett Malduib
do Drostán. Domnall mac Meic-Dubbacín ro báith na h-ule
edbarta ro Drostán ar thabart a [t]hule dó. Ro báith Cathal
15 ar a[n] choir chétna a cuitid thoísig, 7 do-rat proinn chét cec
Nolloce 7 cec Cásc do Dia 7 do Drostán. Cainnech mac
Meic-Dobarcon 7 Cathal do-ratsator Alterin Alla Uethe na
Camss[?]e gonice in beith edar dá Alterin. Do-rat Domnall
7 Cathal Etdanin do Dia 7 do Drostán. Ro báith Cainnec 7
20 Domnall 7 Cathal na h-ule edbarta ri Dia 7 ri Drostán
ó thosach go derad i ssaere ó mormaer 7 ó thésech cu laithi
brátha; [Continued on fo. 4b] 7 bennact in Chomded ar cec
mormar 7 ar cec tosech chomallfas 7 da'n síl da n-éis.

III

Gartnait mac Cannech 7 Ete ingen Gille-Míchél do-ratsat
Pet Mec-Cobrig ri cosecrad eclasi Críst 7 Petir abstoil,
7 do Colum Cille 7 do Drostán, sér ó na h-ulib dolodib,
co n-a nascad do Cormac escob Dúni Callenn, in n-ocmad
5 bliadin rígi Dauíd. Testibus istis:– Nectan escob
Abberdeon, 7 Léot ab Brecini, 7 Mael-Domni[g][1] mac
Mec-Bead, 7 Algune mac Arcill, 7 Ruadrí mormar Marr,
7 Matadín brithem, 7 Gille-Críst mac Cormaic, 7 Mal-Petir
mac Domnaill, 7 Domongart fer léginn Turbruad,
10 7 Gille-Colaim mac Muredig, 7 Dubni mac Mal-Colaim.

IV

Do-rat Gartnait 7 ingen Gille-Mícael Ball Domin i Pet i[n]
Púir do Críst 7 do Colim Cilli 7 do Drostán. Teste Gille-
Callíne sacart, 7 Feradac mac Mal-Bricín, 7 Mal-Girc
mac Trálín.

---

[1] Probably to be so read, see Notes; MS maledomni.

31

The texts and translations

V

Donchad mac Mec-Bead mec Hidid do-rat Acchad Madchor
do Críst acus do Drostán 7 do Choluim Cille in sore go brád.
Mal-[F]échí[n] 7 Comgell 7 Gille-Críst mac Finguni i nn-a
[f]ienasi in testus, 7 Mal-Coluim mac Molíni. Cormac mac
5 Cennédig do-rat gonige Scáli Merlec. Comgell mac
Caennaig, taesec Clande Canan, do-rat do Críst 7 do
Drostán 7 do Choluim Cille gonige in gorthe mór i gginn in
fris is nesu d' Aldín Alenn, ó Dubuci go Lurchari, etar sliab
7 achad, i ssaeri ó thésseach cu bráth; 7 a bennacht ar cach
10 hén chomallfas ar a és cu bráth, 7 a mallact ar cach én
ticfa ris.

VI

Ro báid Colbán in mormér Buchan 7 Éua ingen Garnait a ben
phústa, 7 Donnachac mac Síthig tœsech Clenni Morgainn, na
h-uli edbarta ri Dia 7 ri Drostán 7 ria Colum Cilli 7 ri Petar
apstal, ó na h-ulib dolaidib, ar chuit cetri dabach don-í thíssad
5 ar ard-mandaidib Alban cu cotchenn 7 ar [a] h-ard-chellaib.
Testibus his:– Bróccín, 7 Cormac abb Turbruaid, 7 Morgunn
mac Donnchid, 7 Gilli-Petair mac Donnchaid, 7 Mal-[F]æchín,
7 dá mac Matni, 7 mathe Buchan huli 'n-a [f]iaidnaisse
i nHelain.

VII

Dauíd rex Scottorum omnibus probis hominibus suis salutes.
Sciatis quod clerici de Dér *sint* quieti et immunes ab omni
laicorum officio et exactione indebita, sicut in libro eorum
scribtum est, et dirationauerunt apud Banb 7 iurauerunt apud
5 Abberdeon. Quapropter firmiter precipio ut nullus eis aut
eorum catellis aliquam iniuriam inferre presumat. Teste
Gregorio episcopo de Dún Callden. Teste Andrea episcopo
de Cat*enes*. Teste Samsone episcopo de Brechin. Teste
Doncado comite de Fíb, 7 Mal-Mori d' Athótla,
10 7 Ggille-Bríte comite d' Éngus, 7 Gille-Comded mac Æd,
7 Brócín, 7 Cormac de Turbrud, 7 Ádam mac Ferdomnac,
7 Gille-'ndrias mac Matni, apud Abberdeon.

The texts and translations

For notes on the content, including names, see pp. 37ff.;
on the language, pp. 125ff. Identified place-names are given
here in their modern forms; unidentified ones in italics. All
names are in a normalised spelling.

I

Columba and Drostán son of Coscrach, his disciple, came from
Iona, as God guided them, to Aberdour; and Bede the Pict was
mormaer of Buchan on their arrival; and it is he who bestowed
on them that monastery,[1] in freedom till Doomsday from
5 mormaer and toísech. They came after that to the other
monastery,[2] and it pleased Columba, for it was full of the grace
of God. And he begged the mormaer, that is, Bede, that he
should give it to them, and he did not. And a son of his took
a sickness, after the clerics had been refused, and was all but
10 dead. Thereupon the mormaer went to beseech the clerics that
they should make a prayer on behalf of the boy, that health
might come to him; and he gave to them [land] as a grant from
Cloch in Tiprat[3] as far as *Cloch Peitte Meic-Garnait*.[4] They
made the prayer, and health came to him. Thereupon Columba
15 gave Drostán that monastery, and blessed it, and left the curse
that whoever should go against it should not be full of years or
of success. Drostán's tears [*déra*] came as he was parting from
Columba. Columba said, 'Let Deer be its name from this on.'

II

Comgell son of Aed gave from *Oirte* as far as *Púiréne* to Columba
and to Drostán. Muiredach son of Morgann gave *Pett Meic-*
Garnait and the field of *Toiche Teimne*; and it is he who was
mormaer and was toísech.[5] Matain son of Cairell gave a mor-

---

[1] I.e. Aberdour.
[2] I.e. Deer.
[3] 'The Rock of the Spring.'
[4] 'The Rock of the Estate of Mac-Garnait.'
[5] On the meanings of these titles see pp. 102ff.

5 maer's dues[1] in Altrie and Cú Lí son of Baíthín gave a toísech's
dues. Domnall son of Giric and Mal-Brigte son of Cathal gave
Pett in Muilinn[2] to Drostán. Cathal son of Morgann gave *Achad
na Cléirech*[3] to Drostán. Domnall son of Ruaidrí and Mal-
Coluim son of Cuilén gave Biffie to God and to Drostán.

10 Mal-Coluim son of Cinaed gave a king's dues in Biffie and in
Pett Meic-Gobraig,[4] and two davochs[5] of upper *Ros abard*.
Mal-Coluim son of Mal-Brigte gave Elrick. Mal-Snechta son of
Lulach gave *Pett Malduib*[6] to Drostán. Domnall son of Mac-
Dubaicín 'quenched'[7] all the grants in favour of Drostán in

15 return for giving him[8] his[9] goodwill. Cathal 'quenched' his
toísech's dues on the same terms, and gave a banquet for a
hundred every Christmas and every Easter to God and to
Drostán. Cainnech son of Mac-Dobarchon and Cathal gave
Altrie of the cliff of the birch-tree of the river-bend(?)[10] as far

20 as the birch-tree between the two Altries. Domnall and Cathal
gave Ednie to God and to Drostán. Cainnech and Domnall and
Cathal 'quenched' all the grants in favour of God and of
Drostán from beginning *to end, free from mormaer and toísech
till Doomsday.*[11] AND THE BLESSING OF THE LORD ON

25 EVERY MORMAER AND ON EVERY TOÍSECH WHO SHALL
COMPLY WITH IT, AND TO THEIR DESCENDANTS AFTER
THEM.[12]

III

Gartnait son of Cainnech and Ete daughter of Gille-Míchéil
gave *Pett Meic-Gobraig* for the consecration of a church of
Christ and of Peter the apostle, and to Columba and Drostán,
free of all imposts, with a bond for it to Cormac bishop of

5 Dunkeld, the eighth year of the reign of David. These being the
witnesses: Nechtan bishop of Aberdeen, and Léot abbot of

---

[1] See p. 119.
[2] 'The Estate of the Mill.'
[3] 'The Field of the Clerics.'
[4] 'The Estate of Mac-Gobraig.'
[5] On this term see p. 116.
[6] 'The Estate of Maldub.'
[7] On this term see pp. 120ff.
[8] I.e. Domnall.
[9] I.e. Drostán's, i.e. the monks'.
[10] See pp. 24ff. and Notes to II, 17.
[11] The words in italics are added by Hand C, see p. 13.
[12] The words in small capitals come at the top of fo. 4*b*, after III and IV,
in the same hand as the body of II but written larger; see p. 12.

The texts and translations

Brechin, and Mal-Domnaig (?) son of Mac-Bethad, and Aluine[1] son of Aircill, and Ruaidrí mormaer of Mar, and Mataidín the judge, and Gille-Críst son of Cormac, and Mal-Petair son of
10 Domnall, and Domangart lector of Turriff, and Gille-Coluim son of Muiredach, and Duibne son of Mal-Coluim.

IV

Gartnait and the daughter of Gille-Mícheil gave *Ball Domain*[2] in Pitfour to Christ and to Columba and to Drostán. Witness, Gille-Caillíne the priest, and Feradach son of Mal-Bricín, and Mal-Giric son of Tráillín.

V

Donnchad son of Mac-Bethad son of Ided gave Auchmachar to Christ and to Drostán and to Columba, in freedom till Doomsday. In witness of it, Mal-Fhéichín and Comgell and Gille-Críst son of Finguine, as testimony, and Mal-Coluim son of Moíléne.
5 Cormac son of Cennéitech gave as far as Skillymarno. Comgell son of Cainnech, toísech of Clann Chanann, gave to Christ and to Drostán as far as the great pillar-stone at the end of the thicket nearest to *Ailldín Ailenn*,[3] from *Dubuice* to *Lurchaire*, both rough-grazing and pasture, *free of toísech till Doomsday; and his*
10 *curse on everyone who shall come against it.*[4]

VI

Colbán, mormaer of Buchan, and Éva, daughter of Garnait his wedded wife, and Donnchad son of Síthech, toísech of Clann Morgainn, 'quenched' all the grants from all imposts, in favour of God and of Drostán and of Columba and of Peter the apostle,
5 in return for the dues on four davochs'[-worth] of that which should devolve on the chief religious houses[5] of Scotland in general and on its chief churches. These being the witnesses:

---

[1] Written *Algune*; see Notes.
[2] 'The Deep Spot', i.e. 'The Hollow'.
[3] 'The Little Gully of *Aile*'? See Notes.
[4] The words in italics are added by Hand C; see p. 14.
[5] See Notes.

35   3-2

Bróiccín, and Cormac abbot of Turriff, and Morgann son of
Donnchad, and Gille-Petair son of Donnchad, and Mal-
10 Fhéichín, and the two sons of Maitne, and all the 'good men'[1]
of Buchan in witness of it, at Ellon.

VII

David king of Scots, to all his 'good men',[1] greetings. You are
to know that the clergy of Deer are to be quit and immune from
all lay service and improper exaction, as is written in their book,
and as they proved by argument at Banff and swore at Aberdeen.
5 Wherefore I strictly enjoin that no-one shall dare to do any
harm to them or to their goods. Witness, Gregory bishop of
Dunkeld. Witness, Andrew bishop of Caithness. Witness,
Samson bishop of Brechin. Witness, Donnchad earl of Fife and
Mal-Moire of Atholl and Gille-Brigte earl of Angus, and Gille-
10 Coimded son of Aed, and Bróiccín, and Cormac of Turriff,
and Adam son of Ferdomnach, and Gille-Aindrias son of
Maitne; at Aberdeen.

[1] See Notes.

NOTES ON THE TEXTS

The reference numbers are to the lines of the *edited* texts, and length-marks are given as in those texts. Apart from the Clarendon type lemmata, names are in the same normalised spellings as in the translations. For linguistic forms the Glossarial Index should be further consulted; and for names, the other indexes.

I

1. **Colum Cille**, St Columba. The name means 'The Dove of the Church', cf. Latin *columba*, 'dove'. His real name was Cremthann, and Colum Cille was a nickname; for the anecdote purporting to tell how he got it see Stokes, 'Félire', pp. 144–7; and *ESSH*, I, 22, n. 3. In these texts the name is wrongly spelt twice as *Collum* (see p. 140); on dative *Coluim* see p. 146; on wrong spellings in the derivative *Mal-Coluim* see p. 132.

Drostán, see p. 4.

Cosgreg, genitive; nominative Coscrach. Drostán's father's name does not occur in any other source known to me. For Irish occurrences of the same name see *CGH*, pp. 568f., *AU*, IV, 98, and *AI*, p. 455. In Scotland, note Ferincoskry, formerly the name of the Creich district in Sutherland, = *Ferann Coscraig*, 'Coscrach's Land'; *CPNS*, p. 117. It is an adjectival derivative of *coscur* 'victory, triumph', and therefore means 'Victorious' or 'Triumphant'.

Í, Iona. As is well known, *Iona* is a bogus form, due to misreading the original *Ioua* of Adamnán's 'Life of Columba'. On the relation of the Gaelic *Í* to *Ioua*, cf. *CPNS*, pp. 87ff.; the modern nominative *Í* (for *Éo*) is probably really the dative used as such.

2. **ro [f]alseg**, from the M. Ir. verb *faillsig-*, *foillsig-*, 'reveal'; *Sc. G. fhoillsich* 'revealed'. The lenited *f-*, not being pronounced, is omitted here in the spelling; see p. 138.

doib. On the reason for not printing a length-mark on the *o* see p. 147.

37

gonic'. The full form of the preposition is *gonice*, appearing once in these texts with aphesis of the pretonic syllable as *'nice*, II, 1. Originally a verb-form, meaning 'until you come to', hence taking its 'object' in the accusative.

Abbordoboir, Old Aberdour, on the coast of Buchan, about 6 miles north-west of Deer. Columba and Drostán were perhaps envisaged as arriving by sea. The church of Old Aberdour was dedicated to St Drostán, and his holy well is still there. The early sixteenth-century Breviary of Aberdeen says that he was buried there and that miraculous cures were still performed at his tomb; see p. 4. No other evidence for a Celtic monastery is known.

The name consists of Pictish *aber* 'river-mouth', on which see *PP*, p. 148, and *Dobair* genitive of *Dobar*, the small river which flows into the sea there and is called the Dour, so that the name means 'The Mouth of the Dour'.[1] The word *dobar* (*b* originally = *v*) means 'water', and is on the face of it Gaelic, but could well be Pictish too (probably **duvr*), Gaelicised. Cf. *CPNS*, pp. 462, 465. On Pictish-Gaelic hybrids see further p. 115. *Abirdouer c.* 1329 and *Abirdowyr* in 1336 (*CPNS*, p. 462) show intervocal *-v-* already giving *w*, but Fraser's belief that the form in Deer is 'older than the rest of the document in which it appears' and that the writer 'had access to older documents in which Aberdour was referred to' (*Sc. G. St.*, V, 59) is extraordinary. The 'twelfth-century' spellings such as *Aberdouer* to which he refers are in Latin contexts, where the scribes spelled by ear, or wrote as had become the traditional form of the name in non-Gaelic contexts. In a Gaelic context the spelling with *b* would be perfectly normal at this date and much later.

Bede. This name does not occur in any other source known to me, but a deformation or miscopying of the familiar Pictish name *Bredei, Bridei*, or *Bruide* (see *PP*, p. 161) seems a possibility.

cruthnec, 'the Pict'. The reason for calling him this was presumably that the narrator was well aware that the inhabitants

---

[1] Watson's 'mouth of streamlet' is perhaps dictated by the fact that it is apparently not nowadays called 'the Dour' (cf. *PNA*, p. 3); but it must have been so at one time, and 'mouth of streamlet' is absurd.

Notes on the texts

of Buchan in Columba's time were Picts, not Gaels, and that they were now no longer so; hence the necessity for this comment. It implies that the narrator was writing as a member of the Columban, Gaelic church.

3. **mormær.** For a discussion of this word see pp. 102ff.

Buchan was the north-east region of Aberdeenshire and part of adjacent Banffshire, between the North Sea, the Deveron, and the Ythan. *Buchan* and *Marr* (see Note to III, 7) are given as the two sub-provinces making together one of the main provinces of north-east Scotland in a twelfth-century document edited by Skene, *CPS*, pp. 135ff. (cf. the translation in *ESSH*, I, cxvff.), which probably derives from sources older than the Dalriadic conquest of Pictland; cf. Chadwick, *ES*, pp. 35 and 38ff.

The etymology of the name is obscure, though Watson's suggestion (*CPNS*, p. 119) that it is related to Welsh *buwch* 'cow' might be correct, in which case it would be Pictish. The *bó-cháin* of Hector Boece (*PNA*, p. 26) is fanciful. It is not clear that the *u* is long, in spite of Watson (*loc. cit.*), who supports it with the Old Norse form Búkan, occurring once, which proves little, and the acute accent in Deer, which proves nothing; and of Alexander (*PNA*, p. 26), who says, without naming his authority, that it was long in Braemar Gaelic. The early forms both authorities quote are wholly ambiguous, and the modern local Scots pronunciation is decisively in favour of a short vowel. The name appears to be indeclinable in Deer, since the genitive is *Buchan* here and in VI, 1 and 8; but a genitive *Bucain* is found in the M. Ir. notes to the Félire of Oengus the Culdee, *i Ferann Martain ata i fail Bucain*, 'in Formartin which is beside Buchan' ('Félire', p. 240), and dative *Buchain* is seen in the Old Scottish Chronicle, *occisi sunt in Buchain*, referring to a Viking raid between 954 and 962 (*CPS*, p. 10). It is thus doubtful to what noun-declension it belonged in early Gaelic; it would be indeclinable in Pictish.

ar a ginn. This phrase has *cinn*, modern *cionn* the dative of *ceann*, with 'eclipsis' by the 3rd pl. possessive (Mod. Ir. *ar a*

39

gcionn), see pp. 142ff. The literal meaning is 'before their head', i.e. 'on their arrival; as they found when they got there'.

4. **in gathraig-sain.** Here there is the same 'eclipsis' of initial *c-* by a nasalising proclitic; see pp. 142ff. In speaking of 'that monastery' here and 'the other monastery' in l. 5 the narrator is thinking of the monasteries of Aberdour and Deer as if they already existed (as he was of course very conscious that they later did), instead of doing so only *in posse*. What is meant is respectively 'land for that monastery' and 'where the other monastery now is'.

in saere. On the significance of this see pp. 91ff.

go bráith, a misspelling, see p. 141.

tosec. On the meaning of this word see pp. 110ff. The Sc. G. derivative is *tòiseach*, but this is a secondary development from older *toísech*, as in Mod. Ir. *taoiseach*, and the spellings in Deer suggest that the word was still *toísech* in Buchan in the twelfth century. See pp. 134f.

6. **iar fa llán.** Here *iar* 'after' is no doubt a scribal mistake for *air* 'because'; cf. p. 147. On the *ll-* see p. 144.

do-rodloeg. M. Ir. *do-rothlaig* (or *ro thothlaig*), preterite of *do-thluich-* with the *ro* perfective particle infixed.

7. **go-ndas tabrad,** 'that he should give it', with M. Ir. infixed object pronoun; see Glossarial Index.

8. **na glérec,** with initial *c-* 'eclipsed' by the nasalising definite article; see pp. 142f.

act mad bec, 'all but'; literally 'but if it be a little'.

9. **na glérec,** see note on l. 8.

10. **déndaes,** spelling for *déntais*, see pp. 132 and 136.

do-rat i n-edbairt. *Do-rat*, 'gave', is also the verb used in these contexts for 'gave' in the deeds in the Book of Kells (see pp. 86f.); and moreover, in those documents the verb *ro edpair* 'he granted', plural *ro edpratar*, of which *edbart* is the verbal noun, is also so used. These are evidently Gaelic technical legal terms.

11. **ua Cloic in Tiprat gonice Chloic Pette Mec-Garnait,** 'from the Rock of the Spring to the Rock of the Estate of

Notes on the texts

Mac-Garnait'. These 'rocks' must have been landmarks on the boundaries of the lands believed to have constituted the original grant to the monastery; the second would probably be the boundary mark of a contiguous estate, not the one granted itself. The places cannot be identified. On *pett*, genitive *peitte*, see p. 114. The personal name *Mac-Garnait* appears again in II, 3; it is one of a type of patronymic personal name well-known in Gaelic onomastics. It does not mean 'the son of Garnait' but 'Garnait's-Son', but as a true first name, not a surname; one may compare in English *-son* names used as Christian names, e.g. Bronson Alcott. *Gartnait*, with its later form *Garnait*, is a familiar Pictish name, borne by three legendary and three historical kings of the Picts, as well as by a son of Aedán mac Gabráin the king of Dál Riada who died in 606 or 608, into whose family it had no doubt come by intermarriage with the Picts, like some other Pictish names (including that of this Gartnait's son Cano, cf. the comment on p. 111 below). The etymology is uncertain, but cf. *EIHM*, pp. 365f.

14. **ro-s benact,** with the infixed object pronoun, 'he blessed it'; see the Glossarial Index. *Benact* with final *-t* appears to be a scribal inadvertence for the correct *bennach*, since *bennacht* is the verbal noun; but it is perhaps not impossible that the verbal noun had come to be used locally as the stem of the finite verb, as happened sometimes in other cases (e.g. *gairm-* instead of *gair-* 'call' from the verbal noun *gairm*).

fo-rácaib. M. Ir. *fo-ácaib*, preterite of *fo-ácaib* with the *ro* perfective particle infixed.

i[n] mbréther, lit. 'the word', but *briathar* can mean also 'a phrase, a saying, a promise, a solemn statement, a blessing or curse', and see the RIA *Dict.*, F–*fochraic*, col. 178, ll. 78ff. It is used in this last sense here. On the spelling see p. 133. The MS has i *m*brether, but the Irish idiom is not 'to leave *in* a word' but 'to leave a word', or 'the word', and we must emend to *in mbrether*, taking *in* as the definite article, acc. sg.

15. **blienec.** On the spelling see pp. 131, 133, 139.

41

Notes on the texts

Drostán. For *-án* in place of the expected *-áin* in the genitive see *ZCP*, xvi, 55, and T. Ó Máille, *The Language of the Annals of Ulster* (Manchester, 1910), p. 23.

ar scarthain, 'at, while, on the occasion of, parting', an early example of the confusion of the prepositions *for* and *ar*; cf. RIA *Conts.* A 2, col. 369, iii, and RIA *Dict.*, *fochratae–futhu*, col. 301, (l). Hardly for *iar*, 'after', which does not suit the sense, for one thing.

fri. This older form of the preposition which became *ri* by lenition of the *f-* occurs in these texts only here; otherwise *ri*, etc., see Glossarial Index.

16. **be[d].** The -[d] is required here, since the sense is clearly either future (*bid*) or imperative (*bed, bad*).

Déar, and in vii, 2, *Dér*; other early forms are *Deir* (1246), *Dere* (1321 and 1526), *Der* (1391), see *PNA*, p. 47. On *Nér* see p. 6 above. The etymology is unknown; the 'derivation' in the text is of course worthless, a very typical example of *dinnshenchus*.

[a]. This must be inserted; it has been dropped by the scribe before the *a-* of *anim*, whether by inadvertence or by genuine elision.

anim. One expects *ainm*, and *anim* may be a simple mis-copying of this; it is however just possible that it stands for *ainim* with epenthetic vowel written; see p. 135.

17. **ó [s]hunn.** This is a 'pronunciation-spelling'; *sh-* being pronounced *h*, the scribe has omitted to write the *s-*.

II

The numerous grantors in this document are presumably members of the nobility of north-east Buchan, but few are identifiable. Mal-Coluim son of Cinaed is certainly Malcolm II son of Kenneth II, king of Scotland 1005–34; Mal-Coluim son of Mal-Brigte is no doubt the mormaer of Moray who died in 1029; and Mal-Snechta son of Lulach is certainly the mormaer of Moray who died in 1085. Domnall son of Giric might well be an unknown son of the regent Giric who died in 889, and Mal-Coluim son of Cuilén could be an unidentified son of

42

the King Cuilén who died in 971, since Cuilén is an uncommon name. Some of the names occur more than once, and it is tempting to try to construct pedigrees. Thus Muiredach son of Morgann and Cathal son of Morgann might well have been brothers; Mal-Brigte son of Cathal may have been this Cathal's son. But this is all speculation. The Domnall, Cathal, and Cainnech in the last part of II certainly seem closely connected, and one would suppose they were of the family of the mormaers of Buchan; which would be proved, in the case of Cainnech at least, if Cainnech father of Gartnait in III, 1 was the same person and if Gartnait himself was really mormaer of Buchan. But all this is hypothetical. The idea that Domnall and Cainnech were brothers depends on identifying Mac-Dubaicín with Mac-Dobarchon, which is impossible unless we suppose a gross confusion.

1. **Comgeall**, and *Comgell* in V, 3 and 5. This name is well-known as *Comgall* (cf., e.g., *CGH*, p. 554), but there is some evidence that a by-form *Coimgell*, with palatalised -*mg*-, did exist, apparently particularly in Scotland. St Comgall of Bangor is *Comgellus* in Adamnán's 'Life of Columba', with genitive *Comgilli*, and the usual form of the name, *Comgall*, derives from this with depalatalisation of the *g*. But with alternative spreading of the palatalisation to the *m*, note not only Deer but also the *Senchus Fer nAlban*, with *Comgell*[1] twice for the son of Domangart son of Fergus son of Erc (Adamnán genitive *Comgill*, *VC*, I, 7), from whom comes the name of the region of *Cowal*. The MacFirbis text of the *Senchus* has *Coimgell* in the first case and '*Coimgheall* or *Comghall*' in the second.[2] *Comgell* also occurs in

---

[1] *Sic* the H text; Bannerman, *Celtica*, VII, 154, ll. 13 and 14; the B and L texts have *Comgall* for the first, and the L text the same for the second, though Bannerman does not give these. In l. 63, p. 156, there is *Crích Comgaill*.

[2] *Celtica*, VII, 158, ll. 19, 21. The genealogies which accompany the *Senchus* in the H text have nom. *Comgall* once and gen. *Comgaill* three times for this same person; *Celtica* VIII, 108, ll. 64 and 65, and 109, ll. 99 and 106; and the Annals of Ulster have him as *Comgaill* (genitive) in 538 and 542; so too, the *Duan Albanach* has *Comhgall* for him; see *Celtica*, III, 161, ll. 40, 42, 44.

the early Irish genealogy of the kings of Ossory (*CGH*, p. 109, twice, but genitive *Comgaill* twice, *ibid.*; and p. 110, genitive *Comgill* but also *Comgaill*); compare *Comgell* in the Book of Leinster fo. 353*b*, and the diminutive *Comgellán*, *AU*, 625.

Éda. This is a spelling for *Aeda*, genitive of the name *Aed*; see p. 134.

Orti. Unidentified. The element *ord* is common in place-names in north-east Scotland, meaning a hill (cf. *PNA*, pp. 96 and 344f.), appearing in names as Ord, Ordie, Orda- etc.; the Ord of Caithness is a well-known instance. Watson relates it to Gaelic *ord* 'a hammer', saying 'a hammer-shaped hill (i.e. rounded like a throwing-hammer)' (*CPNS*, p. 140), which is perhaps not very convincing. At any rate *Orti* is probably an example of this word.

'nice Fúréne. On '*nice* for *gonice* see Notes 1, 2, and the Glossarial Index. *Fúréne* is probably for *Púréne*, the *f-* being due to post-verbal lenition (see p. 141f.). Watson suggests in *CPNS*, p. 376 that *Púréne* is a diminutive of his *pòr*; which (substituting *Púr* for this last) it could certainly be; but this can hardly be Pitfour in Old Deer parish, since that name actually occurs, as *Pett in Phúir* (MS *pet ipuir*), in IV, 1, *q.v.* Compare also Watson's Purin in Falkland parish, which was *Pourane* in 1450, and Pitfirrane near Dunfermline, which was *Petfurane* in 1474 (*op. cit.*, p. 377). On all this and on Pitfour, see further the Note to IV, 1. Assuming the *f-* to be original and not the result of lenition, *Fúréne* was identified by Fraser (*Sc. G. St.*, V, 61, n. 4) with Foveran close to Newburgh, about seven miles south of Old Deer, which is attractive at first sight, because certain lands in Foveran parish did belong to the Cistercian abbey and after-wards to the Keiths. But unfortunately this cannot stand, since the early forms *Foverne*, thirteenth century, and *Foveryn*, fifteenth century (Alexander, *PNA*, p. 61), and above all the modern pronunciation, show that we must assume original *fov-*, not *fú-*, in Foveran. Watson's etymology from a diminutive of *fobar* 'well' (*CPNS*, p. 504) is pretty certainly right; Alexander's derivation from *fuarán* (*loc. cit.*) does not suit. The name *Púiréne* or *Fúiréne* remains unidentified.

Notes on the texts

2. **Moridac.** This is a spelling for *Muiredach* (see pp. 129, 131), the name Anglicised as Murray in the surname MacMurray, and meaning 'lord'.

Morcunn. The name is *Morgann* or *Morgant*, spelt in a variety of ways (see pp. 131, 136f.); on the *-nt* see p. 136. Here the genitive is written as if nominative; see p. 132. Other Morganns in Deer, see l. 7, and VI, 2; there is really nothing to show that the Cathal son of Morgann of l. 7 was, or was not, Muiredach's brother. The name is not Gaelic in origin, but Brittonic and probably also Pictish. It is found early in the royal dynasties of Dál Riada, probably under Cumbric influence from Strathclyde, as with some other such names in these sources, and it could have been brought to Buchan as part of the general Gaelic onomastic inheritance at the time of the Gaelic occupation of Pictland. On the other hand it could have been taken from Pictish due to intermarriage between Gaelic and Pictish families in Buchan. The early instance in the Dalriadic family is Morgand grandson of Aedán mac Gabráin, mentioned in the *Senchus Fer nAlban* (*Celtica*, VII, 155, l. 25), who appears also in *AU* where they record the death of his son Tuathal in 663. The name occurs also in the genealogy of the mormaers of Moray descended from Loarn son of Erc of Dál Riada, in the person of the great-great-great-grandfather of the Lulach who appears in l. 12 below (*CGH*, pp. 329 and 330, where the second vowel is wrongly marked long). In the *Genelaig Albanensium* appended to the *Senchus Fer nAlban* in MS H, this man is given as Mongan (*Celtica*, VIII, 109), but the B text reads Morgan, and Mac Firbis has 'Mongan or Morgan or Morónd' (*Celtica*, VII, 151). A somewhat later Morgand is found in an entry in the Annals of Tigernach in 976, which give him as father of one of three mormaers from Scotland killed in Ireland in that year (see p. 104, and *ESSH*, I, 480). According to Alexander, Morgan is 'a thoroughly native surname in Aberdeenshire' at the present day (*PNA*, p. 392; and compare the place-name Tillymorgan, *loc. cit.*).

Pett Mec-Garnait. See Note to I, 11.

3. **Toche Temni.** Unidentified. *Toche* looks like M. Ir. *toiche*

45

'propriety, due order' (cf. RIA *Conts.*, *to–tu*, col. 219), and *Temni* might be *teimne* 'darkness', or the genitive feminine of the adjective *teimen* 'dark'. Or it could possibly be M. Ir. *timna* 'bequest', from O. Ir. *timn(a)e*. Compare the final *-e* written for the M. Ir. descendant of O. Ir. *-ai* in *Mal-Snechte*, II, 12. Anderson suggests 'The Propriety of the Bequest' (*ESSH*, II, 176, n. 3), but it is not clear what meaning he assigns to this; nor is it at all clear that *toiche* can mean 'property' as well as 'propriety', though the second seems meaningless here.

mormaír and **tosec.** On the meaning of these titles see pp. 102ff. On *tosec* as a spelling for *toísech* see p. 134f. It is impossible that this passage can mean that Comgell was mormaer and Muiredach was toísech, as some have thought; it emphasises 'Muiredach gave…; and it was *he* who was mormaer and was toísech'. See p. 112. It does not say what was the province where he was mormaer and toísech, but perhaps Buchan.

4. **Matain,** name unknown. The name occurring in the genitive as *Matni* in VI, 8 and VII, 12 has been taken to be the genitive of it, but it would be difficult to account for this; Anderson's explanation in *ESSH*, II, 181, n. 3 is fanciful. As Matain gave a mormaer's 'share' he was presumably a mormaer; of Buchan?

Caerill; on the spelling see p. 127. This is a known Irish name, *Cairell*; cf. *CGH*, p. 529, and *AU*, index.

cuit, 'share' (also ll. 5, 10 and VI, 4, and *cuitid* in II, 15); see p. 119.

5. **Alteri**, dative; cf. accusative *Alterin* in l. 17, and accusative dual *id.* in l. 18. Evidently an *n*-stem, with 'short' dative; therefore nominative **Ailtere*. One would expect **Ailtre* with syncope, and in fact the *e* is not written, the contraction for *er* being used each time. This is Altrie, formerly the name of the Bruxie area about two miles west of Old Deer, which appears in 1544 as Altre and in 1609 as Altrie. The Lordship of Altrie, which was set up in favour of the Keiths in 1587, was called from this; but it became obsolete when the Keith estates were broken up late in the eighteenth century. It was part of the lands of the Cistercian abbey. Cf. *BD*, p. liii and *PNA*, p. 5.

Notes on the texts

Cú Líi. I do not know this name, but names in Cú plus a qualifying genitive are of course familiar; means 'Hound of Splendour', i.e. 'Glorious Hound'? Or read Culíin, a known name (*CGH*, p. 577; also Cúilíne)? On the misreading *Culn* see the Textual Notes on l. 24. Cú Líi must have been a toísech, but no localisation is given.

Batín. No such name appears to exist, but compare Baetán, a well-known early Scottish and northern Irish name (one of these was an ancestor of the mormaers of Moray). There is also Baethán, Baíthén, Baíthéne (including the one who succeeded Columba as abbot of Iona), Baíthín, and Baíthíne, not connected with Baetán. For these see *CGH*, pp. 514–16. Of these, Baíthín seems the most likely here, and the name is normalised accordingly in the translation on p. 34, and elsewhere in this book.

cuit toíseg. On the meaning see p. 119; on the spelling -*eg*, p. 133.

Domnall mac Giric. The first name is too familiar for comment. Giric is apparently unique[1] except as the name of the mysterious 'regent' or 'usurper' who reigned as king of Scots on behalf of Eochaid son of Run, nephew of the preceding King Aed and grandson of Kenneth mac Alpine, from 878 to 889. His antecedents are unknown, but according to one version of the Chronicle of the Kings of Scotland his father's name was Dungal (*CPS*, p. 191; *ESSH*, I, 357), and according to the Chronicle of Melrose it was Dovenaldus,[2] which is Domnall. If this was Domnall I, brother of Kenneth mac Alpine, it would give Giric a very good claim, of course; but the Gaelic Dungal and Domnall are not the same name, and another explanation is possible. Eochaid's father Run was king of Strathclyde, and *his* grandfather's name was Dumnagual, which is the Old Welsh form of the same name as the Gaelic Domnall, but in written form looks not unlike the Gaelic Dungal. If Giric was son of this Dumnagual he would be Eochaid's maternal great-uncle, and it would be natural that he should act as regent for him if he was

---

[1] Except in so far as it was identified with the name of St Cyricus, see below.
[2] A. O. and M. O. Anderson and W. C. Dickinson, *The Chronicle of Melrose* (London, 1936), p. 10.

a boy, as seems to have been the case. The Domnall son of Giric of our text might well be a son of his in any case, because of the rarity of the name, but this is the more probable if Giric's father was also a 'Domnall'. If so, the granting of *Pett in Muilinn* would probably date between 878 and 889. The name Giric was identified, rightly or wrongly, with that of St Cyricus, and this had evidently already happened by 886–7 (perhaps really 885), since in that year the Chronicle of the Kings of Scotland records an eclipse 'on the very day of St Cyricus', the emphasis of which seems to imply an oblique reference to Giric, and may suggest that Giric regarded him as his patron saint. Ecclesgreig ('the Church of St Cyricus'), now St Cyrus in the Mearns, 'is said to have been founded' in Giric's reign. It may be that Giric popularised the cult of St Cyricus. On all this see *CPS*, pp. cxxxviif. and *ESSH*, I, 357f. and 363f.; and the Note on Mal-Girc in IV below.

6. **Mal-Brigte**, 'Servant of St Bridget'. This is one of the type of name, very common in early Christian Ireland and Scotland, in which the element *mael* 'servant', literally 'crop-head, slave', is prefixed to the name of a saint or other figure of religious significance in the genitive, the whole meaning 'the Servant, or Devotee, of (Saint) X'. The reason for 'crop-head' is that slaves were distinguished by their close-shorn hair; compare the tonsure of the servants of God. The word is sometimes treated as a masculine, in which case it becomes *Maíl-* in the genitive and causes lenition, and sometimes as a feminine (in spite of the fact that these are almost always men's names), in which case it lenites in the nominative and becomes *Maíle-*, non-leniting, in the genitive. Being only secondarily stressed, *Mael-* was very liable to be shortened and reduced, giving *Mal-*, *Mul-*, etc., and this has happened in all the examples in Deer, except that in l. 11 below the genitive *Moíl-Brigte* (for *Maíl-Brigte*) occurs, and that in III, 6 the spelling *Maledomni* of the text (nominative) is probably to be regarded as an error for *Mael-*. Another type of *Mael-* name is seen where the second element is an adjective qualifying the first, such names being no doubt of pre-Christian

origin; an example of this occurs here in the *Maldub*, 'Black Crop-Head' in *Pett Malduib* (genitive) in l. 12. Still another type is found when *Mael-* is qualified by a common-noun in the genitive, e.g. *Mael Dúin*, 'the Servant of the Fort', *Mael na mBó*, 'the Servant of the Cows'. *Mael-Snechtai*, 'the Servant of the Snow', is rather unclear, but it is a known name, and actually occurs here; see Note to l. 12.

There was a Mael-Brigte who was great-grandfather of Mal-Snechta, Mormaer of Moray; see Notes to ll. 11 and 12 below, but his father was not a Cathal.

mac Chathail. See above, the introductory note to the Notes on 11. The name Cathal was a common one.

Pett in Mulenn, 'The Estate of the Mill'. This has sometimes been identified with the old mill on the South Ugie Water just outside the village of Old Deer,[1] which is plausible enough. Pitmillan just north-west of Foveran (Pitmulen *c.* 1315, Petmulane 1514; *CPNS*, p. 411; *PNA*, p. 103) is another possibility; its teinds are recorded as due to the Earl Marischal in 1574 by tack from the Commendator of the abbey of Deer.[2] It is not included however in the possessions of the abbey listed as passing to him at the time of its dissolution in 1587. The identification is therefore uncertain.

7. **Cathal mac Morcunt.** Unidentified. On *Cathal* see the Note on l. 6; on *Morcunt*, that on l. 2.

Achad na Glérec, 'The Field of the Clerics', but evidently a place-name, not a descriptive phrase. Compare *CPNS*, p. 267. Unidentified.

8. **Domnall mac Ruadrí.** Unidentified. There was a Ruaidrí, mormaer of Moray, in the late tenth century, grandfather of Macbeth and great-grandfather of Lulach; if the Cuilén in the next is King Cuilén, Domnall could well have been this Ruaidrí's son. *Ruaidrí* means 'Fierce King'.

Mal-Colum mac Culéon. The spelling *Mal-Colum* is for *Mal-Coluim*, see p. 132; on names in *Mal-* see *Mal-Brigte*, l. 6. *Culéon* is a spelling for *Culéoin*, the genitive of *Cuilén*,

---

[1] E.g. *BD*, p. l.   [2] *ITAAB*, ii, 435.

Notes on the texts

'Whelp' (see p. 133). *Cuilén*, king of Scotland, reigned from 966 to 971, and Mal-Coluim might be an unidentified son of his.

9. **Bidbin**, accusative, and *i bBidbin*, dative, l. 10; clearly Biffie, just south-west of Old Deer (Biffy, 1544, *PNA*, p. 19), which was one of the lands belonging to the Cistercian abbey. It appears to be an *n*-stem, so that the nominative would be *Bidbe (or rather, *Bithbe, as is suggested by the *-ff-*).

Mal-Coloum mac Cinatha. Clearly King Malcolm II, son of Kenneth II, reigned 1005–34. On the spelling *Mal-Coloum* see p. 132; and on *Mal-* names see note to l. 6. 'The Servant of St Columba'. The father's name is nominative *Cinaed*, a quite common one in Ireland and Scotland. It occurs first among names of the Pictish kings, and is probably of Pictish origin, having perhaps found its way to Ireland early, where it appears to have become popular first in the person of Cinaed son of Irgalach, king of Ireland 724–8. The earliest traceable form seems to have been *Ciniod*, genitive *Cinedon*, *Cinadon* (*AU*, 878, *s.a.* 877, *Cinadan*); but was later regarded in Gaelic sources as a compound of the word *aed* 'fire', gen. *aeda*, whence *Cinaed*, with genitive normally *Cinaeda*.[1] Compare *EIHM*, p. 362, n. 8. One would suppose that *Cinatha* here is simply a spelling for this last, if it were not that *Cinadha* occurs also in *AU*, 879 (*s.a.* 878); perhaps under the influence of *Cinadon*? But it might represent reduction in an unstressed syllable; cf. p. 135. The meaning of the first element is doubtful. The form *Kenneth* is simply a Norman spelling, with *k-* to indicate the fact that it is the occlusive, not *s-*, and *th* as a normal way of writing the sound which was still the (voiced) dental spirant in Gaelic when it was adopted. It went out of use later in the Gaelic of Scotland, and the modern treatment whereby *Coinneach* (older *Cainnech*),

---

[1] There is something to be said for Stokes' view (*TPhS*, 1888–90, p. 398) that the Pictish name was originally *Cinioid, genitive *Cinioidon in which *oid, genitive *oidon, would be cognate exactly with Greek *aithōn*, gen. *aithonos*, 'fiery', an *n*-stem derivative of the same Indo-European root as O.Ir. *aed*. If so, *Cinioid* giving *Cinaed* may be due to a knowledge of the meaning among Gaelic speakers.

really quite a different name, is regarded as the equivalent of *Kenneth* is quite secondary.

10. **cuit ríig**, a king's 'share'; see p. 119.

i bBidbin, see Note on l. 9; and on the attempt to spell eclipsis see p. 143.

in Pett Mec-Gobroig, 'in Mac-Gobraig's Estate'. The name occurs again in III, 2, where it is *Pet Mec-Cobrig*. Since -*c* +*g*- giving -*c* + *c*- is more likely than the reverse, we should probably regard the name as being *Mac-Gobraig*, and take *Mac-Cobraig* for a pronunciation-spelling. Neither occurs elsewhere so far as I know, but it is of course a name of the *Mac-* compound type (see Note to I, 11). *Gobrach* is presumably an adjective in -*ach* from *gabar* (also *gobar* already in M. Ir.), 'horse' or 'goat', therefore 'Horsey' or 'Goaty'. On the treatment of the preposition for 'in' see p. 143; on *pett*, pp. 114ff. The place is un-identified, but since it was given to build a subsidiary church in III, 1–2 below, it is not likely to have been very close to Deer, but rather somewhere more outlying in its sphere of influence.

11. **dá dabeg**, 'two davochs'; see p. 116.

Ros abard. The first element is evidently *ros*, 'a wooded ridge or promontory, a heath'. This was an *o*-stem, so that *Ros* must be a spelling for *Rois* (see p. 129), and the name cannot be regarded as *Ros Bard*, 'the Ridge or Heath of the Poets', genitive *Rosa Bard*, as it could be if *ros* was a *u*-stem; unless indeed we read *Rois a[n] Baird*, 'the Ridge (or Heath) of the Poet', with *a* written by error for *an* as in l. 15, which is possible. If not, *abard* must be a single word (because of the doubt about this I print *Ros abard* not *Ros Abard*). An obvious identification which has been proposed by some is Rosehearty, on the coast about three miles north-east of Aberdour. This was *Rossawarty* in 1508 and *Rosaartie* in 1654; cf. *CPNS*, pp. 236f., and *PNA*, p. 109. Watson's explanation of it, however (*loc. cit.*), which is a probable one, *Ros Abartaig*, 'Abhartach's Cape', would de-mand *Rois Abartaig* in Deer. The *rd* for *rt* is perhaps not a serious objection, but the total absence of anything correspond-ing to -*aig* is. Besides, Rosehearty never occurs in any of the

documents bearing on the lands of the abbey. The identification
with *Ros abard* is therefore quite doubtful. One may note the
place-name Auchnavaird in the south-west end of Old Deer
parish. Alexander (*PNA*, p. 12) may be right that this contains
bard 'an enclosed field', and if so it is not relevant to *Ros abard*,
since this *bard* is a loanword from Scots. But it is possible that
Auchnavaird is 'The Field of the Poet'; and if so, 'The
Wooded Ridge, or Heath, of the Poet' – perhaps nearby – is also
possible.

Mal-Colum mac Moíl-Brigte, doubtless the mormaer of
Moray, grandson of the Ruaidrí mentioned in the Note to l. 8
and uncle to the Lulach mentioned in that to l. 12. He died
in 1029, when the Annals of Tighernach call him 'king of
Scotland', an indication of the powerful position of the mormaers of Moray in the eleventh century (cf. p. 109). On the
spelling -*Colum* see p. 132. In *Moíl*-, a spelling for *Maíl*-, we
have the genitive of *Mal*-, in its un-shortened form; on this,
and on *Mal*- names, see the Note on l. 6.

12. **ind Elerc**, 'Elrick'; either Little Elrick about $3\frac{1}{2}$ miles
south-west of Old Deer or Meikle Elrick about $4\frac{1}{2}$ miles south-
south-west of it. Both are mentioned among the abbey lands
granted to the Keiths in 1587. Early editors misunderstood
indelerc, treating it as *in Delerc*, 'The *Delerc*', unidentified (and
no word *delerc* is known). But *ind* is simply a quite normal M. Ir.
spelling for *inn* (or more properly *in n*-, see pp. 140, 143), the
definite article in the accusative. *Elerc*, from O. Ir. *erelc* 'an
ambush', is the word which became later in Sc. G. *eileirig* or
iolairig, 'a deer-trap', i.e. a funnel-shaped defile, natural or
artificial, into which deer were herded and shot down at the end;
and as a place-name it is common in Gaelic Scotland; see *CPNS*,
p. 489. In Deer, *ind Elerc* must be taken as a place-name, one
or both of the Elricks; 'The Elrick', meaning an estate called
after a deer-trap there, since to grant merely a deer-trap would
be very improbable.

Mal-Snecte mac Luloig. On -*Snecte* for M. Ir. -*Snechta*
see p. 131; the name is O. Ir. *Mael-Snechtai*; see Note on l. 6.

Notes on the texts

This was the mormaer of Moray who was defeated by Malcolm III in 1078, and died in 1085, when *AU* calls him 'King of Moray'. His father Lulach was king of Scotland for a few months in 1057–8, when he was killed by Malcolm III; he was son of Macbeth's wife by her first marriage, to the brother of the above Mal-Coluim son of Mal-Brigte. One version of the Chronicle of the Kings of Scotland calls him *fatuus*, 'the half-wit' (*CPS*, p. 152; *ESSH*, I, 603).

Pett Malduib, 'The Estate of Maldub', unidentified. On the name see the Note on l. 6.

13. **Domnall mac Meic-Dubbacín.** The father's name is unknown as such, but the second element must surely be a form of the known name *Dubucán*, for examples of which see *CGH*, p. 603; *Dubacáin*, its genitive, is hardly likely to be intended by the spelling *Dubbacin*, and it is more probably a different diminutive formation, in *-ín*, therefore really *Mac-Dubaicín*. Macbain suggests in *TGSI*, XI, 162, that this may be connected with the Dubucán, mormaer of Angus, who died in 938 according to the Chronicle of the Kings of Scotland (*CPS*, p. 9; *ESSH*, I, 446). If so, we should have to regard Mac-Dubaicín as a patronymic Christian name formed from it, and not suppose, as Macbain appears to, that Domnall was his grandson.

ro báith. On this verb see pp. 120ff.

14. **ro Drostán.** The verb form *ro báith* takes the preposition *ri*, as the other examples show, but there is no need to regard *ro* here as an error, to be corrected, as Fraser does (*Sc. G. St.*, V, 62, n. 4). It is a known, if uncommon, M. Ir. by-form of *ri*; cf. RIA *Dict.*, *fochratae-futhu*, col. 413, l. 71, and add *ri t' múr is ro t' mórmaigin*, E. J. Gwynn, *The Metrical Dindshenchas*, III (Dublin, 1913), 96, l. 12, where the two forms are used side by side in a single sentence. It is interesting to find it here in Deer.

ar thabart a [t]hule dó. Editors prior to Fraser have quite misunderstood the *ar thabart a hule do* of the MS. For example, Stokes, Stuart, Macbain, and Cameron all translate 'giving the whole of it (or, "the whole") to him'; taking *ar thabart* as if 'on giving', *a hule* as 'everything', and *do* as meaning 'to Drostán', i.e. the monastery. Anderson's 'in order to give them to him' dodges the question of *a hule* and takes *ar thabart* as 'for giving'. All this is impossible. Fraser saw this, but his exposition of what is wrong is inadequate. In the first place, as he indicates, *ar thabart* is clearly 'in return for giving', with *ar* in this very common sense. Translating so, *dó* is seen to apply to Domnall, not to Drostán. The construction *ro báid...ar chuit cetri dabach...*, '"quenched"...in return for the "share" of four davochs...', in VI, closely parallels this and shows it to be correct. But above all, *a hule* cannot possibly be 'everything'. This translation is due to misunderstanding the phrase which in modern Sc. G. is wrongly written *a h-uile* but is really *'ah uile* or better *'ach uile*, that is to say, *gach uile*; which however would require *cach ule* or *cech ule* in Deer. 'Everything' could indeed be expressed by *na hule*, and the passage could be so emended, but there is no point in doing this, as this translation makes no sense with 'in return for giving'; nor does it with 'giving' or 'in order to give', since the *edbarta*, the land-grants, had already been given to Drostán and were not now being *given* but being 'quenched'. Fraser's solution, which however he did not discuss, was to read *a [t]hule*, with *tuile* the genitive of *tol* 'will, desire'. He translates 'in return for his favour', by which he must have meant 'in return for Drostán's favour', i.e. the monks'; it could not be Domnall's favour, since this would not be 'in return for' what he had done but would be a benefaction in addition to it. The phrase *tabairt a thuile do X* certainly can mean 'to give his goodwill, affection, love, to X', cf. RIA *Conts.*, *to–tu*, col. 236, ll. 60–1, 63–4, 70; and it is probable that this is the meaning here. There is a special sense of it by which it expresses 'to give his consent to X', cf. *loc. cit.* ll. 24–34; but 'in return for Drostán's (i.e. the monks') consent to it' is pointless, and 'to him' instead of 'to it' is little better when the nature of what is consented to is not defined. It seems, then, we must interpret it that Domnall 'quenched' the grants in return for the goodwill of the monks – for what that may have been worth to him. Possibly he had offended or wronged them in some way, and had even been excommunicated, and now makes peace and restitution. Cf. *Innes Review* (Spring 1970), p. 12, 'Guilty consciences, however, prompted a number of [feudal] benefactions. Malcolm IV granted Kinclaith for remission and absolution of all royal transgressions against the church of Glasgow.'

The *a hule* of the text, for *a thule*, need not imply a pronunciation-spelling; need not imply, that is, that we have the same phenomenon as in *ó hunn* in I, 17; where *sh*, pronounced *h*, is so written. If it did, it would mean that *th* had *already* become the sound *h* in the early part of the twelfth century, as it did later, but this change seems only to have been beginning by the end of that century (see *Ériu*, XVI, 51f., and 93, n. 2). The rather numerous cases of writing *d* for *th* in Deer suggest that *th* was still a dental spirant. Hence *hule* for *thule* may well be due to a mere inadvertent omission of the *t*. Nevertheless, see the Note on *Mec-Bead*, III, 6.

Cathal. See the note at the beginning of the Notes on II.

15. **ar a[n] choir chétna.** The *n* of the definite article is omitted by error, probably either by failure to write, or failure to copy, the contraction-mark for *n* over the *a*; compare the Notes on IV, 1 and V, 3. This is not to be regarded as a Scottish Gaelicism, an example of the Sc. G. dropping of *-n* of the article in this position, which must be much later; and is in any case not peculiar to Sc. G., since spoken Modern Irish does the same. On *an* for *in* see p. 144; and on *choir* for *chor*, Textual Notes and p. 128. 'In the same way' evidently means, in the context, that Cathal too wanted the 'goodwill' of the monastery.

a cuitid thoísig. For *cuitid*, a derivative of *cuid*, cf. 'Félire', p. 110, *ba sí mo chuitid for clár*, 'this was my share on the board'; and Meyer, *Contribb.*, p. 556, spelt with *-ig*.

proinn chét, lit. 'a banquet of a hundred'; evidently a feast given twice a year. If limited to the monks, it implies a large monastery. Stuart thinks it was 'an obligation to entertain a hundred of those of the province of Buchan who were assembled at Deer to celebrate these great festivals' (*BD*, p. liii, n. 1). Perhaps more likely, all the monks plus enough guests to make a hundred. It is worth noting that according to Father Allan McDonald, *pronn ceud* was 'special food reserved for the highest class of gentlemen...A special food left for heroes mentioned in tales.'[1] The term would therefore seem to mean, in modern folklore at any rate, a banquet for distinguished people, not now necessarily a hundred of them. Whether this last was already the case in the twelfth century it is impossible to say, but it seems unlikely.

cec Nolloce 7 cec Cásc, genitives of time. Numerous examples of genitive *Cásc* may be found in the RIA *Conts.*, c, 1, col. 84; cf. Thurneysen, *Gr. O. Ir.*, p. 570, 'treated partly as neut. pl.'.

16. **Cainnech mac Meic-Dobarchon.** On the name *Cainnech* see the Note on l. 9; on names of the type *Mac-Dobarchon*, that on 1, 11. *Mac-Dobarchon* means 'Son of the Otter' (*dobar-chú*, 'water dog'; cf. Note on *Abbordoboir*, 1, 2). *CGH* has no Mac-Dobarchon, but there are several Mael-Dobarchons on p. 688.

17. **Alterin**, see Note on l. 5.

Alla Uethe na Camss[?]e. On this problem see the Textual Notes to ll. 40–1, where it is explained that the scribe seems to have made a mistake in writing the part now read as *na Camss[?]e* and to have erased and re-written it, correcting whatever the mistake had been; and that the reading *ss*, though doubtful, seems to be the least unlikely. If so, the last word looks like a genitive of *camus*, 'bend in a river', which would yield excellent sense; but unfortunately there seems to be no evidence for it as a feminine *ā*-stem with genitive *caimse*, but only as a masculine *o*-stem or *u*-stem with genitive *camais* or *camsa*. However, the other can scarcely be ruled out of court altogether, on these grounds, considering the fact that we are

---

[1] Fr Allan McDonald, *Gaelic Words and Expressions from South Uist and Eriskay*, edited by J. L. Campbell (Dublin, 1958), p. 197. But RIA *Conts. N–O–P*, col. 206, l. 26, '*praind cét*, a meal sufficient for a hundred' (LL, late twelfth-century MS).

dealing with such a remote part of Gaeldom, and that the Middle
Irish period is notoriously one when a good many nouns changed
their declensions.

The rest is more straightforward. *Alla* is surely the genitive
of *all* 'cliff', which actually occurs in this form (RIA *Conts.*, A, 1,
col. 285, l. 43f.). *Uethe* is evidently a spelling for *bethe* with
lenited $b = [v]$; the spelling of this sound with *u* is uncommon
in MSS but by no means really rare. This is the genitive of
beith 'birch-tree', which occurs in the next line. The place-
name phrase would appear to mean, therefore, 'Altrie of the
cliff of the birch-tree of the river-bend(?)', this Altrie being thus
distinguished from the other by this descriptive phase. Diack
objected, in *RC*, XLI, 133, to 'birch-tree', on the ground that
a tree is too ephemeral to be chosen as a landmark in a charter.
But this is untrue; such usages can be closely paralleled in the
contemporary Welsh charters in the Book of Llandaff (see *Ériu*,
XVI, 98, n. 2). Diack's own explanation of *uethe* and *beith* as
a Pictish word for 'road' is purely speculative.

It is perhaps worth suggesting that some of the Alveths
differently explained in *CPNS*, p. 502 might really be *All
Bheithe*.

18. **Domnall 7 Cathal...Cainnec 7 Domnall 7 Cathal.** On
these people see the comments at the beginning of the Notes
on 11.

19. **Etdanin.** It seems very probable that this is Ednie in the
parish of St Fergus, about $3\frac{1}{2}$ miles northwest of Peterhead,
though it is not mentioned among the lands of the Cistercian
abbey. Ednye occurs in 1609 (*PNA*, p. 52; Diack's etymology
quoted there cannot be correct). It would be an *n*-stem, nom.
**Etaine.*

21. **i ssaere...brátha**; see pp. 13 and 89f.

22. **bennact...d' an éis**; see pp. 12 and 85f.

23. **mormar**, see p. 135.

III

The date of this charter is the eighth year of the reign of David I, i.e. between April 1131 and April 1132.

1. **Gartnait mac Cannech 7 Ete ingen Gille-Míchél.** This is evidently the same couple as the grantors of no. IV. Gartnait may well be the father of the Éva of no. VI, but there is nothing to prove this, nor is there anything to prove that he was mormaer of Buchan; nor indeed if he was so, that this was in the right of his wife, since no Gille-Míchéil, mormaer of Buchan, is known. On the contrary, there was a Gille-Míchéil earl of Fife, who died not later than 1136 (*ESSH*, II, 180, n. 3), and Ete may have been his daughter. However, Gartnait may well be the 'Gartnach *comes*' who witnessed the foundation charter of Scone about 1120 (*Lib. Eccl. Scon.*, p. 3)[1] together with the 'Rothri *comes*' who witnesses the present document in l. 7, see the Note below; since the Pictish name Gartnait does sometimes appear in Latin documents, among other corrupt spellings, with final *-ch*. Further, Roger Earl of Buchan confirms, c. 1170–9, a grant of 'Gartenach, *avus meus*',[2] and if this is our Gartnait it would of course strongly suggest, though still not prove, that he too was mormaer of Buchan. The fact that Gartnait grants jointly with his wife *may* mean he held Pett Meic-Gobraig and Ball Domain in the right of his wife, but we hardly know enough about the conditions of land-tenure in Buchan at this period to assert that this is true; nor can we assert the corresponding thing about Colbán and his wife Éva in no. VI, though in this case there is a certain corroboration in the fact that Éva's father Garnait *may* well be the Gartnait of III and IV, and that Colbán is a foreign name.[3] Cainnech, Gartnait's father, might be the Cainnech father of Comgell, toísech of Clann Chanann, of V, 6, and any one of the Cainnnechs in II, but this is purely speculative. On the spelling *Cannech* see

---

[1] But this charter may probably be spurious; see *EC*, pp. 28off.
[2] *Lib. Cart. St. And.*, p. 370; cf. *EC*, p. 347.   [3] Cf. Note to VI, I.

Notes on the texts

pp. 133 and 139. *Gille-Míchéil*, 'Servant of St Michael', is one of a series of names where Irish *Gilla-*, Sc. G. *Gille-*, is prefixed to the name of a saint in the same sense as *Mael-*, *Mal-*; cf. the Index for others in *Gille-*.

2. **Pet Mec-Cobrig.** See II, 10.

cosecrad eclasi Críst 7 Petir abstoil. It is notable that though the land for the church is granted to Columba and Drostán, i.e. to the monastery, in the usual way, the church is to be dedicated to Christ and to St Peter. This is perhaps another sign of the Norman influence which other aspects of the notes in Deer show to have been already visibly on the increase in Buchan in the earlier part of the twelfth century. Compare VI, 3, and p. 4 above.

3. **sér ó na h-ulib dolodib**, 'free of all imposts'. The land is granted from the start in freedom from any of the usual services; cf. pp. 91ff. This is not the same thing as 'quenching', however.

4. **co n-a nascad do Cormac.** Prior to Fraser, editors took this as *co n-a n-ascad*, 'with the gift of them to Cormac'. But the 'gift' is not to the bishop of Dunkeld, which makes no sense; and as Fraser pointed out, *a n-ascad*, which demands a plurality of 'gifts', does not fit the context of a single grant. His reading, *a nascad*, 'its bond' ('under bond to Cormac', Fraser) must be right; a bond, a guarantee, for the due performance of the promise is meant.

Cormac escob Dúni Callenn. Cormac is one of the witnesses of *EC*, no. 74, about 1128, and no. 94, about 1130 (along with 'Alwyn mac Arkil' in the former and 'Alwin mac Archil' in the latter, see below). He was succeeded as bishop by the Gregory of VII, 7, at least as early as about 1135 (cf. *EC*, no. 105).

Dúni Callenn. On the name see *SHR*, XXXIII, 14–16; the older form *Callden* is seen in VII, 7. The etymology 'Fort of the Caledonians' is quite certain. The word *dún* was originally a neuter *o*-stem (hence the early Latinisations as *dunum*), but later became an *s*-stem, as here.

in n-ocmad bliadin rígi Dauíd. The eighth year of the reign of David I was from April 1131 to April 1132. The words

59

in n-ocmad are in the accusative – an accusative of time – and hence the nasalisation by the definite article. Whether *ocm* for *octm*, or better *ochtm*, is a mere scribal slip, or whether it represents a genuine pronunciation, the simplification of the difficult consonant group, cannot be determined. It can hardly represent the Sc. G. development of *cht to chc*, since that does not appear till the latter part of the seventeenth century (the Wardlaw MS).

5. **Testibus istis.** The presence of these Latin words has been taken as evidence that the scribe was copying and largely translating a Latin original. But, as anyone who knows anything about early Celtic MSS is aware, monastic scribes constantly mingled Latin and the vernacular, very often without the slightest apparent reason; this is conspicuous in, e.g., the Old Welsh deeds in the Book of St Chad (see p. 85). The most that the present example can be held to prove is that the writer was familiar with the formulæ of Norman Latin charters, which is not surprising considering his probable history as a scribe (see p. 14), and that he used this Latin formula here rather like a rubric.

Nectan escob. He was the first recorded bishop of Aberdeen, from 1125 till a date not later than 1150. Nechtan is a familiar name, both in Irish and Pictish (see *PP*, p. 145).

6. **Abberdeon**, Aberdeen. The MS has *abb* with suspension-mark, but in VII, 5 and 12 the *-deon* is written out in full (the *e* suprascript in l. 5), with the contraction for *er*; and there can be little doubt of the correct expansion (*Abbor-* in I, 2 is really irregular). The name is purely Pictish. The first element is *aber* 'river-mouth', as in Welsh. The second element is Ptolemy's *Devana*, Ravennas' *Devoni*, representing an early Pictish **Dēwonā* (with close *ę̄*). This is of course not the Dee but the Don, at whose mouth the town of Old Aberdeen stands; the name means 'the Goddess' (compare the Gaulish river *Dīvonā*), as also does that of the Aberdeenshire and Cheshire rivers *Dee*, from **Dēwā*. In Pictish of the historical period one would expect either *Aber Dēwon* or *Aber Duiwon* (cf. *PP*, p. 162), but in any case the river-name was borrowed by the Gaels at the stage of

Notes on the texts

Dēwon, with their own subsequent loss of intervocal *w* and shortening of long vowels in hiatus, giving *Aber Dĕ-on*, which is what is seen in Deer. The modern Gaelic for *Don* is *Deathan*, in which the unstressed *o* has regularly become *a*, and the hiatus between the vowels is shown by writing the (silent) *th*. On the name see further *CPNS*, p. 211, and *EIHM*, p. 383; and on the development of *Deon* to *Don* and *-deen*, see M. Förster, *Der Flussname Themse und seine Sippe* (Sitzungsb. d. Bayerischen Akad. der Wiss., Phil.-Hist. Abt., 1941, vol. 1; Munich, 1941), pp. 179ff. The form in Deer is absolutely correct early Gaelic. The account in *PNA*, pp. 1f. is not satisfactory, partly owing to Alexander's general tendency to take Diack seriously.

Léot ab Brecini. The name is Norse *Ljótr*, which was borrowed as *Léod* and has survived in the surname Mac Leòid, 'Macleod'. For other Scandinavian names in Deer see Algune mac Arcill below, and Colbán in VI, 1. *Leod* abbot of *Brechin* witnesses *EC*, no. 134, *c.* 1141 (with Gregory, bishop of Dunkeld, 'Earl Duncan', probably the earl of Fife, see note on VII, 9, and others); no. 161, 1143–7 (*Brechin*; with 'Earl Dunecan' and others); and no. 224, *c.* 1150 (N.B., *Breichin*; with Gregory bishop of Dunkeld, Andrew bishop of Caithness, Earl Duncan, Alwyn filius Archil, and others).

Brecini. Brechin is far outside the modern Gaelic-speaking area, and the real Gaelic form of the name seems not to be recorded. Early forms are genitive *Brechne* in the Chronicle of the Kings of Scotland between 971 and 995 (*tribuit magnam civitatem Brechne Domino*; *CPS*, p. 10), and *Brecini* in the present instance; dative *de Brechine*, *Reg. Episc. Brechin.*, I, 3 and passim; *de Brechin* in VII, 8 below; *de Breychin*, *Reg. Episc. Brechin.*, I, 4; *de Breichin*, *EC*, no. 224 as above. It is not clear, therefore, what noun declension the word belonged to, partly because one cannot tell in the Latin documents whether the scribe was treating it as undeclinable in his Latin context, or giving a genuine Gaelic case-form. On the whole the evidence suggests an *ā*-stem, nominative *Breichen (or perhaps dative *Breichin* used for nominative, as often with *ā*-stems in M. Ir.);

61

genitive *Breichne* (or, lacking syncope, *Breichine*, as here in Deer, unless this is a secondary form with epenthetic vowel); dative *Breichin*. Watson quotes no modern Gaelic forms, or any others in addition to the above; *CPNS*, pp. 111f. He gives the commonly repeated, but exceedingly uncertain, suggestion that the *aduan Brecheinawc*, 'region of Brecheinawc' of the Book of Taliesin[1] refers to Brechin. If *Brecheinawc* is to be explained as he thinks, it would be a form with the regional-name suffix *-iawg* derived, with vowel-affection, from a personal name which would probably be **Brochan* in Pictish. Watson attempts to explain *Brechin* as 'a shortened Gaelic form on the analogy of the numerous Irish names in *-ne*'. It is not quite clear what he thinks it was 'shortened' from, though he evidently supposes an antecedent Pictish form with Pictish vowel-affection; and two serious objections are that the name seems *not* to be the *Breichne* which his theory would demand, and that his forms in *-ne* are names of tribes (and hence of districts), and never of towns.

Mael-Domni[g]. The text reads Maledomni; curiously misread by some editors (see the Textual Notes). Hand D uses here the contraction for *m* which he also used in Domnall two lines below. He has also two other contractions for *m*, but he never uses this one for *n*. Watson and Fraser read correctly *Maledomni*; Anderson's *Maelduin* is unwarranted. Analogy would demand *Mal-Edomni* for this, a name with the prefix *Mael-* reduced to *Mal-* as in the others in Deer (see Note on II, 6, *Mal-Brigte*); but *Edomni* is unknown and inexplicable. It looks very much like the known name *Mael-Domnig*,[2] in which the final *-g*, pronounced as English *y*, could be virtually inaudible after the *i* and therefore not written. *Male-* could be a scribal slip for *Mael-*, perhaps under the unconscious influence of the fact that *Mal-* is normal in Deer. This is evidently

---

[1] See J. E. C. Williams, *The Poems of Taliesin* (Dublin, 1968), p. 128.

[2] Compare Mael-Brigte son of Mael-Domnaigh, abbot of Lismore in Ireland, who died in 912 (*AU*); Maol-Domhnaigh son of Maine, grandfather of the first earl of Lennox in the pedigree mentioned in the note on Algune mac Arcill below; and the place-name Pet Muldonych near Struan, 1504, *CPNS*, p. 238.

Notes on the texts

the same person as the man who appears in the great charter to Dunfermline about 1128 as *Maldoueni mac Ocbeth*[1] (*Reg. Dunferm.*, p. 4 = *EC*, no. 74; a *Maldoueni de Scona* also occurs in this), and as *Meldoinneth filium Machedath*[2] *iudicem bonum et discretum* in *EC*, no. 80, also *c.* 1128; no doubt this is the same as the *Maldoueni iudice* of *EC*, no. 68, *c.* 1126. In the first, second, and fourth of these, the final spirant *gh* is dropped in the same way as in Deer; in the third it is represented by *th*, which is a familiar spelling in Norman Latin for the Celtic guttural spirants *ch* and *gh*.

mac Mec-Bead. This is clearly the name Mac-Bethad, 'Son of Life' (i.e. 'Saved', not 'Damned'); that is, Macbeth; compare the previous Note. The name Mac-Bethad occurs twice in *CGH*, p. 680, twice in *AU*, and once in *AI*, apart from King Macbeth. It is curious that here, and in v, 1, as well as in Norman Latin documents, of course (where it is less unexpected), the intervocal -*th*-, which was still almost certainly the voiceless dental spirant of English '*th*ink', has apparently disappeared. Compare the Note on II, 14, *a hule*, where it is pointed out that the development of this sound to [*h*] is not probable so early (still less a subsequent complete loss). It is more likely that in Mac-Bead for Mac-Bethad = [*beθəð*], where *th* was the sound just described and *d* was the same as *th* in English '*th*at', there was a haplology of the two dental spirants, so that the first disappeared under the influence of the second. That is, this is a special case, not a general one. The Norman Latin and English *Macbeth* would represent *Mac-Be(th)ad* not *Mac-Beth(ad)*.

7. **Algune mac Arcill.** This man is well-known in documents of the reign of David I and Malcolm IV, in which he occurs a number of times. The son's name is found four times as *Alfwin* (*EC*, nos. 136, *c.* 1141; 55, *c.* 1143; 164, *c.* 1144; and *Reg. Reg. Scott.*, I, no. 29, *c.* 1136–47); once as *Alfuin* (*EC*, no. 225, *c.* 1150); six times as *Alwyn* (*EC*, nos. 74, *c.* 1128; 128,

[1] Must be an error for *mac Macbeth*. Maldoueni is *nominative*, so that Lawrie's *Maldouenus* (p. 327) is wrong and misleading.
[2] Presumably an error for *Macbedath*.

63

c. 1140; 209, *c.* 1150; 221, *c.* 1150; 224, *c.* 1150; and *Reg. Reg. Scott.* I, no. 117, 1153–9); once as *Ælwyn* (*Reg. Reg. Scott.*, I, no. 118, 1154–9); ten times as *Alwin* (*EC*, nos. 94, *c.* 1130; 103, *c.* 1133; 110, *c.* 1136; 125 and 126, *c.* 1139–41; 159, *c.* 1143; 171, *c.* 1144; 175, *c.* 1144; 207, *c.* 1150; and *Reg. Reg. Scott.*, I, no. 125, 1153–62); and once as *Algune* (Deer). The father's name is *Arkil* three times (*EC*, no. 74; *Reg. Reg. Scott.*, I, nos. 118, 125); *Archill* three times (*EC*, nos. 136, 164, 175); *Arcill* once (Deer); *Archil* thirteen times (*EC*, nos. 94, 103, 110, 125, 126, 128, 155, 159, 171, 207, 221, 224, 225); *Arch-* once (*Reg. Reg. Scott.*, I, no. 29). *Arkil* is an Old Danish name (also Old Swedish; Old Norse *Arnketell, Arnkell*), and appears in early mediaeval English sources as *Arncel, Arcel, Arcil*, etc.;[1] *Archel, Archil, Archillus*, etc., are well-known in Domesday Book.[2] *Alfwin*, etc., is Anglo-Saxon *Ælfwine*, Domesday Book *Alfuuinus, Aluuinus*, etc.,[3] but it seems to have been borrowed into Old Danish as early as the eleventh century, no doubt in England.[4] The spelling *Algune* is evidently intended for *Alguine*, for *Alwine*, with the sound *w* rendered by *gu*. This however is very peculiar. It is not a Gaelic usage to do so, and though it is of course extremely common in Old Welsh, Old Cornish, and Old Breton, which cannot be relevant here, there is no evidence at all for it in Pictish[5] (nor would Pictish be relevant at this late date even if there were). Germanic *w* regularly became *gw* in loanwords in the Romance languages, as in *wise* borrowed as French *guise*, and one would naturally take *Algu[i]ne* for a Norman spelling if it were not for the fact that this phonetic development in Romance is found in initial position only, not internally. However, though the Normans would not pronounce *Alwin* with *gw* it is possible that a spelling-confusion owing to their initial *gw* might arise on the part of a Gaelic scribe (whose own language had no *w*) with some knowledge of Norman French; and this must be the most likely explanation.

[1] *NPE*, p. 8. [2] *PCPN*, p. 163; *SPLY*, pp. 14ff. [3] *PCPN*, p. 181.
[4] Cf. R. Hornby, 'Fornavne i Danmark i Middelalderen', in *Nordisk Kultur*, VII (Stockholm, 1947). I owe this reference to the kindness of Dr Pálsson.
[5] See *PP*, p. 163. Original *w* apparently remained unchanged in Pictish.

Notes on the texts

It has been suggested that Alwin was a Northumbrian noble,[1] his name having been taken to be English. But the evidence on his name and his father's suggests rather that he was of Anglo-Danish descent. A charter of David I[2] speaks of *terram quam Arkil tenuit* between Haddington and Athelstaneford. This may or may not be our Arcill; if it is, he had East Lothian connections. However, in the twenty-two Latin documents mentioned above, in the phrase 'Alwin son of Arkil' (or other spellings) the word for 'son' is *mac* in no fewer than eleven (*EC*, nos. 74, 94, 125, 126, 128, 155, 159, 221; *Reg. Reg. Scott.*, I, nos. 29, 117, and 125; otherwise *filius*). This must mean that whatever its remoter antecedents, the family was thoroughly acclimatised in a Gaelic context by his own time. He was probably a Scottish noble of Danish or Anglo-Danish descent, whether in the male or female line, who belonged in his own day to some one of the Gaelic regions of Scotland. For other such people compare *Colbán* in VI, 1. There is nothing surprising about a Danish or Norse background to the nobility of Scotland at this time; compare the Arkil who had land between Haddington and Athelstaneford, if he is not the same person, or the Thor son of Swain who was lord of Tranent and probably sheriff of Lothian (*Reg. Reg. Scott.*, I, 46).

Professor Barrow has suggested that our Alwin may have been a royal official, of the Celtic traditional type, if he is the same person as Aluuinus Rennere of *EC*, no. 104, *c*. 1134, the Elwyn Renner of no. 228, *c*. 1150, and the Elwinus Renner of *Reg. Reg. Scott.*, I, no. 164, 1153–62 (see *op. cit.*, pp. 32f.; *rannaire* 'distributor of food, dispenser, butler, carver'); which would account for his continual presence at court and witnessing of royal charters. For the idea that he was ancestor of the earls of Lennox, in the female line, see L. McKenna, *Aithdioghluim Dána* (The Irish Texts Society, vol. XXXVII; Dublin, 1939), I, 172. The first earl of Lennox, who flourished in the second half of the twelfth and the beginning of the thirteenth century, was

---

[1] Cf. *EC*, p. 327. 'Northumbrian' apparently purely on the grounds that this is the part of England nearest to Scotland.   [2] *EC*, no. 186.

Alwynn, called in Irish *Alún* or *Ailín,* and the Irish bardic poem addressed to him by Muireadhach Albanach makes his (unnamed) mother daughter of one *Ailín* (see *loc. cit.*). This last could be Alwin son of Arkil chronologically, and the name could be borrowed into Gaelic in either form (in the second case, assimilated to the native name *Ailíne* or *Ailéne*); but whether it is at all probable is another matter. The Irish genealogy quoted by Skene (*Celtic Scotland* [Edinburgh, 1890], III, 476) and McKenna, *loc. cit.,* makes Alwynn son of Muireadhach (as does the poem) son of Maol-Domhnaigh, son of Maine, son of Corc, son of Lughaidh. Maine son (really grandson) of Corc son of Lughaidh is a character of Irish genealogical legend,[1] but the pedigree is very likely to be reliable as far back as Maol-Domhnaigh, and it shows that Alwin son of Arkil cannot have been Alwynn's ancestor in the male line.

Ruadrí mormar Marr. On the name see Note on II, 8. 'Rotheri *comes*' witnesses the great charter of Dunfermline *c.* 1128 (*Reg. Dunferm.,* p. 4 = *EC,* no. 74), along with Cormac bishop of Dunkeld, 'Maldoueni mac Ocbeth', 'Madeth *comes*', 'Alwyn mac Arkil', and others (see Notes on III, 4, 6, 7); and 'Rothri *comes*' witnesses the foundation charter of Scone along with 'Gartnach *comes*' and others (see Note on III, 1). Ruadrí, Rotheri, and Rothri are no doubt all the same person. On *mormar* see pp. 102ff. and 135 (17*e*). *Marr* is the province of Mar or Marr, the country between the Dee and the Don. It is not certain whether *Marr* or *Már* is the correct Gaelic form, since early spellings conflict (*Marr* in the present instance is for genitive *Mairr*). See *OG,* p. 536, for the evidence, which on the whole supports *Marr,* in spite of (genitive) *Mair* in a good source like *AU,* 1014; and this was the opinion of Watson, *CPNS,* p. 115.

8. **Matadín brithem.** Unidentified. The name is clearly 'Little Tyke', from *matad* 'cur' with diminutive *-ín* suffix; compare

---

[1] The prehistoric part of one of the pedigrees of the Éoganacht of Munster; see *CGH,* pp. 220, 222, 226. This is not the only Scottish genealogy which purports to derive from Munster ancestors, of course.

Notes on the texts

Matudán, the same with *-án* diminutive suffix, in *CGH*, p. 698 (seven instances); three in *AI* in the tenth and eleventh centuries; and several in *AU* in the mid-ninth, late tenth and early eleventh centuries. A *Cospatric mac Madethyn* occurs as recipient of a grant by William Comyn, earl of Buchan, in the earlier part of the thirteenth century,[1] and although this cannot be the same person the name is evidently the same. The *d*- and *th*-sounds (the second as in English *the*), written respectively *t* and *d* in Deer in the normal Gaelic way, are rendered exactly by ear in the Latin charter. *Brithem* is the regular O. Ir. for 'judge', becoming later *breithem*, but the older form survives here.

Gille-Críst mac Cormaic. Unidentified; 'Servant of Christ'; cf. Note on III, 1 and V, 3. There are several Irish Gilla-Crísts in *CGH* and the index of *AU*.

Mal-Petir mac Domnaill. Unidentified; 'Servant of St Peter'; cf. the Note on II, 6. *Mael-Petair* is not found in *CGH*, but occurs a number of times in *AU* and *AI*. In Scotland, there was a Malpeder (not son of a Domnall), earl of Mearns, at the end of the eleventh century (*ESSH*, II, 90).

9. **Domongart fer léginn Turbruad.** There are three *Domangarts* or *Domongarts* in *AU* (one of them also in *AI*), all members of the royal family of Dál Riada; of whom Domangart son of Fergus son of Erc is probably the best known, the other two being his great-grandson and great-great-great-grandson; while the Senchus Fer nAlban has three others, one a grandson of the same Domangart son of Fergus and the other two great-great-grandsons (*Celtica*, VII, 154f., ll. 16, 20, 24). *CGH* gives three others, all Irish. *Fer léginn*, 'man of reading', is defined by the RIA *Conts.*, I, col. 84, as '*professor of sacred scripture and theology in a monastic school*, often a bishop, abbot, or "airchinnech" [monastic steward]'. 'Head of a monastic school' would be perhaps a little less narrowly limited; it is often rendered 'lector'. *Turbruad* (spelling for genitive *Turbruaid*, as in VI, 6) is Turriff, about 16 miles west of Old Deer; early forms are *Turuered*, 1207 and 1250; *Tufred*, 1211; *Turref* and *Turrech*, 1272 (*PNA*,

---

[1] *Reg. Episc. Aber.*, I, 14.

pp. 129f.). This passage, and VI, 6 (cf. VII, 11), constitute the only clear evidence for the existence of a Celtic monastery at Turriff, but scepticism about it on these grounds is exaggerated and quite unwarranted, as in the case of the scepticism about a monastery at Deer prior to the Cistercian one (pp. 98ff.). As even Lawrie himself noted, the charter of Alexander Comyn, earl of Buchan, of 1272, founding a *domus elemosinarum* there, mentions a *via monachorum* which may well refer, as he puts it, 'to an old religious house' (see *EC*, p. 347.)

10. **Gille-Colaim mac Muredig.** Unidentified; 'Servant of St Columba', see the note on *Gille-Críst* above. There is one Irish Gilla-Coluim, son of a Gilla-Críst, in *CGH*, in the Fermanagh genealogy on p. 184. On the name *Muiredach* see the Note on II, 2.

Dubni mac Mal-Colaim. Unidentified. The son's name *Duibne* is almost unique,[1] but it does occur in the late M. Ir. text *Acallamh na Senórach* (ed. W. Stokes in Stokes and Windisch, *Irische Texte*, IV, i), l. 4558, where it refers to a legendary king of Bregia and Meath. For *Mal-Colaim*, 'Servant of St Columba', see the Note on II, 6.

IV

1. **Gartnait 7 ingen Gille-Mícael**, see III, 1.

Ball Domin, literally 'the Deep Spot', presumably a hollow. Unidentified. There is a *Baldovan* near Dundee, evidently the same name, but clearly not the same place.

i Pet i[n] Púir; text *ipet ipuir*; see the Textual Notes. Evidently Pitfour, about a mile north-north-east of Old Deer; early forms, see *PNA*, p. 102. Diack's '*fúr*', and his whole note on the word in *RC*, XLI, 120ff., are characteristically fanciful and wrong-headed. The name stands for *Pett in Phúir*, with the word *púr* seen in names such as Dochfour near Inverness; Delfour (Gaelic *Dail a' Phùir*) in Kincraig and Cromdale; Pitfour in Rogart, Kilmuir Easter, and Avoch; Balfour in Tully-

---

[1] The *Duibne* of *Diarmait ua Duibne* is probably genitive of a goddess's name **Duiben*.

nessle, Edzell, and Markinch; Tillyfour in Monymusk; Tilly-
fourie in Cluny; Pourie in Murroes; Purin in Falkland;
Trinafour (Gaelic *Trian a' Phùir*) in Struan; *Tom a' Phùir* in
Glenartney forest; Tirafuir (Gaelic *Tìr a' Phùir*) in Lismore;
Pennyfuir (Gaelic *Peighinn a' Phùir*), near Oban; and others,
see Watson, *CPNS*, pp. 376f. It is clear that this is a word *púr*,
a masculine *o*-stem, occurring early with the definite article, in
the genitive, as in *Phúir*, modern Gaelic *a' Phùir*, qualifying
a preceding word like *pett, baile, dail, dabach, tulach*, etc. Those
cases where there is now no trace of the article in the Gaelic
form, such as *Baile Phùir* in Rogart or *Dabhach Phùir* near
Inverness, have simply dropped this unstressed element; in
Anglicised forms like *Pitfour, Tillyfour*, this naturally happens
a fortiori. According to Watson (*loc. cit.*), *púir* is the genitive of
pór, which he renders 'pasture' and regards as a British loanword (perhaps rather, Pictish), but this is not the meaning of
Gaelic *pòr* which means 'seed, grain, crops', and its genitive is
not, and could not possibly be, *pùir*, but *pòir*. However, *pùr*
for *pòr* could be analogous to *pùsta* for *pósta* (see Note on VI, I).
Nevertheless the meaning of *púr* remains uncertain; possibly
'crop-land'. In our text, *ipuir* is evidently for *in Phúir*, with
i written for *in* by the same kind of error as in the omission of *n*
in *Mal-[F]échi[n]* in V, 3; and compare the Note on II, 15.
The meaning is 'The Estate of the *Púr* (Crop-Land?)'. Compare the Note on *Fúréne* in II, 1.

2. **Gille-Callíne.** Unidentified. On names in *Gille-* prefixed to
those of saints see Note on III, 1. The saint here is St Caillín,
patron of the monastery of Fenagh in Leitrim, who was said to
have been a contemporary of St Columba; on him, see Kenney,
SEHI, p. 400; and cf. *AU*, 1377, 1428. The name also takes the
forms *Caillíne* and *Cailléne* (*CGH*, p. 529), the three diminutive
suffixes *-ín, -ine*, and *-éne* being more or less interchangeable.

    Feradac mac Mal-Bricín. Unidentified. *Feradach* is a
common name. *Mal-Bricín* is another name in *Mael-*, see Note
on II, 6. *Bricín* is St Bricín, abbot of Tuaim Drecain; see Kenney,
SEHI, p. 782; compare also Briccéni abbot of Lorrha, *AU*, 844.

Notes on the texts

3. **Mal-Girc mac Trálín.** Unidentified. A name in *Mael-*;
cf. Note on II, 6, and Irish *Mael-Giric* in *CGH*, p. 690. The
Girc is no doubt St Cyricus; see the Note, II, 5. The name
Trálín seems to be unknown, but could be a diminutive of the
word *tráill* 'thrall' (from the Old Norse or English) which
occurs as early as Cormac's Glossary; see RIA *Conts.*, *to–tu*,
col. 273. On this assumption, I have marked the *a* long, and
spelt it with *ll* in the translation. Compare names like Matadín,
III, 8, for the meaning.

V

1. **Donchad mac Mec-Bead mec Hidid.** Unidentified. The
name *Donnchad*, perhaps 'Battle-Prince', Anglicised as Duncan,
is very common; in Deer, cf. VI, 7 (2), and VII, 9, and specially
Donnachac, VI, 2. On the name Mac-Bead, see Note on p. 63.
Ided or *Idad* (the *H-* is purely graphic) seems an unknown name,
unless we can compare it with *Idath* or *Idad* the father of the
Irish legendary fairy prince Froech (W. Meid, *Táin Bó Fraích*,
l. 1; Dublin, 1967).

Acchad Madchor. Evidently Auchmachar, about $2\frac{1}{2}$ miles
north-west of Old Deer; meaning, 'The Field of Madchar'.

2. **in sore go brád.** On these spellings see pp. 135 and 138.

3. **Mal-[F]échí[n]**, unidentified. Text *malechi*. There seems to
be no such name as *Malechi* or *Mal-Echi*, or *Echi*, and it is very
probable, as Watson suggests (*CPNS*, p. 322), that it is the
same as the *Mal-[F]æchín* of VI, 7; on the failure to write the *-n*
see Notes on II, 15 and IV, 1. Compare Mael-Féchéni, abbot of
Moville, *AU*, 944. A name in *Mael-* (cf. Note on II, 6); the
saint's name is evidently *Féichín* (on the failure to write the
lenited *f* see p. 138), i.e. St Féichín of Fore, on whom see
SEHI, pp. 458f.

Comgell. Unidentified. See Note on II, 1.

Gille-Críst mac Finguni. Unidentified. For *Gille-Críst* see
Note on III, 8. *Finguine* is a fairly common name; cf. *CGH*,
p. 645, and the indexes to *AU*, *AI*, and *ESSH*. It appears to
have been used in Pictish as well as Gaelic; the four in *ESSH*
are all Picts, late seventh to eighth centuries.

Notes on the texts

i nn-a [f]ienasi. For the omission of lenited *f* see p. 138, and for that of *d* before *n*, p. 139. Standard M. Ir. spelling would be *i n-a fiadnaise*.

4. Mal-Coluim mac Molíni. Unidentified. On the name Mal-Coluim see Note on II, 9. *Molíne* seems to be an unknown name, but compare *Mailéne* or *Muiléne* in *CGH*, p. 704, *Mailín* in *AI* Index, apparently 'Little Bald One', from *mael* 'bald'. If so, we should read *Moilíni* or *Moelíni* here (on the spelling *o* for *ai* see p. 134), and I have so emended it, in the translation; but it is of course uncertain.

Cormac mac Cennédig. Unidentified. Both names are common; the second is Anglicised as 'Kennedy'.

5. Scáli Merlec. There can be no question but that this is Skillymarno, about 3 miles north of Old Deer. Early forms are *Skillemarnocht*, 1554; *Skalymarnoth*, 1558; *Skillimarne*, 1608; *Skillymarnoch*, 1752; see *PNA*, p. 115. The first word is a loan from Old Norse *skáli* 'hut', which was borrowed into Irish as *scál*, diminutive *scálán*, but in Scottish Gaelic in forms closer to the Norse, *sgàile* (which is what we have here), *sgàil*, and diminutives *sgàilean* and *sgàileag* (also *sgàlan* = Irish *scálán*). *Merlec* is clearly *meirlech* (genitive plural of *id.*), 'of the robbers'; therefore 'The Hut of the Robbers'. In Skillymarno, the *á* is reduced because only lightly stressed; *meirlech* must have given *meàrlach*, as it has in some Sc. G. dialects; the *n* is probably the result of partial assimilation at a distance to the nasal *m*; and *-o* is a very common Anglicisation of final *-ach* in names, cf. *CPNS*, p. 379 bottom. There is no point in Alexander's doubts, *PNA*, p. 115, and his *mo Ernoc* would not give *-marno*.

Comgell mac Caennaig. Unidentified. On *Comgell* see Note on II, 1. *Caennaig* (spelling for *Cainnig*, see pp. 127 and 133) is genitive of *Cainnech*, see Notes on II, 9, 18 and III, 1.

6. taesec Clande Canan. See pp. 111ff.

7. gonige in gorthe mór. *Gorthe* has been read by previous writers, including the present one, as *gort lie*, and rendered 'Great-Rock-field' (Stokes, Stuart, etc.), or as a place-name,

71

Notes on the texts

significantly untranslated (Macbain, Cameron), though Anderson suggests reading *gort liath mór* 'large grey cornfield', which is not a happy emendation or interpretation. Fraser however read *gort/he*, which is certainly correct; and I followed this reading in *Ériu*, XVI, 95, while emending to *gort lie*, taking this as *lie* for *liaic*, nominative for accusative (which is of course possible at this date), and regarding it (though not explicitly) as 'field-stone', which is preferable to 'rock-field'. But though Fraser did not comment on his *gorthe* it is clear from his translation, 'up to the great standing stone', that he took it as *coirthe*, 'pillar-stone, standing stone, menhir', with eclipsis of *c*- after the definite article in the accusative, spelt *g*- (cf. *i gginn* just below, and p. 143); cf. Auchencorth near Edinburgh, *Achadh na Coirthe*,[1] *CPNS*, p. 143. This is certainly right.

There are a number of megalithic monuments in the neighbourhood of Deer. The 'Standing Stone' at Gaval, about 2½ miles north of Old Deer, on the 1″ Ordnance Map is an obvious candidate at first sight; but the 6″ map of 1872 calls this 'Stone Circle' (the other stones must have been removed in the interval), which seems to rule it out. A stone circle could not attract the name *coirthe* (unless perhaps it was one of the type with a circle of small stones and one much larger one outside it). Another possibility is the place Auchorthie (= the above *Achadh na Coirthe* or *an Choirthe*) about 4 miles north-west of Old Deer. There appears to be no standing stone there now, but there must have been one once, and presumably a conspicuous one, to give its name to the place.

i gginn in fris. In *i gginn*, 'at the end', the nasalised *c*- is spelt *gg*-; see pp. 142f. Spelt in M. Ir. *i cinn*, Mod. Ir. *i gcionn*. The word *fris* was always read as *fius*, and not unnaturally left untranslated, or treated as a (peculiar) place-name, 'the Pius' or 'the Fius', though Stokes, followed by Stuart, guessed, without any apparent basis, that *in fius* might mean 'the hither'. Fraser however saw that the true reading is almost certainly

[1] Or *in Choirthe*; the word is both masc. and fem. early. In the present passage *mór* in the accusative suggests it is masc.

in fris,[1] though he was unable to translate it, and there can be little doubt he was right; see the Textual Notes. It is evident that *in fris* is a spelling for *in phris* (cf. p. 137), genitive of *pres* 'thicket, copse' (as was suggested to me by A. O. Anderson in a letter of 29 March 1953); a Scottish Gaelic word; cf. *CPNS*, pp. 419f. The whole phrase means, therefore, 'at the end of the thicket'.

8. **is nesu d' Aldín Alenn** (text *aldin*), 'which is nearest to A.A.'. *Aldin* has naturally been identified with Aden in Old Deer, which was *Alden* in 1365, *Aldene* in 1406; and *Auldane, Audane, Auden, Aden*, etc., from 1492 on (*PNA*, p. 3). For an Irish place-name which could be the same cf. *Ailldin* in County Cork (*OG*, p. 20). But in that case, with *Aldin* of the text a place-name, it would then be difficult to account for the addition of *Alenn*. Such an addition would be either an adjective or a qualifying genitive, and in either case its purpose would be to define more clearly the place-name, such definition often implying a contrast; as it might be **Aldin Mór*, 'Great Aldin' by contrast with **Aldin Bec*, 'Little Aldin', or **Aldin Buchan*, 'Aldin of Buchan',[2] and not some other *Aldin*. But no such adjective is known, nor any regional name of the sort. *Alenn* looks like the genitive of an *n*-stem, therefore with nominative **Aile*, but this gets us no further; by his 'of the meadow' (*PNA*, p. 3) Alexander seems to be thinking of the Sc. G. *àilean*, whose genitive would in any case be *alein*, and at any rate hardly *alenn*, in Deer. One thinks of Ailenn the capital of the kings of Leinster, but the genitive of this is *Ailinne*.

Another explanation has occurred to some, that *aldin* may be for *ailltín*, diminutive of *allt*. This word means 'height, cliff' in Irish, but in Sc. G. it developed in meaning to 'a rocky gully with a stream flowing down it', and this was probably so when the various *Garvalds* in the Anglian part of S.E. Scotland were named in the tenth to twelfth centuries. It still retains to the present day, in some dialects, the sense of 'a stream between steep

[1] See above, p. 27.
[2] Cf., for example, Irish *Temair Luachra*, 'Tara of [the district of] Luachair'.

banks',[1] though in others (and in standard Sc. G.) it now means simply 'a burn', regardless of the surroundings. Compare *CPNS*, p. 140. If so, then the meaning would be 'The Rocky Gully of *Aile*', or whatever *alenn* represents. The only difficulty here is the *ld* for *lt* or *llt*; but this is easily explained. In most Gaelic dialects 'pre-aspiration' developed in the *llt* group, so that *allt* is /*auLht*/ or /*aL:ht*/, but in some it did not, including the dialects now spoken nearest to Buchan, those of Strathspey, Moray, and Nairnshire. In such cases the representation of *t* is a voiceless non-aspirate lenis, which is phonemically /*d*/, so that the spelling *aldin* for *ailltín* is quite natural. Moreover, it can be paralleled in a Latin charter for Aberdeenshire, one of Malcolm (?III), in which the Clachie Burn near Bennachie is called *Alde Clothi* (*Reg. Reg. Scott.*, I, 162), and compare a sixteenth-century source quoted in *PNA*, p. 210, *Alde Clothi quod sonat Latine 'rivulus petrosus'*. This is early Gaelic *Allt Clochaidh*. The explanation of *aldin* as a derivative of *allt* was proposed by Diack in *RC*, XLI, 110ff., and, though most of his article on it is without value, the suggestion is sound. But if *aldin alenn* is 'The Little Gully of Aile', the place cannot be Aden, Diack notwithstanding. Kinaldie or Kinnadie near the source of the Stuartfield Burn about three miles south of Old Deer is very likely *Ceann Alltaidh*; cf. *PNA*, p. 75; but that is no reason to identify the *allt* in question with the *aldin* of Deer. The '*thicket* which is nearest to the Little Gully of Aile' cannot of course be identified.

ó Dubuci go Lurchari. Neither place is identified, nor is it possible to explain the names. Fraser suggests that *Dubuci* might be *dubbuci* 'black mire', but without explanation (*Sc. G. St.*, v, 63, n. 5). He probably meant *dub* 'black' and *buice*, which however is an abstract noun meaning 'softness', etc., and there is no evidence known to me for a concrete sense, 'mire' or other.

etar sliab 7 achad, 'both moor (or "rough-grazing") and

---

[1] E.g. with some of the informants used by the writer in collecting material for the Linguistic Survey of Scotland.

Notes on the texts

(pasture-)field'. The idiom *etar...acus...* 'both...and...' is of course familiar; 'between...and...' (Macbain, Cameron) is wrong here.

9 i ssaeri, etc., see pp. 14, 21 and 89f.

7 a bennacht...ticfa ris. On these words see pp. 12 and 85f. On the phrase *ticfa ris* see the Glossarial Index, *s.v. tic-*. Compare also the deeds in the Book of Kells (see pp. 86f.), two of which similarly have a curse on anyone who shall 'come against' their provisions, using the verbal phrase *tic i n-agid*.

VI

1. **Colbán.** 'Earl Colbanus' witnessed a St Andrews grant;[1] took part in the attack on England by William the Lion in 1173;[2] and witnessed a Lindores charter between 1178 and 1182.[3] Magnus son of Earl Colbanus witnessed a St Andrews grant,[4] and one by William Comyn, earl of Buchan, between 1219 and 1233, in which he is called son of 'Earl Colbeyn'.[5] Colbán is no doubt the Old Norse name *Kolbeinn*, Old Danish *Kulben* and Old Swedish *Kolben*, which appears in Domesday Book as *Colben* and in the Durham *Liber Vitae* as *Colbain, Colbein, Colben*, and *Colbanus*.[6] Magnus is of course a well-known Norse name. It looks very much as if Colbán was of Scandinavian origin or descent.[7] Compare the Note to III, 7, on Algune son of Arcill.

in mormér Buchan. This is the reading of the text, not *Colbain mormér Buchan*; see Textual Notes. This involves an unusual use of the definite article (*mormaer Buchan* would be regular for 'the mormaer of Buchan'), but one that is by no means unknown in the early language; cf. RIA *Conts., I,* 2, col. 188. On *Buchan* as genitive see the Note on 1, 3.

[1] *Lib. Cart. St. And.*, pp. 259f. [2] *ESSH*, II, 278n.
[3] *ESSH*, II, 180, n. 3. [4] *Lib. Cart. St. And.*, p. 270.
[5] *ITAAB*, II, 428.
[6] *NPE*, p. 83; *PCPN*, p. 306; *SPLY*, p. 177.
[7] Thurneysen notes in *ZCP*, XIX, 209, that the early Irish **Columbán* should have become **Colbán* regularly, and that the actual *Colmán* is irregular. Nevertheless, Colmán is common and **Colbán* never occurs in Irish, so that it is unlikely we should regard Colbán here as Gaelic.

75

Notes on the texts

Éua ingen Garnait. It is usually assumed that her father was the Gartnait of III, I, and IV, I; that this Gartnait was mormaer of Buchan; and that Colbán was mormaer of Buchan in the right of his wife. This may be probable, and is supported by the likelihood that his family was of Scandinavian origin, but can hardly be said to be certain; cf. the Note on III, I. *Éua* is the Latin, from the Hebrew. *Garnait* is a secondary form of *Gartnait*, with *rtn* simplified to *rn*; see p. 136.

a ben phústa. The normal form of this is of course *pósta*, from *pós-*, but in some modern Sc. G. dialects the verb is *pùs-*, and as it is also *poos-* in Manx, participle *poost*, this development is likely to be quite old; and may well be genuine here. Cf. O'Rahilly, *Irish Dialects Past and Present* (Dublin, 1932), p. 138n.; but his suggested Norse influence seems improbable.

2. Donnachac mac Síthig, unidentified. The first name is peculiar. It seems like a form of *Donnchad* (see Note on V, I), and curiously enough, it does look remarkably like what would be the modern pronunciation of the name in dialects not very far removed from Buchan. In all Irish and Scottish Gaelic dialect an epenthetic vowel developed between the *n* and the *ch*; and in the Scottish Gaelic of northern mainland Inverness-shire, and almost all mainland Ross-shire final *-adh* has become -[ǝk], phonemically -/ǝg/, for which *-ac* would be a very natural spelling. However, in Strathspey, partly in Nairnshire and Moray, in the Gaelic-speaking region of Banff-shire, and in Braemar the whole syllable was lost; but this could have been secondary to the development to -/ǝg/. Nevertheless, all this is almost certainly a coincidence. There is no really clear evidence that epenthesis can have been as old as the earlier twelfth century (but see p. 135); and as for the development to -/ǝg/, this itself presupposes the prior change of /ð/ to /γ/ (of which there is no other trace in Deer), which happened first everywhere in Gaeldom, but which was scarcely beginning before the late twelfth century. It is not probable therefore that *Donnachac* can be explained in this way, particularly since the ordinary spelling occurs elsewhere in Deer four times, two of them in no. VI itself; see below. The explanation may be, rather that this is some sort of hypocoristic form of a name in *Donn-* (very likely of *Donnchad* itself), comparable to the known *Donnacán* (*CGH*, pp. 593f.). The *ch* might well be a misspelling for *c*, and the *-ac* might perhaps be for *-ác* from *-óc*, if this development is early enough; supposing therefore a hypocoristic **Donnacóc*.

Síthech is evidently from the adjective *sídach*, *síthach*, *síthech*, 'peaceful', etc. As a name, it seems not to occur in Irish, except in the surname *Mac Síthigh*, 'Mac Sheehy', a family of Scottish gallowglasses who claimed descent from Síthech, great-grandson of Domhnall the eponymous ancestor of the Scottish Mac-Donnells. The personal name appears as *Sythach*, a *nativus* of Badenoch, in a composition between Walter Comyn and the bishop of Moray, 1232–42; *Reg. Episc. Morav.* no. 76, p. 84.

tœsech Clenni Morgainn. On this see p. 110.

3. **ria Colum Cilli.** *Ria* is a fairly common M. Ir. by-form of the preposition *ri*, much commoner than the rare *ro* which is found in II, 14.

4. **ar chuit cetri dabach.** It is clear that the sense of *ar* here is the common one of 'in exchange for', as in the other examples with this verb. Macbain, who took *ro báid* as 'dedicated', translated *ar* as 'on', though it is difficult to see what sense he extracted from that; Cameron followed, and suggested that the monastic lands were freed from all exactions except 'the proportion of four davochs on which a tax was payable to the King' (*CL*, p. 242). Anderson, who translated 'upon the extent of four dabachs', thought it meant the monks were immune from taxation on four davochs only, the rest of their property being liable to the same taxation as other monasteries and churches (*ESSH*, II, 180f.). Fraser's 'in consideration of' must be right, and the meaning must be 'in return for the dues payable (= *cuit*) on four davochs'; in other words, Colbán and Éva 'quenched' all the grants, and their price for doing so was that the monastery paid them the *cuit*, the dues, chargeable on four davochs'-worth of the tax described in the next words. See pp. 116f., 119, 121ff.

don-í thíssad ar, 'of that which should devolve on' (*don-í*, preposition *do/de* 'of' plus definite article plus demonstrative *í*; past-subjunctive of *tic ar* 'falls on, devolves on, pertains to', see RIA *Conts.*, *dodénta–dúus*, col. 301, ll. 25ff.). Cf. Fraser's 'of the payments due in respect of'. That is to say, of those taxes which fall on, are payable by, due from.

5. **ar ard-mandaidib Alban cu cotechenn 7 ar [a] h-ard-chellaib.** The word written *mandaidib* is no doubt the dative plural of *mennat*, with original *nn* spelt *nd*, as very commonly in M. Ir.; *d* written for *t* (= [*d*]) by pronunciation-spelling, which is not rare in M. Ir.; and unexpected *a* for *e*, on which see p. 129. According to the RIA *Conts.*, *M*, col. 104, l. 31, the meaning is '*a place of abode* in wide sense (of locality or district, not of dwelling house)'. This is slightly ambiguous; certainly it does not mean a house in the sense of bricks and mortar, but the examples show that it *can* mean 'house', etc., in the sense of the place where one dwells, and not only 'locality or district'. In the present case the meaning appears to be an ecclesiastical foundation, but distinct from a church, presumably therefore a monastery – not the buildings, but in the abstract the monastery as a 'going concern', a home of monks. Professor Donaldson points out that this is exactly the meaning of '[religious] house'. One may translate therefore 'on the chief [religious] houses of Scotland in general and on its chief churches'. These would be monasteries and churches which had dependent foundations. Stuart notes in *BD*, p. ciiin. that the church of Kinkell had seven subordinate churches, and that of Mortlach had a subordinate monastery at Cloveth, and five churches. On the meaning of the whole passage see pp. 123f.

6. **Bróccín**, evidently the same person as the Brócín of VII, 11. A royal judge called *Brocin* appears in Latin documents between about 1150 and 1173 (*SHR*, XLV, 1966, 21), and it is highly probable he is the same person. Anderson treats the name as the diminutive of *brocc*, 'badger' (*ESSH*, II, 181, n. 2), but this would need *Bruiccín*, and the *o* must be long: compare the Irish *Bróccíne*, *Bróccéne*, *Bróccán*, *CGH*, p. 526; *Brócán*, *AI*, p. 449.

Notes on the texts

Cormac abb Turbruaid. See Notes on III, 9, and VII, 11. He is apparently not otherwise known.

Morgunn mac Donnchid 7 Gilli-Petair mac Donnchaid. Unidentified. On the name *Morgunn* see Note on II, 2; on *Donnchad*, that on V, 1; *Gille-Petair*, 'Servant of St Peter', is a name in *Gille-*, see Note on III, 1. These two sons of Donnchad are very likely brothers, and as they are mentioned first among the lay witnesses they may perhaps be sons of the toísech of Clann Morgainn of the beginning of VI.

7. **Mal-[F]æchín.** Unidentified, but see Note on V, 3.

8. **dá mac Matni.** Unidentified, but compare Gille-'ndrias mac Matni in VII, 12, who may well be one of these two sons. The name is obscure; the *Maithne* of *CGH*, p. 697 can hardly be compared as it seems to be a spelling for the familiar *Maine*. Nor is it likely to be the genitive of the *Matain* of II, 4; see Note.

mathe Buchan 'the good men (i.e. "nobles", etc.) of Buchan', a common usage. It is the equivalent of the *probi homines* of VII, 1.

'n-a [f]iaidnaisse. On the omitted *f* see p. 138.

9. **i nHelain.** Ellon, the chief town of Buchan. Early forms are *Ellon*, 1157; *Helin*, 1165, 1183; *Elone*, 1328 (*PNA*, p. 53); the *H-* is purely graphic. Ellon in Strathspey is *eilean* 'island', but this is from older *ailén*, *oilén*, and the form in Deer can hardly stand for this. On Alexander's *àilein* (= *àilean*), see Note on V, 8; the *ài-* of this would hardly be spelt *e-*, nor the *-ean* spelt *-ain*. Dative *Elain* rather suggests an *n*-stem, nominative **Ela* (which would of course rule out Alexander's *eilean* or *àilein*), but no etymology suggests itself.

On the significance of this document see pp. 88f.

1. **omnibus probis hominibus**; i.e. nobles, clerics, burgesses, and other responsible, politically and socially significant members of society.

2. **sciatis.** Cf. *Reg. Reg. Scott.*, I, 75f.

quieti et immunes, 'quit and immune', i.e. 'free'.

3. **laicorum officio et exactione indebita**: on the meaning of these phrases see pp. 93f.

4. **Banb**, Banff. The name appears to be *banbh*, 'sucking-pig', originally perhaps a river-name (alternative name for the Deveron?); the Welsh cognate *banw* occurs as the name of streams. See *CPNS*, pp. 231f.

5. **Abberdeon**, Aberdeen. On the name and its form see Note on III, 6.

6. For the constantly repeated **teste** compare the *testis* following the names of every witness to the document no. 4 in the Book of St Chad discussed on p. 85.

7. **Gregorio episcopo de Dún Callden.** Gregory occurs already as bishop of Dunkeld (on the place-name see the Note on III, 4) in a document of *c.* 1135[1] (*EC*, no. 105), and died in 1169 (see *ESSH*, II, 267). He had therefore become bishop not later than *c.* 1135, but his predecessor Cormac was still alive in 1130 (see Note to III, 4).

    Andrea episcopo de Catenes. Andrew became bishop of Caithness not later than 1146, and died in 1184; *ESSH*, II, 182, n. 2, and 308. He witnesses, e.g. *EC*, no. 189, 1147–50; also *EC*, 207 and 224, and is grantee in 221, witnessed by the above Gregory, Earl Duncan (see Note on l. 9 below), Gillandres of Scone (cf. Note on l. 12 below), and Alwyn mac Archil; all three *c.* 1150. *EC*, 221 and 224 are witnessed also by Gregory bishop of Dunkeld and Earl Duncan, among others. The exact expansion of the *cāt* of the text is not clear, but *Catenes* is the most probable, cf. *Cateness* in *Reg. Episc. Brechin.*, I, no. 1; *Katenes* in *EC*, 221 and 224, *Cateneis* in no. 207, and *Cathanesia* in the *De Situ Albanie* (cf. *CPS*, p. 135, *CPNS*, p. 108).

8. **Samsone episcopo de Brechin.** He is not known to have been bishop before King David's death in 1153, and the first document outside Deer in which his name occurs as such is not earlier than 1156 (*ESSH*, II, 182, n. 3). But there is no reason to suppose he was not bishop earlier than this. Professor Barrow

---

[1] Anderson gives him as already bishop at some time between 1131 and 1136, referring to *EC*, no. 134 (*ESSH*, II, 182, n. 1); which however Lawrie dates *c.* 1141.

notes (by letter) that David I granted a market to the bishop and céili Dé of Brechin about 1150, which shows that there *was* a bishop there before David's death, and that if it was not Samson we must suppose some previous, unknown bishop who has left no trace.

9. **Doncado comite ¦de Fíb.** On the name see Note on V, 1. *Fíb* is the normal early Gaelic for Fife, modern *Fíobh*. Duncan became earl of Fife not later than 1136, died in 1154 and was succeeded by another Duncan (*ESSH*, II, 182, n. 4, and 362, n. 4; and *EC*, p. 318). He may have been son of the Gille-Mícheil earl of Fife of *EC*, n. 84, *c.* 1130, and cf. *ESSH*, II, 318; and Note on III, 1, above. Earl Duncan is known in documents of King David's time (e.g. he witnesses *EC*, 221, *c.* 1150, grant to Andrew bishop of Caithness, along with Gregory bishop of Dunkeld, Gillandres of Scone, and Alwyn mac Archil; and *EC*, 224, *c.* 1150, along with Leod abbot of Brechin and Alwyn filius Archil); but Deer appears to be the only place where his earldom is named, cf. Lawrie in *EC*, p. 425.

Mal-Mori d' Athótla. *Mal-Moire*, 'Servant of St Mary'; see Note on II, 6. *D' Athotla*: *d'* for *de* is unexpected in a Latin document, and what we have here and below is clearly the M. Ir. *de*, the vowel of which is commonly elided before another vowel in M.Ir. *Athótla*, spelling for *Athfhótla*, 'New Ireland', i.e. Atholl; see *CPNS*, pp. 228f.

According to the Orkneyinga Saga, the father of Matad, earl of Atholl, was a Mael-Muire, who was brother of King Malcolm III; cf. Anderson, *ESSH*, II, 182, n. 5, who doubts the relation to Malcolm, but hesitatingly accepts that the present 'Mal-Mori' was this Mael-Muire and father of Matad (on the ground that he is here called *d' Athótla*; he does not envisage the possibility of any other member of this family being meant). The question of dates is important here. Matad is earl of Atholl in the Orkneyinga Saga in years identified as 1134, 1136, and not earlier than 1139[1] (see *ESSH*, II, 139, n. 2 – p. 140, where

---

[1] Dr A. B. Taylor, translator of the Orkneyinga Saga (Edinburgh, 1938), kindly tells me that he thinks it cannot have been much after 1139 if at all.

Notes on the texts

Anderson says that this 'has no great historical value'; and *op cit.*, pp. 192f.). *Madeth comes* witnesses two Dunfermline charters, the former (*EC*, no. 74) dated by Lawrie *c.* 1128 and the latter (*EC*, no. 94) dated by him 1130 (but Anderson, *ESSH*, II, 139, n. 2 puts both between 1128 and 1136); and *Maddoc comes*, presumably intended for the same, witnesses another Dunfermline charter (*EC*, no. 127), dated by Lawrie *c.* 1140 and by Anderson, *loc. cit.*, as between 1128 and 1147. He also witnessed the original charter of foundation of Melrose, the date of which is *c.* 1136 (*EC*, 141; cf. *Reg. Reg. Scott.*, I, no. 41; Professor Barrow kindly informs me that Anderson's (and Lawrie's) date 1143–4 in *ESSH*, II, 182, n. 5, l. 4, was inferred because he mistakenly assumed that the set of witnesses in which '*Madd-*' occurs belonged to the second foundation charter of Melrose, not the first. '*Maduc consul*' witnesses a grant by David I, *EC*, no. 100, and '*Madd- comes*' another, *ibid.* no. 101; but neither of these can be dated, though they are evidently not earlier than 1136 (see *EC*, p. 341). Richard of Hexham *s.a.* 1139 lists hostages given in that year to King Stephen as the sons of Earl Gospatric, of Hugh de Moreville, and of Earl Fergus (of Galloway) and the sons of two earls of Scottia (i.e. Scotland north of the Forth), namely Earl *Mal-* and Earl *Mac-* (Anderson, *Scottish Annals from English Chroniclers*, London, 1908, pp. 214f.). Professor Barrow suggests to me that the first is Malise of Strathearn and the second Matad of Atholl (though the contraction is that usual for *-us*, therefore *Macus*, a known Scottish name, of course); and since sons given as hostages were only so given while their fathers were alive, this would mean that Matad was still living in 1139. Professor Barrow (by letter) thinks Matad died soon after 1139,[1] and left two young sons; Malcolm, perhaps born about 1132, who succeeded Matad as earl of Atholl, and Harold, perhaps born about 1134, who afterwards became earl of Orkney, these dates being indicated by the fact that Scandinavian sources suggest

[1] He notes that the fact Matad does not witness the second foundation charter of Melrose, 1143–4, suggests that he was dead by this time.

Notes on the texts

Harold was about five years old in 1139. He notes that between about 1139 and about 1154 or later the records are silent about earls of Atholl. He makes the ingenious suggestion, which removes the difficulty of an improbably early date for no. VII, that its *Mal-Mori* is not Mael-Muire father of Matad but an unknown younger brother of Matad's, called after his father, who was acting as guardian for his young nephews and as *de facto* earl of Atholl but not *de jure*; which would account for his being named as witness in VII between the earls of Fife and Angus, but being called 'of Atholl', not 'earl of Atholl'. If so, this would put no. VII not before the accession of Matad but after his death. One should add that in *ESSH*, II, 139, n. 2, Anderson says that Matad died between 1152 and 1161, and p. 182, n. 5, that he was earl in 1143 or 1144 and 'still in ?1152'; but unfortunately he leaves his source in darkness, and there appears to be no evidence whatever for this.

10. **Ggille-Bríte comite d' Éngus.** Gille-Brigte earl of Angus; 'Servant of St Bridget' (a name in *Gille-*, see Note on III, 1). The *Gg-* is peculiar, but the scribe wrote the same at first in *Gille-Comded* in l. 10, though he corrected this afterwards. *Bríte* for *Brigte* is a pronunciation-spelling; see p. 140. On the spelling *Éngus* for *Oengus* or *Aengus* see p. 135. Gille-Brigte is known to have been earl in sources as old as a time not earlier than 1157 and not later than 1159, and to have died after 1187 (*ESSH*, II, 182, n. 6); he is not otherwise known to have been so in David I's reign, but this does not, of course, mean that he was not.

Gille-Comded mac Æd. Apparently unidentified. Another *Gille-* name; the second element is *Coimde*, genitive *Coimded*, 'the Lord', compare *AU*, 1225, *Gilla in Coimdeg* (spelling for *Coimded*). *Æd*: the genitive *Æda* would be expected (as appears correctly, spelt *Eda*, in II, 1); but in a Latin document the scribe might feel some embarrassment about giving a Gaelic genitive, and yet could not bring himself to Latinise it as *Ædi* or the like. He does the same with *Ferdomnach* in l. 11, and cf. *Gille-'ndrias* for *Gille-'ndréis*, l. 12. However, he did write *mac* instead

83

of *filius*, as was often done in Latin charters at this time (cf. Note on Algune mac Arcill, III, 7).

11. **Brócín.** See the Note on VI, 6. There is nothing to show that he was *not* flourishing earlier than *c.* 1150.

Cormac de Turbrud, abbot of Turriff, see the Note on VI, 6. *Turbrud* is a spelling for *Turbruad* (see Note on III, 9); the Latin scribe probably did not trouble very much about the correct orthography. Nothing is known about his dates, outside Deer.

Ádam mac Ferdomnac. Unidentified. The name *Ferdomnach* is well evidenced in Ireland, see *CGH*, p. 630 and *AU* and *AI* indexes. Like *Æd* above, it is given here in the nominative instead of the genitive, *Ferdomnaig*, in the Latin context.

12. **Gille-'ndrias mac Matni.** Unidentified, but see the Note on VI, 8; also for the father's name. Gillandres of Scone, who witnesses *EC*, no. 221, *c.* 1150, the grant to Andrew bishop of Caithness mentioned above, may be the same person, but he looks like a cleric, whereas the present one seems rather to be a layman. A name in *Gille-* (see Note on III, 1), plus *Aindrias*, 'St Andrew' (but the genitive, *Gille-Aindréis*, would be expected; cf. Note on l. 10). The name is Anglicised as Gillanders.

Abberdeon. See Note on III, 6.

HISTORICAL COMMENTARY

I. PURPOSE, DATE AND GENUINENESS OF THE NOTES

What was the purpose of the Gaelic entries in the Book of Deer, and when were they written? Why should the monks wish to write up a record of the grants of land and immunities previously made to their monastery at the time they did, whenever that may have been?

In Anglo-Saxon England the writing of charters and other formal deeds, often granting land to religious bodies, in Latin or Anglo-Saxon, properly witnessed by clerical and lay notables, frequently dated, commonly detailing the boundaries of the lands granted, and sometimes invoking blessings on those who fulfil their provisions and curses on those who violate them, are a familiar feature.[1] The earliest are as old as the late seventh century. Something of the same sort is found contemporaneously in Wales. There are several deeds written in the ninth and even late eighth centuries, in a mixture of Latin and Old Welsh, in the Book of St Chad, an eighth-century illuminated manuscript of the Gospels belonging at the time to one of the Welsh monasteries of St Teilo;[2] and of the numerous mixed Latin and Old Welsh deeds in the mid twelfth-century Book of Llandaff, most appear to be copies or adaptations of older ones. An interesting example is the Chad document no. 4,[3] of the ninth century, telling how a certain Ris and others (names illegible) gave a piece of land, whose boundaries and the dues to which it is subject are briefly described in Old Welsh. The names of the clerical and lay witnesses (headed by *Deus omnipotens*) are then listed,

---

[1] See for instance F. Harmer, *English Historical Documents of the Ninth and Tenth Centuries* (Cambridge, 1914). Examples with a curse are nos. III, p. 6; IV, p. 8; X, p. 15.

[2] See for these, and for the Llandaff deeds, J. G. Evans and J. Rhys, *The Text of the Book of Llan Dav* (Oxford, 1893). On the dates of the Chad documents see *LHEB*, pp. 46f.

[3] Evans and Rhys, p. xlv.

each name followed by '*testis*'; and it ends, in Latin, 'Whoever shall keep [these provisions] shall be blessed, and who shall break them shall be accursed of God.'

No such documents are known among the Gaelic peoples before the eleventh and twelfth centuries, and it is likely that it was not their custom previously, any more than this was *generally* the case with the Welsh, to preserve formal written records, having legal force, of the gifts of land, etc., granted to corporations and individuals. They possessed them, and were known to possess them, and that was enough. The Normans, of course, with their strong sense of the necessity for proper legal forms, brought with them eventually to all parts of the British Isles the use of the regular Latin charter, fully witnessed, and it is generally supposed that the appearance of such written grants in Ireland and Scotland is entirely due to Norman influence. The oldest extant regular Norman-Latin charters in Scotland are granted by the sons of Malcolm III; that is, by Kings Duncan II in 1094 and Edgar (1097–1107); and by Alexander I (1107–24) and David I (1124–53); but they do not become common till the time of David I. However, notes on older grants (in Latin) are preserved, such as those by Macbeth (1040–57) to the Céili Dé of Loch Leven, and such notes continue to the time of Edgar. According to Liam Price,[1] the practice was brought to Ireland in the twelfth century by the newly arrived monastic orders, of which the first house was Mellifont, founded soon after 1142. The oldest Irish instances of recorded grants are found in the famous Book of Kells, like the Book of St Chad an illuminated manuscript of the Gospels of the eighth century, the greatest manuscript belonging to the Columban church in Ireland. Here records of seven land-grants, to or by, or records of purchases by, the monks of Kells have been written in Irish in blank spaces on fos. 6, 7 and 27;[2] and a further five, evidently originally in the same manuscript on pages now lost,

---

[1] *Celtica*, VI, 123.

[2] Edited and translated by J. O'Donovan, *Miscellany of the Irish Archaeological Society*, I (1846), 128ff., and edited by Mac Niocaill, *NLC*, pp. 10ff.; see also *SEHI*, pp. 753ff.

are known in an early seventeenth-century copy in the British Museum.[1] They were apparently all entered at the same time, in the late twelfth century, though the dates referred to are various, the earliest being between 1033 and 1049 and the latest between 1160 and 1166.[2] Of the seven still extant in the Book of Kells, all but this last one belong ostensibly to a time before 1142, and even if they were entered into Kells after the foundation of Mellifont it seems highly probable that these are copies from genuine older records. In one of them, the earliest, King Conchobor Ua Mael-Shechlaind, having violated the protection of the monastery, makes atonement by granting the church of Kildalkey and its lands 'to God and to Columba till Doomsday', exempt from a variety of dues and services detailed. There follows a list of the sureties (N.B., not merely witnesses) who according to Irish legal practice guaranteed the observance of the conditions; and it ends with a blessing on every king who keeps them and a curse on every king who violates them. Another, dating from between 1128 and 1140,[3] and therefore more or less contemporary with the documents in Deer, as we shall see, records a grant by the monastery of Kells of two townlands 'to God and to Columba and to Bishop Ua Cellaig'. The representative grantors are the abbot, the priest, the *fer légind*, and the vice-steward, and it was done 'in the witness of'[4] the king of Breifne and other nobles.

It is to be noted that most of the above mentioned Welsh and Irish deeds are not written on separate parchments or engrossed in cartularies, but were entered in blank spaces or margins in some one of the relevant monastery's most valuable religious manuscripts, where they would be safely preserved by virtue of the careful preservation of the sacrosanct manuscript itself. Their existence would be well-known to the monks, and they could easily be produced whenever necessary. It was not, of

---

[1] Edited by Mac Niocaill, *op. cit.*
[2] See Kenney, *SEHI, loc. cit.*, and *NLC*, p. 34n. Mac Niocaill dates this one 1161; see p. 92 n. 4 below. The latest of the five newly edited copies from British Museum Add 4791 is not later than 1161; the earliest, not earlier than 1106.   [3] 1133, according to *NLC*, p. 28.   [4] *I fiadnaise.*

course, a Norman practice to record deeds in this fashion, though it was an Anglo-Saxon one. Indeed the latest editor of the Kells grants emphasises their close similarity to the Anglo-Saxon ones.[1] The upshot of all that has been said is that though the full charter as we know it in later mediaeval times is certainly of Norman origin, the Celtic peoples did occasionally[2] make written records of deeds, with the names of grantors and grantees, land-boundaries, mention of dues, lists of witnesses, and formulae of blesses and curses, before the period of probable or possible Norman influence, though not indeed before that of Anglo-Saxon. Moreover, the relevance of it all to the entries in the Book of Deer is very striking, particularly the Welsh examples, both the early ones in the Book of St Chad and the later ones in the Book of Llandaff. Some of the technical phraseology in Deer is closely like or identical with that in the Book of Kells (a monastery which, like Deer, belonged to the Columban church). Set in this context, there is nothing unusual or surprising about Deer (apart from certain of the formulations peculiar to it, to be discussed below), and the only surprising thing is the fact that these notes have been preserved at all, and from such a remote region, when all else has been lost.

The clue to the questions asked at the beginning of this section lies in entry no. VII. In this, the king firmly lays it down that the monastery is to be *free* ('quit and immune') from every kind of render of 'lay service', and from attempts to extort payments to which the claimants had no right.[3] It is evident that this charter is the culmination of a legal process which had been carried on for some time by the monks, who had previously argued their case in a court held at Banff and sworn oaths to its truth at a later court at Aberdeen; that they had been in fact suffering from improper extortions; and that part of the evi-

---

[1] *NLC*, pp. 8ff.

[2] Mac Niocaill quotes evidence which shows that the Irish clergy at least knew what a formal written grant was, as early as the eighth century, though it hardly proves that they made use of them; *NCL*, pp. 6ff.

[3] Compare e.g. the supposed grant by King Hungus to St Regulus of St Andrews, giving liberty to the inhabitants from the obligation to various services and *de inquietatione omnium saecularium exactionum* (*CPS*, p. 187).

dence produced by them was the Gaelic entries in the Book of Deer themselves, which must be what is meant by 'as is written in their book'. 'Lay service' here means the payment of taxes and tributes, and the performance of certain tasks such as repairing roads and bridges, normally due from lay tenants to their overlords; and the exaction of these is implicitly declared by the king to be improper – which is clearly what the monastery had been claiming. Finally, this is a true charter, or an approximation to one, in the sense that it is fully witnessed, by high clerical and lay witnesses.

As regards the date of no. VII, it is possible to infer this, within limits, from internal evidence, for details of which see the Notes to it. Unluckily, although something is known about the dates of many of the witnesses, very little of it helps us to give any sort of firm date. However, its granting must fall within the reign of David I, 1124–53, and since VII is unquestionably later than III, the last Gaelic entry (with IV) chronologically, it would not be older than 1131. Further, there is reason to think that the Mael-Muire of Atholl mentioned in it became guardian to the young sons of Earl Matad in or after 1139, and that he is witnessing it in this capacity (see the Note to VII, 9). It would be fair enough to date VII in broad terms between about 1140 and 1153. But it may be possible to pin it down to an exact year. It is probable that David I must have been present at the courts held at Banff and Aberdeen, and the only occasion when it seems fairly certain he was in the north-east is at the time of the foundation of Kinloss Abbey, the date of which may have been 1150.[1] It may be, therefore, that the successful culmination of the efforts by the monks of Deer to get their rights and immunities confirmed by royal charter came in the year 1150.

Seen in this light, the entries in the book, and particularly some of their peculiar features, begin to make sense. First, the fact that Hand C made two significant additions to what had been written before, as we have seen.[2] He rubbed out the last couple of words at the end of the present II on fo. 4*a* ('11*a*'), and

---

[1] *Reg. Reg. Scott.*, I, 114.   [2] See pp. 13f.

.aving re-written them smaller, squeezed in the words 'free from mormaer and toísech till Doomsday'. At the end of v he added two further lines, 'free of toísech till Doomsday; and his curse on everyone who shall come against it'. It is true that the first grant in v is explicitly stated to be 'in freedom till Doomsday'; but the second was not, as written by Hand B, and C felt obliged to add this. Further, C's own main entry, no. vi, not only makes it clear that the deed of 'quenching' of which it consists frees the monastery from all imposts (other than a defined payment in lieu of them), but also gives a list of witnesses, ending with 'all the "good men" of Buchan', and locates the act at Ellon. Again, the list of grants written by Hand A as contained in ii makes no mention anywhere at all of 'freedom', nor does it name any witnesses whatever. Moreover, as we have seen, the original closing section of ii ('ii*b*') was erased by Hand D, the last scribe to enter Gaelic material in the book. Why should he have done this? Not to make room for his own iii and iv, as there is plenty of room elsewhere in blanks in the MS, not to mention margins. It is highly improbable that D would coolly remove for good an account of a further gift or gifts to the monastery, since all record of them would thus be permanently lost. Yet the whole context, and the closing formula at the top of fo. 4*b*, shows clearly that what was removed must have been such a record. The only solution which makes sense is that D *re-wrote* what was already written here; and that the reason why he did this is that what was there before was unsatisfactorily worded. The analogy of what has just been noted suggests strongly that the reason why it was unsatisfactory was that it made no explicit mention in iii of the grant as being '*free* of all imposts', and that the witnesses of both iii and iv had been omitted, or perhaps rather, inadequately given. This last is the more likely, since even if we allow for Hand A's much larger writing he would still not have filled the page if he gave no witnesses at all. What D did was to repair these omissions after he had carefully rubbed out A's unsatisfactory account.

What is happening is, then, that at a certain stage some

aspects of the description of the monastery's possessions, of the conditions under which they came into its hands, and of the proof they really belonged to it, were felt to be unsatisfactorily set out; set out in such a way that they might not stand up in court, or at least in the new Norman type of court which the Celtic monks had to face at Banff and Aberdeen. So, quite simply, they emended the material entered by A and B – 'forged' would perhaps be too strong a word. The inadequacies may have been of two kinds. First, the names of the witnesses had been omitted, or some of them; or not given in proper style, saying who was abbot, who mormaer, and so on; or the grants had never been formally witnessed at all, and this had to be 'put right'. The fact that there is no attempt to name witnesses to the grants in 'IIa' may mean that D's corrections in his III and IV were quite genuine additions of real facts which had however been left out or incompletely stated by A. And then, there is this obviously all-important emphasis by C and D on the 'freedom' of the grants, something that A had wholly ignored and B partly so. This matter of 'freedom' was something that was much concerning the clergy in Wales, Ireland and Scotland, notably in the twelfth century. It may have represented to some degree an extension to the Celtic countries of the so-called 'Investiture Controversy' which was carried on in Europe in the late eleventh and early twelfth centuries, the struggle to free the church from lay control and from the usurpation of ecclesiastical offices by lay princes which had troubled it during the Dark Ages.[1] But the Celtic monasteries of the pre-Norman period had been notoriously liable to lay interference and control, and the 'lay abbot' is a well-known character. Hence a stress on 'freedom' is found in documents earlier than the last quarter of the eleventh century, notably in the grant of Kildalkey between 1033 and 1049 in the Book of Kells, which was made to the monastery explicitly 'without tax, without tribute, without military service, without the quartering of men upon it by king or toísech'. The

---

[1] I am indebted to Monsignor David McRoberts for information about the 'Investiture Controversy'.

charters in the Book of Llandaff constantly lay weight on the 'freedom' of the lands granted;[1] and the Old Welsh document in it known as the Privilege of St Teilo,[2] which details the rights and immunities claimed by the monastery of Llandaff, says that these were granted 'free of every service to an earthly king without [exactions by] bailiff or royal steward, without [liability to] public court within the territory or outside it, without hosting, without distraint, without the duty of watch and ward', and adds that one of the privileges is the right to have a wharf for ships 'free from king and from everyone except for St Teilo and his church of Llandaff'. In Ireland about the same time the Synod of Cashel of 1101 tried to free the church from the obligation to pay tribute or tax to king or chief till Doomsday, but attempts in this direction were being made for some years before this Synod and continued after it.[3] At a later period, the latest deed in the Book of Kells, between 1160 and 1166, records how the High King of Ireland and the king of Meath induced the king of the Uí Loegaire to sell his claim to certain dues from the church of Ardbraccan, and it continues that the church with its lands is now free, both because of the general freedom of all churches and because of this purchase. In 1161, according to the Annals of Ulster, the head of the Columban church in Ireland 'freed' his churches in Meath and Leinster, and their tribute and control were put in his hands, 'for they were in subjection before that', i.e. were subject to secular lords. The 'general freedom of all churches' just referred to would be either that asserted at Cashel in 1101 or this 'freeing' of 1161.[4] In Scotland one may quote from the Latin grant[5] by Ethelred, earl of Fife, to the Céili Dé of Lochleven, given 'cum...omni libertate et sine exactione et petitione cuiusquam *in mundo episcopi vel regis vel comitis*'. Much later, William the Lion (1165–1214)

---

[1] E.g. *libera ab omni regali et seculari servitio; cum omni sua libertate sine ullo censu terreno*, etc.   [2] Evans–Rhys edition, pp. 120f.

[3] Cf. K. Hughes, *The Church in Early Irish Society* (London, 1966), pp. 263f.

[4] This is why Mac Niocaill dates this document 1161; cf. p. 87 n. 2. *EC*, no. 14, dated by Lawrie 1093–1107.

granted lands to Glasgow Cathedral 'free, quit, and absolved from every service and secular exaction and the claim of all men',[1] a phrase which was a common form in charters.

But the freedom of the church had become a matter of serious importance in Scotland already in the time of the regent Giric (878–89). According to some versions of the Chronicle of the Kings of Scots, he was 'the first to give liberty to the Scottish [i.e. Gaelic] Church, which was in servitude at that time after the custom and fashion of the Picts'.[2] This seems to mean that it had been the Pictish practice that lands held by the church were liable to pay secular dues and taxes; that this had not been the case with the Gaelic church; and that when the Gaels occupied Pictland the Gaelic church of the new 'Scot-land' within the bounds of the old Pictland came under the old Pictish dispensation, and continued under it until Giric freed it a generation later. If so, the Pictish custom must have re-asserted itself again, at any rate in Buchan, before the time when the notes in Deer were written; and secular lords had succeeded in re-imposing their claims on church lands, or were attempting to do so.

Since Hand A, the first scribe to enter Gaelic notes in Deer, makes no mention of 'freedom', it is a question whether he is a good deal older than the rest, not concerned with this, and writing long before the matter of the legal suit about the rights of Deer was envisaged. The facts that this hand is earlier in *type* than the others, that the datable grants in II were made by people living in the eleventh century, and that I has ostensibly little connection with the property of the monastery, have probably been responsible for what seems to be the generally held opinion that this is the case. The legend of the foundation of Deer could have been copied relatively early, at any time consistent with the probable dates of the script; and the brief, scrappy notes of gifts which constitute II could be made from memoranda which had been jotted down from time to time, also early, contemporaneously with their actual granting. If so, this copy could nevertheless not have been written before 1058, when Lulach,

---

[1] Cf. *Innes Review* (Spring 1970), p. 7.   [2] Cf. *ESSH*, I, 364f.

father of Mal-Snechta, died and his son became mormaer of
Moray, in which capacity he made his grant. This is all quite
reasonable; but it would seem not to be correct, for all that. We
have seen that III is almost certainly a re-writing of an older
version entered by Hand A; but III dates itself in the eighth year
of the reign of David I, or 1131–2. It follows that A was writing
in or after that year, and there is no palaeographical objection to
this. The fact that the language of all the entries is consistent with
the first half of the twelfth century is discussed below, pp. 151f.,
and there is nothing about it which must be as old as the eleventh.

If so, how do we explain what happened? I think it is probable
that all the entries were written with a view to bringing the
lawsuit – that they were the depositions, the visible evidence,
'written in their book' for this purpose. In that case, the history
of the Gaelic entries would be explained as follows: the first
thing the monks would do would be to establish the credentials
of their monastery and its foundation, as an ancient and honour-
able one on the part of none other than the original father of the
Columban, the Gaelic, church in Scotland, by writing up the
authentic account of how he and his disciple came to establish
it, on land granted by the mormaer of Buchan of the day 'in
freedom till Doomsday'. This was done by Hand A. It is a quite
typical Celtic foundation-legend. It could, of course, have been
modernised from an older written source or translated from
Latin, but there is no trace of evidence for this, and it is very
likely derived from the well-known oral tradition of the monastery. If its source was an older written one, it is at any rate improbable that it was as old as the Pictish period before the middle
of the ninth century, or it would hardly have described Bede
as 'the Pict'. Next, the writer listed brief notes describing about
a dozen land-grants made in the past to the monastery, three
instances of lords foregoing their dues, three 'quenchings',
and two annual feasts.[1] These were mere jottings, evidently

[1] The extraordinary idea, stated as a fact by Cameron (*CL*, p. 234) that II
'relates to the refounding of the Abbey of Deer in the tenth century' is
entirely baseless, nor does he advance any evidence in its support. Such
a 'refounding' is quite imaginary.

based on the common knowledge and tradition of the monastery's holdings among the monks, particularly no doubt the monastic steward. He would know from daily familiarity the names of all the various estates, and those of the grantors; but if there had ever been any formal witnesses, which is very doubtful, these were by now forgotten. If any prior or contemporary written accounts of any or all of the grants in II had existed when A wrote they would surely have been rather fuller than this, and copied out here in full to make them more impressive. The way they are noted strikes the reader as chaotic, without any proper chronological order, and this is just what would be expected of notes written up from oral information.[1] At a slightly later stage in the development of the preparations for the suit, the monks were brought to appreciate the importance of establishing the names of witnesses wherever possible, and of stressing the fact (or inventing the claim) that many of the grants were 'free' of all the taxes and other imposts summarised in note VII as 'lay service'. As a result, Hand B, whose training as a scribe was evidently in the same school as and contemporary with A's, wrote note v following immediately on A's II (including his lost '11*b*'), in which he mentions two deeds, one of them 'in freedom till Doomsday' and the other with a rather amateurish list of witnesses, among whom no clerics are specified. Subsequently, Hand C, of a slightly different type, wrote an important charter by the mormaer of Buchan and his wife and the toísech of Clann Morgainn, 'quenching' all the grants [in freedom] from all imposts, properly witnessed by an abbot, several lay witnesses, and all the nobles of Buchan, and given at the provincial capital of Ellon. By this time the importance of the claim to 'freedom' was so much appreciated that C fudged two previous documents by inserting this, at the end of '11*a*' and at the end of v. Finally, Hand D, probably a younger man who was more in touch than the older generation of Celtic scribes at Deer with the new movement towards Normanisation in the

---

[1] Macbain's idea (*TGSI*, XI, 140) that it is to be explained as due to 'Pictish influence in the succession' cannot be taken seriously.

North, rubbed out all that part of II which was on the lower half of fo. 4*a* (i.e., all '11*b*' except the closing formula on the next page), which had consisted of the record of two land-grants by Gartnait, who may have been mormaer of Buchan, and his wife Ete, daughter of Gille-Mícheíl; and re-wrote them so that they were more satisfactorily worded from the point of view of the lawsuit – mainly, perhaps, with a fuller and better-worded list of witnesses, and the clear statement that the first was 'free of all imposts'. Then last of all we have the record of the royal judgement at Aberdeen, in more or less proper Norman charter style, written by E, probably a younger scribe trained at Deer who had afterwards come far more completely under Norman influence than D had.[1]

For the dating of the whole process, the evidence on that of no. VII discussed on p. 89, though inconclusive, suggests that it was between about 1140 and 1153, and quite possibly in 1150. We have seen also that '11*b*' was apparently written by Hand A at some time in or after 1131 – not necessarily soon after. Indeed if Colbán the mormaer of Buchan of no. VI was really the successor as such of the Gartnait of III and IV, on which see the Notes, some time would presumably have to be allowed for the latter to have died before VI was written. It is not by any means to be supposed that the preparations for the suit must have occupied nearly twenty years. Still, litigation of this kind is something which could have extended over quite a number of years, especially in those leisurely days, and a space of say ten years or so between A and E would not be in the least surprising, particularly if the monks had to wait much longer than they had originally expected for a royal visit to the North-East by David I. Perhaps we may conclude by suggesting a date between the late 1130s and about 1150 for the whole procedure from A to E. It is not possible to attempt to pin it all down more narrowly; and to propose a broad 'median' dating such as '*c.* 1145' is impossible when we are dealing with a series of documents probably covering a good many years, with a beginning and an end each of

[1] Cf. pp. 15f.

which might in theory be separately datable. Such a date is perfectly consistent with the scribal and linguistic evidence.

It might be said that if the purpose of all this was to provide visible proof of the holdings and immunities of Deer for the purpose of bringing a lawsuit, it would have been done in Latin; we could compare Fraser's argument for the genuineness of the entries, that the use of Gaelic shows they were not fabricated for production in court under the feudal system.[1] But here we must distinguish. Fraser was thinking of a fully feudal court of the type well established in the North after its complete Normanisation; and specifically, after the re-foundation of Deer in 1219. But at the time when the notes were written this process had hardly begun in northern Scotland. The monks were following the firm tradition of Celtic law, and were writing their evidence in the only language intelligible to those who, in their eyes, would constitute the mass of any probable court, the 'good men of Buchan'. We have the close parallel of the more or less contemporary deeds in the Book of Kells, as well as the striking fact that many Anglo-Saxon charters, even those recording gifts to ecclesiastical bodies, are in the vernacular. Moreover, we need not assume that the scribes were writing with a view to any definite occasion already fixed. Rather, they may have felt, 'Obviously we are going to have to go to law sooner or later about all this lay oppression, when the king visits these parts, and we had better get our rights down on parchment now', without appreciating that the new kind of royal court which had perhaps not yet made its appearance in Aberdeenshire might expect its proceedings to be in Latin. Incidentally this would fit well with the opinion just expressed that the process of preparation may have been quite a long one.

Some doubt has been thrown by certain writers on the genuineness of the entries in the Book of Deer. It is of course a fact that early charters were sometimes forgeries, with the object of establishing 'proof' of the right of the holder to the lands, etc., that he held; and reacting against this, students of charters have

[1] *Sc. G. St.*, v, 65.

sometimes tended to take the line that all must be regarded as forged unless there is positive proof that they are genuine, though one might be forgiven for thinking that this may be pushing scepticism to extremes. The chief source for this attitude to Deer was Lawrie. He consistently cried down the importance and reliability of the Gaelic notes in it. According to him,[1] their value has been exaggerated. They are meagre, and there is little evidence on the date of any of them (both of which objections are true), and it is not safe to draw conclusions from them about the state of the church and people prior to the twelfth century. The grants are to 'an unnamed church of St. Drostan', and he doubts whether there was a monastery at Deer at all before the Cistercian foundation of 1219, on the grounds that there is no trace of it at all in records[2] and no local tradition about it at Deer. Moreover, the only thing which connects the notes with Deer is no. VII, which is itself perhaps spurious. On this, he says elsewhere[3] that he suspects it is a fabrication, though he cannot suggest why or when it should have been so fabricated; he considers it unlikely that the Gospel book had been seen by the king and his chancellor, and very unlikely that he would confirm such informal writings, which were mainly the tradition of the church. If we ask, then, how the notes ever came to exist, Lawrie's answer is,[4] 'These notitiae may have been written by an Irishman, one of the secular clergy serving at Aberdour or Deer, in the twelfth century, who may have collected the traditions of grants of lands to Drostan's churches, written in Irish and using titles – Mormaer and Toisech – known in Ireland.'

Lawrie's influence was bound to be considerable. A. O. Anderson seriously entertained the possibility that the Gaelic notes are forgeries of the period later than 1219, apparently impressed by the fact that there is no independent evidence that a monastery existed at Deer in David's reign. He thinks the script of nos. I–VI is probably later than 1219, and perhaps belongs to the end of the thirteenth century; and while that of VII

---

[1] *EC*, p. 220.   [2] This is perhaps not quite correct; see p. 6 above.
[3] *EC*, p. 425.   [4] *EC*, p. 220.

can hardly be later than the beginning of the thirteenth century it is abnormal, and difficult to judge. 'If it is forged, the previous numbers are probably also forged. But neither it nor they can be proved not to be copies of genuine documents.'[1] So too D. E. Easson, following Lawrie and Anderson, thinks the evidence for a Celtic monastery at Deer in the time of David I is uncertain.[2]

On the other hand, J. Cameron objected[3] to Lawrie's views as being a result of want of appreciation and knowledge of the language of the notes, and to his criticisms of their subject matter as being without authority and deficient in historical accuracy. More cogently, Fraser, without mentioning Lawrie or Anderson, points out[4] that as regards the absence of the names of witnesses and seals, the notes in Deer are no worse off than other 'charters' of the time; that the grants are attested by the only kind of document or deed then in use;[5] and that Deer is nowhere named in the grants, which is strongly against the theory that they represent an attempt by the Cistercian monastery to manufacture a traditional authority for their title to the lands.

As Cameron suggests, Lawrie's attitude is wrong-headed, and indeed in some points it is rather absurd. He evidently believed there was never a monastery at Deer before 1219; that the royal 'charter' was a forgery; and that I–VI represent traditions about grants to the *churches* of Aberdour and Deer collected in the twelfth century by an Irish secular priest at one or other of these churches. His 'Irish' priest in Buchan may well strike one as a little ridiculous. The reason for this notion is evidently twofold, though nowhere stated. Someone who knew Scottish Gaelic must have told Lawrie that the notes are not (modern) Scottish Gaelic but 'Irish', by which he meant, as Scottish Gaelic speakers often do, the literary language known in

---

[1] *ESSH*, ii, 181, n. 5.
[2] *Mediaeval Religious Houses in Scotland* (London, 1957), p. 191.
[3] *CL*, p. 204.   [4] *Sc. G. St.*, v, 64ff.
[5] Cf. Innes, *National MSS* (full reference, see no. (5), Preface above), i, viif.

Scotland in recent centuries as such but in fact being originally
the 'Common Gaelic' written language of all the Gaelic world,
of Scotland as much as Ireland. Indeed, as we shall see, Scottish
Gaelic had barely even begun to differentiate itself from Irish
in the twelfth century. The second reason was probably unconscious. In Lawrie's day, Celtic sources, particularly those
in the vernacular, were still regarded with grave suspicion by
serious historians, especially those of the 'Whig' historical tradition; it was common, for instance, to call Irish documents 'wild
tales'; and to ascribe a text to an Irishman was subtly to dis-
credit it. The attitude of historians to Celtic material has changed
a good deal in the more than half a century since Lawrie wrote,
and nowadays they are prepared to treat it on its merits just
like any other such. It is difficult to believe that so many nobles,
and even a king, would have made extensive grants of lands and
immunities to two small and unimportant secular churches; and
the reasoning, which seems to commend itself to some, that
the existence of a Celtic monastery at Deer is nowhere inde-
pendently corroborated and that therefore it is spurious is simply
an *argumentum ex silentio*. In the same way, the Deer entries are
the only explicit evidence we possess that there ever was a
monastery at Turriff, but if there was *not*, it would be an extraordinary way of forging an 'authentic' document to say that it
was witnessed by the abbot of a monastery which everyone
knew had never existed. As to the objection that there is no
modern local tradition about a Celtic monastery at Deer, such
a tradition, if it existed, would have been quite worthless, as
Lawrie himself would have been the first to point out. There
were 'Celtic' monasteries in various parts of Scotland before
the Normanisation of the Church, and there is no reason why
there should not have been one in Buchan. To complain that
there is no evidence for it is really not to disprove its existence,
but merely to state the well-known fact that Scotland is exceedingly deficient in documents of any sort belonging to the
pre-Norman period. The Gaelic *notitiae* mention by name several
estates which are later known to have belonged to the Cistercian

abbey, and it would be more natural to conclude that they simply passed to it when the Celtic monastery was refounded in 1219 as a Norman one than to suppose that they had previously belonged to the churches of Aberdour and Deer. One wonders why Lawrie's Irishman should have bothered to amuse himself by collecting these things at all, and particularly to write them in 'Irish'. Lastly, Lawrie is quite mistaken in implying that the use of the titles *mormaer* and *toísech* is evidence of Irish origin. Both were of course familiar in Scotland, and the first is not even an Irish title at all, as we shall see.

As to the theory that no. VII is a 'fabrication', Lawrie himself was unable to account for it. Certainly, it is not quite cast in the form of a regular feudal confirmation, but has the air of a piece of reportage by one of the scribes of Deer well versed in Norman scribal practice, for the information of the present and future monks and others; but that does not automatically prove it a forgery. The objection that the royal officials would not accept evidence of this sort does not take account of the fact that such evidence would be all there ever was in the way of written proof of anything in Buchan at this time; or of another, that it was 'proved by argument' – that is, oral evidence, always acceptable in any court – and supported by oaths – always taken seriously in law. The fact that it was in Gaelic would be no objection in a court where many of the proceedings must have been carried on in Gaelic. There is absolutely nothing in Anderson's theory that the script of I–VI is probably later than 1219; and moreover, the language of the Gaelic entries cannot be so late as this. If we are to take Anderson's line that all the entries may be spurious and written after 1219, with a view to providing the Cistercian abbey with 'early' authority for its estates and its privileges, we should have to explain not merely why I–VI never mention Deer (as Fraser points out) but also why they are not written in Latin and in the feudal style, as they certainly would have been; and why much more play is not made with names like those of Mal-Snechta the mormaer of Moray, and above all King Malcolm II, in no. II. These documents are wholly unlike what an early thirteenth-century forgery would be like. And besides, if we go further and deny that a Celtic monastery ever existed, how could the Cistercian monks claim to hold lands by right of such a monastery when everyone would know it never had? And in any case if they did not get, e.g., Biffie, which we know they later held, from the Celtic monastery because there never was a Celtic monastery, the only reasonable alternative is that it was granted them by William Comyn in 1219; but if so, they would have a proper charter for it and for the rest, and the elaborate fabrication of spurious older gifts would be unnecessary.

One can only conclude that scepticism about the existence of a Celtic monastery at Deer has been grossly exaggerated and ill-argued, and that it is without any adequate foundation;[1] also that although the Gaelic documents were admittedly slightly tampered with by the scribes, for the rest they are perfectly genuine, and that VII is an authentic summary of the judgement of the court at Aberdeen and list of the witnesses (who are most of them people well-known as dignitaries and witnesses in other contemporary documents). Remembering that the historical context is a Celtic one in which Norman feudalisation had scarcely begun, the 'irregular' character of no. VII which has worried traditional historians is perfectly natural.

2 SOCIAL STATUS IN THE BOOK OF DEER

Apart from 'king', which needs no special commentary here, two other Celtic ranks of nobility are mentioned in our source; the 'mormaer' and the toísech.

It is clear that mormaer is the title given to the highest rank of Gaelic nobility in Scotland under the king, and that they were each set over a large given territorial region. In Latin sources the equivalent is *comes*, otherwise used as equivalent

---

[1] The fact that no. I gives a story of its origin which is obviously legendary is wholly without significance. The story of the foundation of St Andrews, to mention only this one, is equally legendary, but no one doubts that it existed before the Normans came.

Historical commentary

or translation of 'earl'. This is seen already twice in our no. VII, where Donnchad *comes* of Fife and Gille-Brigte *comes* of Angus are witnesses. The Ruaidrí who is described in Deer no. III as mormaer of Mar is called *Rotheri comes* in the great charter of Dunfermline and *Rothri comes* in the foundation charter of Scone (see Notes on p. 66). In a poem to Alwyn, first earl of Lennox, composed by Muireadhach Albanach Ó Dálaigh early in the thirteenth century,[1] he is called *mórmhaor Leamhna*, 'earl of Lennox'. A particularly clear example from a later time is the entry in the Annals of Connacht for 1306, *Roberd a Briuis, mormaer Cargi, do gabail rige a nAlbain*;[2] 'Robert Bruce, earl of Carrick, becomes king in Scotland.' Later still, the title *iarla*, a loanword from Norse *jarl*, came to be adopted in Gaelic in Scotland, and *mormaer* acquired its vaguer modern meaning of 'lord'.[3] The equation of this Celtic rank with the Anglo-Saxon one of 'earl' is very likely not exact, but it must have been approximate. In the generation before the Norman Conquest the English earl was a hereditary royal official who was joint president, with the bishop, of the shire court and commanded the shire militia, functioning as the representative of the king. He received one third of the court fines and one third of the customs paid by the burghs, and in some regions there is evidence for estates permanently assigned to his maintenance. Besides the earl there was also the sheriff, a new official at this time, chosen by and responsible to the king alone for the administration of local finance and the execution of justice in his shire.[4]

The probability that the mormaer was some kind of high royal *official*, and more than merely a noble, is greatly increased by the etymological meaning of this compound word. The second element is Old and Middle Irish *maer*, 'an official or steward'.

---

[1] See L. McKenna, *Aithdioghluim Dána* (Irish Texts Society, Dublin, 1939), I, 172ff. and II, 102f.   [2] *RC*, LI, 100.

[3] Cf. Angus Matheson, *Éigse*, VI, 67.

[4] On all this see F. M. Stenton, *Anglo-Saxon England* (London, 1947), pp. 539ff. Unlike the sheriff's, the earl's powers might extend over several shires.

Historical commentary

Until fairly recently the first element was always regarded as *mór* 'great', so that it would mean 'great officer, High Steward', which very well suits what has just been said about the Anglo-Saxon earl. The occurrences of the word – it does not exist in Modern Irish – quoted in the Royal Irish Academy's *Contributions to a Dictionary of the Irish Language*, M, cols. 172f., are as follows. (1) Four examples from the book of Deer itself, where the accents are of course irrelevant, as we have seen (p. 17). (2) *Nad farcbath ri na mormoer di suidibh*, Annals of Ulster, year 918, 'but neither king nor mormaer of them [the Scots] was killed'. (3) *Gilla-Comgan mac Mael-Brighde, mormaer Murebe*, Annals of Ulster, year 1032, 'G.-C. son of M.-B., mormaer of Moray'. (4) *Mormaer Leamna do milliudh a fell lé righ Alban*, Annals of Ulster, year 1425, 'the earl of Lennox[1] was destroyed through treachery by the king of Scotland'. (5) The Annals of Tigernach, 976, mention Cellach son of Findghaine, Cellach son of Bairidh, and Donnchad son of Morgand, as *tri mormair Alban*, 'three mormaers of Scotland', present on a raid in Ireland.[2] (6) *Domnall mac Emin, mormaer Alban*, GG, p. 174, 'D. son of E., a mormaer from Scotland' (fought at Clontarf in 1014). (7) The Cotton Titus annals refer to this same person as present at that battle, calling him *Domnall mac Emini meic Cannaich Móir.i.mórmáer i nAlbain* (*RC*, XLI, 328), 'D. son of E. son of Big C., that is, a mormaer in Scotland'. Two later Scottish examples are (8), *inghen morbair Moireogh*, 'daughter of the earl of Moray' (seventeenth century; Cameron, *Reliquae Celticae*, II, 164); and (9) *ar morbhair-ne a bfer faire*, 'our lord their watchman' (after 1680; *TGSI*, XXIX, 224). One may also add as cases not given in the RIA *Contributions* not only the reference to Alwyn, earl of Lennox, quoted above, but also Annals of Ulster, year 1014, *Domhnall mac Eimhin mic Cainnigh, mormhaer Mair i nAlbain*, 'D. son of E. son of C., mormaer of Mar in Scotland' (fell at Clontarf); and Annals of Ulster, year 1216, *Muiredach mac mórmair Lemhnach*, 'M. son of the earl of Lennox'. It will be noticed that every one of these instances has reference

---

[1] Not, of course, 'of Leven' with the RIA *Conts*.   [2] *RC*, XVII, 359.

Historical commentary

to Scottish lords, and the only one given by the RIA *Conts.* that has not is in *GG*, p. 168, *Da coirgead deich mormair Briain co n-a ngall-socraitib*, 'the ten mormaers of Brian [Boru] were drawn up with their Norse allies' (at the battle of Clontarf). The fact is that all the evidence suggests that the mormaer was a Scottish official, not an Irish one, and a few rare examples applied to Ireland are probably due in some way to Scottish influence. It is true that a similar compound occurs sometimes with reference to Ireland, *ard-maer*, 'high steward, chief-officer',[1] but this is not so much the title of a rank but a mere common-noun – as it were, not 'Chief-Officer' but 'chief officer'.

It will also be noticed that in only three cases above is the vowel of the first syllable marked long. The fact that in the others there is no length-mark does not, of course, prove that it was short, since length-marks were often omitted. Nevertheless, its rarity is notable. What is even more striking, however, is the fact that it is short in modern Scottish Gaelic. The word is now spelt *morair*, the history of which, leaving aside the question of the first vowel, is as follows. The *-rmaer* of the early *mormaer*, which was $-/r\tilde{v}(aɪ{:})r/$, developed a svarabhakti vowel $/ə/$ between the $/r/$ and the $/\tilde{v}/$ which by subsequent vowel harmony came to be identical with the vowel of the first syllable; the nasal spirant was de-nasalised (hence the late spelling *morbhar*[2] for *mormhar*); the diphthong was shortened in the un-stressed syllable; the intervocal *v* was dropped with hiatus; and the genitive with palatalised final *-r* came to be used for the nominative. That is to say, assuming that the first vowel was short, original $/mɔr\tilde{v}(aɪ{:})r/$ went through the following changes: $> /mɔrə\tilde{v}(aɪ{:})r/ > /m(ɔrɔ)v(aɪ{:})r/ > /m(ɔrɔ)var/ > /m(ɔrɔ)-ar/ > /m(ɔrɔ)-ar'/$, which last is the usual pronunciation of what is now spelt *morair*. In some regions, including all the Gaelic-

[1] Cf. RIA *Conts.*, M, col. 22, ll. 83–5.

[2] The RIA *Conts.* seem to say that Anderson told the editress that the 'Scottish form' of the word was *morbhar*; if it is implied that this was originally so, it is incorrect. But it was probably not implied, cf. his note in *SHR*, xxix mentioned below.

speaking country nearest to Buchan, the hiatus has been contracted, giving $/m(\mathrm{ərə})r'/$, $/m(\mathrm{əra})r'/$, etc.; and in some the final r is non-palatal, either because the last stage mentioned above never took place or more likely because the region now has no $/r'/$ phoneme.

This shortness of the o of *mor-* in modern Scottish Gaelic was responsible for the view generally held at present that it is not *mór* 'great' at all. This was first suggested by Watson in his *Bàrdachd Ghàidhlig*[1] (he did not mention the rarity of the length-mark over the o). He took it to be '*mor-*, compositional form of [Irish and Scottish Gaelic] *muir*, sea', and explained the compound as meaning 'sea-steward, sea-officer', suggesting it is comparable to the Romano-British *Comes Litoris*, the commanding officer charged with the defence of the eastern and southern shores of Britain against the Saxons at the end of the Roman rule there. This was adopted by A. O. Anderson in *SHR*, xxix (1949), 85, who rejects 'High Steward', but unlike Watson he does not treat *mor-* as the compositional form of Gaelic *muir* but as from the British **mori* 'sea', and the whole from Brit. **mori-mair- (sic)*; which etymology, curiously enough, he appears to attribute to Watson.[2] He says that 'other evidence points the same way', but as the other evidence is not specified this is not very helpful. He suggests that both early and late spellings with the length mark are due to a very natural false popular etymology on the assumption that the first element was really *mór* 'great'. The RIA *Conts.*, *M*, mentioned above, adopted these theories of Anderson's, which had been communicated to the compiler by letter. They also quote him as saying that 'the Scottish form seems to have been [originally] *morbhar (-mhar)*', which is certainly incorrect, as Deer shows, and was evidently abandoned by Anderson himself by the time he wrote in *SHR*, xxix. Another idea in the RIA *Conts.*, associated with the preceding, and apparently derived from Anderson and rightly abandoned by him in *SHR*, is that the second element (his

[1] First published 1918; see third edition (Stirling, 1959), p. 378.
[2] But this is probably simply that Anderson expressed himself awkwardly here.

Historical commentary

'-*bhar*') was not really *maer* at all but was secondarily interpreted as such.

In an article in *RC*, xxxv (1914), 401ff. (see particularly 404, 407, 408), Fraser, naturally taking it for granted that the first element was *mór*, entered into a complicated and unconvincing argument that the vowel was secondarily shortened when the word was [quasi-]proclitic in titles, and that this affected the pronunciation where it was stressed. This is criticised by Anderson (*SHR*, xxix), who seems, however, not to have followed Fraser's (admittedly obscure) reasoning. The discussion does however bring out the important point that in words with a long vowel in the first syllable svarabhakti does not develop at all; and for Fraser, believing that the vowel was long, this was what had to be explained. An alternative explanation, and the one generally accepted at present, is of course that the vowel in the word was never long, and that Watson was right.

Nevertheless, there are certain questions which raise doubts in one's mind about Watson's 'Sea-Officer'. There is no evidence whatever that such an official ever existed. If he did, against whom would his activities be aimed? Why should such a post become transformed into one which could be identified with that of an earl; in some cases, moreover, such as Mar, with their earldoms a long way from the sea? Moreover, there are linguistic objections to Watson's theory. The composition-form of the Goidelic **mori* is not *mor-* but *muir-* or *mur-*, the correct development, phonologically, from **mori-*;[1] as may easily be seen by checking through the Royal Irish Academy *Contributions*. There are, it is true, a few rare cases where *mor-* seems to occur. But some are secondary Sc. G. deformations, such as *morbhach*, *mormhach*, or *mormhaich*, 'low-lying land along the sea', which is from *murbach*;[2] or *morghath* 'fish-spear', which is from *murga*. The etymology of others is obscure; and at least

---

[1] This is perhaps the reason why Anderson suggests that the word contains British **mori* 'sea', since the Welsh for 'sea' is in fact *mor* (not *muir*).

[2] See Gwynn, *Sc. G. St.*, II, 105. Watson was mistaken in taking the word as a compound of *magh* 'plain'; *CPNS*, p. 501.

one other (*morlo* 'seal', appearing in dictionaries) is Welsh. It must be admitted that 'Great Steward' is intrinsically much more probable, if only the short *o* and the svarabhakti in *morair*, and the possible shortness of the *o* in earlier sources, could be accounted for. One may point out that the rule that in words with svarabhakti the first vowel was never originally long is not without at least one exception in Sc. G., the name Aonghus. This was /ɑ́:nyəs/ at an earlier stage, but is now /(ɑ́Nɑ́)-əs/, with shortening of the first vowel and svarabhakti; which provides an exact parallel for deriving /m(ɔrɔ)-ar'/ from an older /mɔ:rṽ(aɪ:)r/ consisting of *mór* 'great' and *maer* 'steward'. However, only one such parallel may not be thought enough, and the very common omission of the length-mark in early sources may be taken seriously (in which case its occasional appearance would indeed be due to popular association with *mór* 'great'). But if so, there is a quite different possible solution. The first mormaers recorded in Scottish documents all belong to the North-East, to the old Pictland, and none are found at any later time in what were the original Gaelic regions except the border one of Lennox; and the office and its functions could easily have been one inherited from the Pictish system of administration when the Gaels occupied Pictland in the middle of the ninth century.[1] There need be nothing difficult about this; the royal administration in Pictland is likely to have been at least as sophisticated as anything the Gaels had; and as a parallel, compare the note on the davoch and its possible Pictish origin, pp. 116ff. Now the Pictish for 'great' would probably have been *mōr*, with long *o*, and like all the other early Celtic languages, its word for 'official' would doubtless be *maer*, which is a loan from Latin. It is likely, however, that this would not give *mōrṽaer* but *morṽaer*, with short *o*, shortened before the following group of two consonants; would give, that is to say, exactly the form required to explain the development of modern Sc. G. *morair*. So if we accept this, 'Great Steward'

---

[1] The RIA *Conts.*, *s.v. mormaer*, already suggest it is 'probably of indigenous (?Pictish) origin', doubtless following Anderson in this.

is after all the solution; and it is the one which fits the facts best. Incidentally, it would provide a simple explanation of why the title was not used in Ireland.

As regards the functions and duties of the mormaer, the probable meaning of the word would seem to suggest that he was a royal official, the highest rank of such, the king's deputy in his district and having the duty of collecting the royal revenues, or some of them, since acting as a 'factor' is one of the primary functions of the Celtic *maer*. He was apparently entitled to his share of these dues, his 'cut', as we shall see (p. 119). Early Scottish sources show that he was a *territorial* magnate, and held his position by hereditary right, whatever the original position may have been; and in this he was comparable to the late Anglo-Saxon earl. Some mormaers would naturally be more powerful than others. There was a time in the history of the development of the Scottish monarchy, in the tenth century, when the 'men of Moray' caused a good deal of trouble to the Crown and behaved as if they claimed to be an independent kingdom. In fact when their mormaer Finnlaech was killed in 1020, the Annals of Ulster call him *rí Alban*, 'king of Scotland'; and his nephew Malcolm son of Mal-Brigte, also mormaer, was called by the same title in the Annals of Tigernach when they recorded his death in 1029 (*RC,* xvii, 369), so that some Scots at any rate, presumably those of Moray, regarded the mormaers of Moray at this period as kings. This might account for the fact that at least once in the Book of Deer a mormaer of Moray is found granting an estate in the territory of another mormaer, him of Buchan, when the above Malcolm son of Mal-Brigte gave Elrick to the monastery; but we have no reason to think that mormaers could not hold private estates outside their mormaerdoms.

In Deer we have five instances of men actually called mormaer. In I, Bede is mormaer of Buchan; in II Muiredach son of Morgann is 'mormaer' (and toísech, on which see below), and so evidently is Matain son of Cairell, but of what region is not stated in either case; in III Ruaidrí is mormaer of Mar;

in VI, Colbán is mormaer of Buchan; while in VII Donnchad is *comes* of Fife and Gille-Brigte *comes* of Angus.

There is another title of rank or office in the notes in the Book of Deer, that of *toísech*.[1] There is no real doubt about the etymological meaning of this word, namely 'leader'.[2] Already in early Irish texts this has become slightly enlarged; side by side with 'leader' in the sense of 'one who leads' it can be 'chief' or 'ruler' of a people, territory, etc.,[3] as in the grant of Kildalkey in the Book of Kells.[4] It is used in this way of the chief of a noble family-grouping, the head of what in Scottish terminology is called a 'clan' or 'sept'. This is the meaning of *tòiseach* in Sc. G. also, but here it is a rather rare and literary word, the idea being normally expressed otherwise. However, in the Book of Deer there are two cases where it appears to occur in exactly that sense. In no. V, Comgell son of Cainnech is toísech of Clann Chanann, and in no. VI, Donnchad son of Síthech is toísech of Clann Morgainn. *Clann* means 'the noble kindred, the ruling family-group descended from a common ancestor', rather comparable to what is implied when one speaks of 'the Howards' or 'the Percies'. It does this also in early Irish family-names like Clann Carthaig 'the McCarthys', Clann Cellaig 'the O'Kellys', Clann Domnaill 'the MacDonnells of Antrim', Clann Aeda Buide 'Clanaboy', and so on; a usage which can be traced back to the early tenth century. Irish has other words for this general idea, such as *cinél* and *síl*, and so has Sc. G., particularly *cinneadh*. All such family-names consist of a word like *cinél* or *clann* followed by the name of the eponymous ancestor in the genitive, the ancestor in such cases being generally but not always a known character of the historical period. In the two instances in Deer, *toísech clainne* certainly appears to mean 'chief of a noble kindred', a concept

---

[1] On the probability that *toísech* is correct in Deer, not *tòisech*, see p. 134f.
[2] Cf. H. Pedersen, *Vergleichende Grammatik der Keltischen Sprachen* (Göttingen, 1909), I, 136 (differently but less convincingly p. 308; cf. Vendryes in *RC*, XXXI, 513).
[3] See examples in the RIA *Conts.*, *to–tu*, col. 234.   [4] See p. 91.

Historical commentary

later expressed in Sc. G. by *ceann cinnidh*. In mediaeval Scottish documents[1] *caput progeniei* is obviously the Latin rendering of this, and *kenkynolle* also occurs, clearly *cenn cinéoil* with the same meaning.

How far *clann* in Deer implies a large, all-embracing group with several sub-divisions, or one of these smaller sub-divisions themselves, is not apparent. Nor can we tell who the two *clann*'s were, and where their territory lay. One might suppose that one was the ruling family of Buchan and the other that of Moray, and since Ruaidrí the first known mormaer of Moray, grandfather of Macbeth, was grandson of a Morgann, descended from Loarn son of Erc, Clann Morgainn might well be thought to be the ruling noble kindred of Moray.[2] Against this, Donnchad the toísech of Clann Morgainn is associated in no. VI with Colbán the mormaer of Buchan and all the nobles of Buchan, and this could imply that Clann Morgainn belonged to Buchan. Not necessarily so, however, since this deed is one 'quenching' all the grants, apparently all those ever made to Deer which stood in need of this, and it would therefore be natural that a representative of the rulers of Moray (and perhaps two of his sons, see Note on VI, 6) should join in it with the ruler of Buchan. As to Clann Chanann, the second word is the genitive of the name *Cano*, a rare one and probably of Pictish origin; and there was a well-known Cano, grandson of Aedán mac Gabráin of Dál Riada, living in the seventh century, from whom this Buchan kindred might have derived its name. At any rate, however all that may be, it looks as if toísech is used in these two instances in Deer in the well-established sense of chief of a noble kindred, a *clann*. We should perhaps conclude that on the whole Clann Morgainn and Clann Chanann do not represent the families of the mormaers of Moray and Buchan as such, but rather some smaller divisions of them, since if their toísechs were mormaers of either region, that title would surely have been given them.

[1] E.g. *Reg. Mag. Sig.*, I, nos. 508, 509 (1372, pp, 185f.).
[2] There can of course be no connection with the much later 'Clan Morgan', the Mackays of Sutherland.

Side by side with this, however, the other occurrences of the word in Deer suggest that *toísech* could also bear a quite different meaning. In I, Bede gives Aberdour in freedom from mormaer and toísech. In II, Cu Lí gives a toísech's dues, contrasted with Matain who gives a mormaer's; Cathal 'quenches' his toísech's dues; and Cainnech and others 'quench' all the grants in freedom from mormaer and toísech. In V, Comgell, himself a toísech, gives land free of toísech till Doomsday. These occurrences suggest some kind of official, with dues payable to him from lands, similar but perhaps inferior to a mormaer. The status of toísech was not, however, incompatible with that of mormaer, since in II we are told of Muiredach that 'it is he who was mormaer and was toísech'.[1] There was clearly therefore some difference, distinct from the one being merely higher than the other. In the passages where mormaer and toísech are contrasted, toísech (N.B., without *clainne*) can hardly be being used in the sense of 'chief of a kindred', since anyone who was mormaer of, e.g. Moray would surely also, in Celtic custom, be chief of the ruling family of Moray. One possible suggestion is that in these cases toísech has its etymological meaning of 'leader'; that is to say, he was the general of the tribal army in the field, whereas the mormaer, who was the highest ranking royal territorial official in the region, was also ruler of the whole tribe. It would follow, in Celtic society, that all mormaers were *toísig clainne* but not all *toísig clainne*, or *toísig* unqualified by *clainne*, were mormaers.

Just as the *mormaer* was identified with the *comes*, the *earl*, so the *toísech* was identified in early Scottish terminology with the *thane*, the title of another Anglo-Saxon official borrowed from England like that of the *earl*. The Scottish thane was a subordinate officer of (usually) the king, or of an earl, set over

---

[1] Some editors (including Stokes in his edition of 1872 but not that of 1866), puzzled by what seems an incompatibility, have tried to take *mormaer* as referring to the previously-mentioned Comgell and the *toísech* to Muiredach. But this is quite impossible; the wording goes out of its way to be explicit that Muiredach held both these ranks. See Note to II, 3.

a stated territory of his lord's lands, holding his position heredi-
tarily, and charged with duties in connection with the administration of his thanedom and with its military organisation, the
collection of its taxes, and the administration of justice there.[1]
Like the mormaer, he was entitled to his share of the dues
collected; twelfth-century charters show that certain dues were
paid to the thane in Angus and the Mearns from which the
beneficiaries of the charters might be granted exemption, or
which could be diverted to their use,[2] and this is strongly
reminiscent of the toísech's 'cut' in Deer, on which see below,
p. 119. It seems likely that the toísech in this sense was a deputy
official comparable to the mormaer, but at a lower level and with
different duties, not however incompatible with the rank of
mormaer ('it is he who was mormaer and was toísech'); and
that with the coming of Anglo-Saxon influence to Scotland
under Malcolm Canmore and 'the sons of Margaret' he was
identified with the thane, whether the correspondence was exact
or only partial. It is to be noted that whereas mormaers are
territorially linked, and so are thanes, there is nothing in Deer to
show that toísechs were, though this may be quite accidental.
If all this is so, it would appear that we must distinguish quite
clearly between *toísech*, the royal or other officer, and *toísech
clainne*, the hereditary head of a noble kindred.[3] The second is
a typically Gaelic concept, quite familiar in Ireland, whereas
the other has no Irish parallel; whether this suggests that he
was part of the Pictish social organisation, as the mormaer may
perhaps have been, or whether he was really the Anglo-Saxon
thane borrowed and accommodated with a vaguely appropriate

---

[1] Cf. Cosmo Innes, *Lectures on Scotch Legal Antiquities* (Edinburgh, 1872),
p. 80.

[2] As Professor Barrow kindly tells me. E.g. *Liber Sancti Thome de Aber-
brothoc* (Bannatyne Club, Edinburgh, 1848), I, 38, 39 (= *Reg. Reg. Scott.*,
II, 243, no. 186); *Reg. Reg. Scott.*, II, 346, no. 344; 347, no. 345; and 482,
no. 590.

[3] The name Macintosh presumably means 'Son of the Toísech' in the first
sense, which would be a natural type of surname (cf. Macnab, 'Son of
the Abbot') whereas 'Son of the (Clan) Chief' would not, since all the
nobility were sons or at least descendants of chiefs.

Gaelic title, cannot be determined. It is remarkable, at any rate, as Professor Donaldson points out to me, that the known Scottish thanages are almost all in the former Pictland.

3. LAND-HOLDING AND LAND-GRANTING IN THE BOOK OF DEER

On the nature of land-holding and land-granting in north-east Celtic Scotland in the eleventh and twelfth centuries the Book of Deer throws a good deal of light,[1] some of it rather dim light, but more perhaps than on any other aspect of the social system. The basic socio-economic unit in farming seems to have been the *pett*, a term which it is almost impossible to translate with one single word. 'Estate' or 'parcel of land' expresses its territorial aspect, but it probably meant more than this – not merely a unit of land but a unit of population, not just an area but also the village community which lived in and worked it. The mediaeval 'manor' is perhaps as good a one-word translation as any, but this has been avoided in this book because its feudal connotations would make it misleading; 'township' might make it appear to some too exclusively a question of population. There could hardly be any fixed size or any approximation to it, any more than there was with the feudal 'manor', but it is at least of interest that there is some reason to think that one of the *pett*'s in Deer was about 100 acres in extent (p. 118). It is well-known that *pett* is a Pictish word; that the etymological meaning is 'piece', i.e. 'parcel of land', cognate with the Welsh *peth* 'thing', the Gaulish **petia* 'piece' (whence French *pièce*; and note late Lat. *petia terrae* 'parcel of land', very much the meaning of *pett*), and the Gaelic *cuid* 'share'; that the modern map of Scotland north of the Forth, east of the Grampians, and south of the Dornoch Firth (i.e., the heart of historical Pictland) is peppered with settlement-names in *Pit-*; and that in a number of cases there is an interchange between such names and a

---

[1] *Pace* Lawrie; see p. 98. Compare rather Stuart, *BD*, p. lviii, 'It is clear that the population and institutions of Buchan were wholly Celtic in the time of David I.'

Historical commentary

Gaelic form in *Baile-*.[1] For instance, Pitlochry is Gaelic *Baile Chloichrigh*; Pitfour in Sutherland is *Baile Phùir*, and the same is true of Pitfour in the Black Isle; and Pitgersie a few miles south-east of Deer was interchangeably Pitgerso and Balgerso in English as late as last century.[2] This means that the Gaelic speakers who settled in Pictland after the occupation under Kenneth mac Alpine and his successors identified the native *pett* with their own *baile*.[3] As a common-noun the oldest meaning of *baile* was 'place', but in place-names in early Ireland when followed by a group-name in the genitive plural it meant 'territory of a small tribal group or family'; and in the Norman period when qualified by the name of an individual in the genitive it was 'land held by a feudal tenant'; 'farmstead' and 'village' developed from this.[4] With the Norman usage one might compare English names of farms, common in Sussex and elsewhere, such as 'Jordans', meaning 'farm once belonging to a man called Jordan'.

The interchange between Pit- and Baile- in names suggests at first sight that the Gaelic incomers regarded the two as identical in meaning; but the fact that such an enormous number of Pit- names have survived without substitution of Baile- may imply, rather, that there *was* some difference, probably small but significant, in the constitution of a *pett* from that of a *baile*, which was felt to exist. A large number of Pit- names have a Gaelic second element, which probably means they represent re-foundations by the Gaelic immigrants to Pictland, with new lords, but held on the same terms, or constituted in the same manner, as under the Picts and hence preserving the first element of the original settlement-name. In the Deer notes there are five *pett* names, all obviously meaning 'estate, parcel of land, manor', doubtless with the population unit inhabiting it

---

[1] On all this, and for a map of Pit- names, see the writer's note in *PP*, pp. 146ff.   [2] *PNA*, p. 102.

[3] *Pett* was *not* borrowed into Gaelic as a common-noun, any more than *ville*, so common in forming American village names, has really been borrowed into American as such, though the *meaning* is known.

[4] See L. Price in *Celtica*, VI, 119ff.

implied. They fall into two types. First those followed by the name of an individual in the genitive, exactly the 'Jordans' type; these are Pett Meic-Garnait in I and II; Pett Malduib in II; and Pett Meic-Gobraig in II and III; that is, 'Mac-Garnait's *pett*', 'Maldub's *pett*', and 'Mac-Gobraig's *pett*'. The other type is exactly comparable to one of the late developments of *baile* names in Ireland and Scotland, locally descriptive ones such as Irish *Baile na hAbha* 'the farmstead of the river', or Scots Ballencrieff, i.e. *Baile na Craoibhe*, 'the farmstead of the tree'. These are Pett in Muilinn 'the *Pett* of the Mill' in II and Pett in Phúir 'the *Pett* of the Crop-land(?)'[1] in IV.

The other unit of land-holding seen in the Book of Deer is the well-known *dabhach*, Anglicised as *davoch*, which is quite a different matter from the *pett*. It occurs in II, where Malcolm II gave the monastery two davochs in 'upper *Ros abard*', and in VI, where the mormaer of Buchan and others 'quench' grants in return for a payment chargeable on four davochs-worth of certain taxes. The meaning of the term has often been discussed.[2] The original meaning is 'a large vat';[3] the application to land is not found at all in Ireland, however, but only in Scotland. Just how a word meaning a vat should come to be used of land is not quite clear, but this could have arisen if the term was applied to that amount of land necessary to produce, or to require for sowing it, a fixed amount of grain, enough to fill a large vat of a fixed size; this being perhaps not the total yield of grain but only the proportion of it due as a fixed render of tax. This would explain the fact that when it can be checked, in later times, the actual acreage is seen to vary considerably in various parts of the country, exactly as in the case of the mediaeval bovate and ploughgate, and for the same reason. If it was originally purely a measure of arable land, it had ceased

[1] See Notes to IV, I.
[2] See in particular G. W. S. Barrow in *Scottish Studies*, VI, 131ff.; also W. J. Watson, *CPNS*, pp. 253f.; W. E. Levie, *Sc. G. St.*, III, 99ff.; and other references given in these sources.
[3] The supposed derivation from *dam* 'ox' given by some is fanciful.

to mean this later, and applied to pastoral land and rough mountain grazing as well. According to Professor Barrow it meant, by the twelfth century, a definite quantity of land with fixed boundaries, being roughly 200 Scottish acres in extent in north-east Scotland; and it was the basis of the assessment of certain pre-feudal dues. Incidentally it may be significant that it is associated chiefly with the old Pictish country; possibly it is, once again, an aspect of the Pictish socio-economic system adopted by the incoming Gaels? One would be anxious to avoid the imputation of 'Pictomania', but we should remember that Pictland had presumably been an agriculturally much richer, and doubtless on the whole a more populous and powerful country, than the old Dál Riada, and it would be not in the least unnatural that the immigrant Gaels should adopt various of the customs of these people among whom they settled. The fact that the church in Pictland remained 'in servitude...after the custom and fashion of the Picts' for a generation after the Gaelic occupation[1] would be a case in point; another would be the borrowing of the term *pett*, and another that of *mormaer* and official *toisech* if this is really what happened. In connection with Deer, it is interesting to note that the customary endowment of a subordinate church in Aberdeenshire and Moray in the twelfth century was apparently half a davoch,[2] as a ploughgate was in the south; the royal gift of two davochs to the important monastery of Deer is thus quite in proportion.

There appear to be three chief types of grant made to the monastery of Deer. The first, and commonest, is a simple gift of a fixed piece of land, an estate, the boundaries being sometimes sketchily mentioned. No. II is made up largely and no. V wholly of such, and the original grant for the site and support of the monastery itself, in I, is another. Giving lands like this would mean that the monks now either farmed them themselves or leased them for rent to tenants, paying no rent proper themselves to the lord who had granted them. But it seems that they

---

[1] See p. 93.   [2] See Cowan in *SHR*, XL, 48.

did not own them in freehold, but, in the usual mediaeval
manner, on terms of rendering certain fixed dues and services
to the overlord. These will be discussed below. In some cases
the gift is made by more than one person. So in II Domnall and
Mal-Coluim give Biffie; Cainnech and Cathal give Altrie, or
part of it; Domnall and Cathal give Ednie. In these cases, both
grantors must presumably have had an interest in the place, or
have been joint owners.[1] In III and IV Gartnait and his wife
Ete give respectively *Pett Meic-Gobraig* and a place called *Ball
Domain* in Pitfour. Under the feudal system this would mean
that Gartnait owned these lands in right of his wife, to whom
they had belonged by inheritance as an heiress; but we cannot
assert that this would necessarily have been the case in Gaelic
law. The grant of *Pett Meic-Gobraig*, incidentally, was made for
the purpose of founding and supporting a church – being a *pett*
it must have been much more than a mere site for a church. If
the remark about the endowment of subordinate churches in
Aberdeenshire and Moray just above is applicable here, one
would suppose that *Pett Meic-Gobraig* was half a davoch,
therefore very roughly 100 acres, and this casts an interesting
light on what the size of a *pett* might be, though obviously they
would vary very greatly.

It will be noticed that one of the land-grants is made by a
king, Malcolm II; and three are by mormaers, Bede who gave
the land for the monastery in I, and Mal-Coluim son of Mal-
Brigte and Mal-Snechta son of Lulach who made grants in II.
Both the last two are known to have been mormaers of Moray,
though neither is specified here as such.[2] The Muiredach son
of Morgann who gave Pett Meic-Garnait and the field of Toiche
Teimne is said to be both mormaer and toísech; but no land-
grants are made explicitly by a mere toísech, though a *toísech
clainne*, Comgell son of Cainnech of Clann Chanann, makes
such a gift in V. All the other estates are given by people whose

---

[1] Stuart's suggestion (*BD*, p. l) that one grants as mormaer and the other
as toísech is speculative.

[2] On the question whether the Gartnait of III and IV was a mormaer, see the
Note to III, 1.

Historical commentary

rank is unspecified, though the cases of the two mormaers of Moray just mentioned suggest that some of them may well have been mormaers or toísechs.

The second type of grant consists not of lands and the basic rents from their tenants but of the grantor's 'share', his *cuit*, what has been rendered above by the almost homophonous colloquial English 'cut'. So in no. II, King Malcolm II gives a 'king's share' in Biffie and in Pett Meic-Gobraig; Matain son of Cairell gives a 'mormaer's share' in Altrie; and Cú Lí son of Baíthín gives a 'toísech's share', apparently also in Altrie. What this means is not stated, but it is evident that *cuit* was the dues and services liable to be rendered by the tenants of the estates named, to the king, and also to the mormaer and the toísech under whose authority they were, not as landlord but in virtue of their office. To put it differently, each of these ranks and officers was entitled to his own 'cut' from the estates concerned, in the form of taxes and services; and every piece of land was liable to these payments unless remitted. To 'give' his *cuit* would seem to mean that he now renounced it. If the lands already belonged to the monks, they simply now no longer rendered him these dues; if not, what the grantor is doing is assigning to them the dues which came to him from estates still belonging to him and *not* themselves now granted to the monastery. We seem to have an example of the first of these in no. II, if the order of the grants is really chronological, where Malcolm II gives his king's dues in Biffie, an estate previously granted to the monks by Domnall son of Ruaidrí and Mal-Coluim son of Cuilén but obviously still liable to render the royal *cuit* until freed of it by the king. The payments in question no doubt included the *kain*, a fixed payment in kind, and the *conveth*, dues for maintenance, which are well-known as burdens on land in later Scottish documents.[1]

---

[1] Respectively Gaelic *cáin* and *coinnmheadh*.

Historical commentary

The third sort of grant mentioned in the Book of Deer is the peculiar one whereby a grantor is said to have 'quenched' certain things. Etymologically, the verb in question means 'drowned, submerged, quenched', and the meaning in the passages in Deer is probably literally 'extinguished, exterminated'.[1] Some previous editors have translated 'merged', probably thinking of 'submerged'; and others 'mortmained'. 'Merged' however is clearly wrong, since this implies joining together things which were originally separate, particularly the fusing of a smaller thing with a larger, but this does not fit the examples. Nor will 'mortmained' serve. 'To mortmain' means to make a grant to a corporation, which does not die, is never under age, does not marry, etc., and from which therefore, under feudal law, it could never pass away again; it is now forever in the grip of the corporation's 'dead hand'. But this does not suit either, since *all* the simple land-grants and gifts of 'shares' already discussed are by definition already mortmained to the monastery, whereas this is evidently something different. Moreover, most previous editors have mistranslated some of the phrases associated with this verb,[2] so that what is really happening is obscured.

To take the examples first. In II, Domnall 'quenched' all the grants in favour of Drostán (i.e. the monastery) in return for the monks' giving him (Domnall) his (Drostán's, i.e. the monastery's) goodwill;[3] and Cainnech and Domnall and Cathal 'quenched' all the grants in favour of God and of Drostán from beginning to end, free from mormaer and toísech till Doomsday (but this last phrase is a subsequent addition in the text). In VI, Colbán, mormaer of Buchan, and Eva his wife, and Donnchad the toísech of Clann Chanann, join in 'quenching' all the grants

[1] The translation 'quench' is used throughout this book rather than 'extinguish', which might have seemed called for at first sight; because 'extinguish' is used in a technical sense in English terminology, of dues, not grants, whereas in Deer the verb applies to the grants (e.g. '"quenched" all the grants from all imposts', in VI). The result is the same in any case, that the dues were extinguished.   [2] See the appropriate Notes.
[3] On the meaning of this see the Note to II, 14.

'from all imposts, in favour of God and of Drostán and of Columba and of Peter the apostle', in return for four davochs'-worth of certain rents or taxes (a point discussed below). Also in II, the 'quenching' by Cathal is rather different; he quenches his toísech's dues,[1] 'on the same terms' as the above Domnall, i.e. presumably in favour of the monks and in return for their goodwill. Note that no estate is specified as the one burdened by the dues in question.

These instances show that 'quenching' is something which is done on behalf of the monastery; that the grantor expects and is given a return for it (which would however be less than the value of the 'quenching', since otherwise no benefit would be conferred); that it is defined as bringing freedom from all imposts (note 'quenched from all imposts', not 'quenched, in freedom from all imposts'); and that it mostly applies to 'all the grants'. But alternatively, a lord may quench his dues; no single estate being mentioned in this connection, it probably means all the dues at present rendered to him from any of the monastery lands, particularly since the other uses of the verb apply to a plurality. In fact, none of the 'quenchings' are specifically associated with any estates.

The 'quenching' of the lord's *cuit*, his dues, is at first sight the more readily intelligible of the two types. It looks as if it means that he forewent in perpetuity the taxes, etc., due to him as toísech, and as just said, on any and all estates hitherto liable to pay him this *cuit*. How this differs from the 'giving' of a lord's *cuit* on a single specified estate, as discussed on p. 119, is not clear; but it may be that when he remitted his dues on *all* his lands this distinction was felt to require a different, and more emphatic (or perhaps more permanent) verb.

The other type, the 'quenching' of 'all the grants', is less clear. If it meant the donor remitted all the dues on all the monastic estates to which he himself was entitled, this would be the same as the above-described 'quenching' of his *cuit*, and

---

[1] So that in this case the English 'extinguish' would be a satisfactory translation.

would surely therefore be phrased in the same way. One would suppose it must mean rather that he undertook himself to render in future all taxes, services, etc., due from the monastery to toísech, mormaer, and perhaps king from all the estates hitherto granted to it.[1] Not only the analogy of the type just discussed, but also the phrase '"quenched" all the grants *from all imposts*', would suggest this. The words 'free from mormaer and toísech till Doomsday' were added secondarily to the act of 'quenching' by Cainnech, Domnall, and Cathal in II, but this is no doubt an attempt to insist more explicitly on this aspect of a 'quenching' rather than to assert an extra claim not normally inherent in such. But if so, why should Cainnech, Domnall, and Cathal '"quench" all the grants' (emphatically stated to be 'from beginning to end') when this had already been done by Domnall son of Mac-Dubaicín earlier in the same list; and why should the mormaer of Buchan and others do the same thing in no. VI? The answer may be that fresh acts of 'quenching' became necessary from time to time because in the interval secular lords had been re-asserting their claims to receive their 'cut'; we have seen, after all, that such re-assertions are implicit in the situation in Deer in view of the general 'freeing' of the Church which appears to have been enacted in the time of Giric. Perhaps the heirs of Domnall son of Mac-Dubaicín and subsequently those of Cainnech, Domnall, and Cathal, had repudiated the deed of their predecessors. One should note that a 'quenching' of 'all the grants' appears to require the joint action of more than one lord, in two of the three cases; in the last case, of the mormaer of Buchan and his wife and an important *toísech clainne*, as well as the general witness of all the nobles of Buchan. These were presumably big affairs, particularly the third, much more so than a mere grant of a small manor. Moreover, the return made by the monastery in the last case, as discussed below, was by no means nominal. In the others the 'goodwill' of the monks may imply that the

[1] Such undertakings are a known feature in feudal land-granting also; cf. the *Innes Review* (Spring 1970), p. 8.

donator had offended them, and wished to be reconciled. On this see the Note to II, 14. Finally, there is the fact that the Cathal who 'quenched' his toísech's dues also gave funds for a banquet for a hundred people twice yearly, at Christmas and Easter; in other words, he founded a 'college feast' – a good way, no doubt, of earning the 'goodwill' which he too seems to have required.

The last problem in connection with the grants to Deer is raised by the fact that the 'quenching' in no. VI was done 'in return for the dues on four davochs'[-worth] of that which should devolve on the chief [religious] houses of Scotland in general and on its chief churches'.[1] 'That which should devolve', etc., would seem to mean a national tax payable by all the chief monasteries and mother-churches of Scotland, presumably to the king. Deer must have been one of the chief monasteries in question, and no doubt these and the 'chief churches' raised contributions from their dependent foundations towards it. The tax reminds one of the feudal 'common aid' normally rendered to the king by all estates, whether lay or ecclesiastical, which was levied apparently on the basis of an assessment by davochs.[2] The dues mentioned (the word is *cuit*) as payable on four davochs would perhaps be those chargeable on four davochs of the monastery's lands as part of their contribution towards this tax. But what happened to them under this deed of 'quenching'? They could hardly now have been diverted from the king to the mormaer of Buchan, his wife, and the toísech of Clann Morgainn, since they could not bind him to this. If, however, we can take 'in return for' in this case as the equivalent of 'except', it would give good sense. By quenching all the grants, the mormaer and his associates were apparently undertaking themselves, in future, all the dues previously payable from all

---

[1] See the Notes for a discussion of details in the meaning of this phrase. The translations and discussions of previous editors are put rather astray by misrendering the phrases translated here as 'in return for' and 'should devolve on'.

[2] Compare e.g. *Lib. Eccl. Scon.*, p. 42, no. 67, where Alexander II reduces the rates for 'common aid' due from the canons of Scone for Blairgowrie from those on 6 davochs to those on 5.

the monastery's estates to toísech, mormaer, and king. Bu a 'return' for this was expected; and this time it took the form not of a (smaller) recompense by the monastery direct to the grantors, but of its continuing to render, and thus freeing the grantors from undertaking to render, a fixed part of this 'common aid' normally paid by Deer in its capacity as one of the chief monasteries of Scotland. This exception would be the *equivalent* of a counter-payment by the monks to the grantors for the benefit to them of the otherwise total 'quenching' of their dues, without actually being paid them; so that the 'in return for' formula remains applicable.

ORTHOGRAPHY AND LANGUAGE

I. THE SPELLING OF THE SCRIBES OF DEER

Essentially the spelling of the Gaelic notes in Deer is the same as that of the ordinary late Middle Irish to which they belong; but though there are inconsistencies in M. Ir., there are far more of such in Deer. Many of them can be paralleled in M. Ir., but one would not expect to find them in such profusion in any one text. Moreover, in addition to gross inconsistencies there are sometimes wholly 'wrong' or even fantastic spellings. For example, while failure to indicate a palatalised consonant or consonants between vowels, by writing *i* before it, where this is not strictly necessary, is well-known in M. Ir., the scribes of Deer sometimes leave out the *i*, where it *is* necessary, before a final consonant or consonants; with the result in some cases that a nominative appears to have been written for a genitive, and so on, as in *mac Morcunn*, II, 2. There is in fact considerable hesitation about how to write the vowels of unstressed syllables. These were by now all phonemically /ə/, but allophonically [ə], [ɪ], or [i]; and the regular late M. Ir. usage, which is derived from an older one where unstressed vowels were not yet reduced to /ə/, is as follows:[1] (1) internal [-ə-], *a*; sometimes *o* or *u*, due to historical reasons; (2) internal [-ɪ·], *ai* or *ui* (the *i* sometimes omitted in non-final syllables), sometimes *i*; (3) internal [·ə-], *e* or *iu*; (4) internal [·i·], *i*; (5) final [-ə], *a*; sometimes *ae* or *ai*, or *o*, or *u*, due to historical reasons; (6) final [·ə], *e* or *i*; sometimes *iu*, due to historical reasons. In Deer, the variations are much more marked, resulting in things like *dorodloeg* for *dorodlaig*, *dolodib* for *dolaidib*, *brether* for *brethir*, *Cannech* and *Caennaig* for *Cainnich* or *Cainnig*, and so on (see details below), some of which give a wrong impression of the quality of the consonants and some even of the true grammatical form. Again,

---

[1] Here - before or after a vowel stands for a neutral or velarised consonant, and ɪ for a palatalised consonant.

the voiced stops /*b*, *d*, *g*/ are regularly written *p*, *t*, *c* internally and finally in M. Ir., for historical reasons, though sometimes *b*, *d*, *g* (in Mod. Ir. always *b*, *d*, *g*); but in Deer the *b*, *d*, *g* spellings are plainly commoner, though *p*, *t*, *c* are also common. The result of these and the other 'abnormal' spellings analysed here is that at first sight the notes in Deer strike the eye as distinctly unlike Middle Irish, and this was taken by Macbain[1] as evidence that the Gaelic of Scotland in the twelfth century had already become differentiated from that of Ireland, and was considerably more 'evolved' than Irish. But Macbain was under a misapprehension; the spellings in Deer which he took for evidence of phonetic change having happened at a faster rate in Scotland than in Ireland are purely a matter of orthography, and the changes in question had happened just as much in Ireland as in Scotland.[2] It is merely that the Irish scribes spelt in a more traditional manner and the Scottish ones more 'by ear', like an English-speaking child who writes *enuf* for *enough*. The question how far Deer does really show any traces of purely Scottish linguistic peculiarities is discussed below, pp. 149ff.

In fact this is the explanation of the whole thing. Irish scribes were well trained in the long tradition of how to write. The Scottish scribes were also trained in the usual way, of how to write the Common Gaelic language, as is natural in the circumstances of the common Columban church; but they were imperfectly trained, their spelling was not very 'good', in the sense that they did not know the traditional spelling very well, and tended therefore to strange hesitations, pronunciation-spellings, or mere mistakes. This is not at all unnatural, considering that Deer is on the remotest edge of the Common Gaelic civilisation-area; its writing-masters must have been out of touch and poorly qualified. One may compare the extraordinary corruption and provincialism of the illuminations in

[1] *TGSI*, XI, 142.
[2] A good many of Macbain's linguistic and orthographic notes are misconceived and quite untrustworthy.

Orthography and language

the MS, which may well be evidence that these, and also the exceedingly corrupt original text of the Gospels, were produced at Deer, some centuries earlier.

In the following analysis of the orthography of Deer in relation to that of contemporary M. Ir., spellings which are perfectly normal in M. Ir. are in some cases not even discussed. Thus stressed /-a-/ or /-a:-/ is always written *a* in Deer,[1] as in M. Ir. (e.g. *mac*, passim), and the nasal *v* phoneme is always written *m*, also as in M. Ir. (and is therefore not distinguished from /*m*/); and there would be no point in saying so and occupying space unnecessarily with examples. This is an account of how Deer differs from Irish rather than a complete description of its spelling.

N.B.: apart from capital letters to show proper names, and the expansion of contractions, the spellings in sections (1) to (26) below are those of the diplomatic text. On the meaningless acute accents (omitted here) which pepper the texts in the MS, see p. 17.

Stressed vowels

(1) /-a$^{\iota}$/ when short, /-a$:^{\iota}$/ when long. In M. Ir. normally respectively *ai* and *ái*, but in a non-final syllable sometimes *a* and *á*. In Deer, the commonest *in non-final syllables* is *a*. So, short, *roalseg*, I, 2; *athle*, I, 5; *doraten*, I, 5; *Alteri*, II, 5; *Cannech*, III, 1; *Gille-Calline*, IV, 2; *Clande*, V, 6; *Alenn*, V, 8; *mathe*, VI, 8; etc. Long, *slante*, I, 10, 12; *tanic*, I, 12; *Scali*, V, 5; etc. The *ai* spelling is not common; note *Cainnec(h)*, II, 16, 19; *laithi*, II, 21. The rare *ae* is not meant for the diphthong, no. (17) below, but simply for *ai*; *Caerill*, II, 4; *Caennaig*, V, 6. The spelling *e* occurs once, in *Clenni*, VI, 2; by contrast with *Clande* just before. But it is possible that this represents a genuine phonetic development which also took place in Ireland, whereby /-a$^{\iota}$/ became /-ö$^{\iota}$/ in some words, in circumstances which are not perfectly clear, though rounding in contact with labials accounts for

---

[1] In I, 4, *braith* for *brath* is simply a slip.

some. In Ireland this became later $/-e^1/$ or $/-i^1/$, spelt in some cases *oi*, the second also *ui*. In most Scottish dialects it has given $/-ɤ-/$, e.g. in this very word, *cloinne*, but in those nearest to Buchan it is now often $/-e^1/$.[1] The *e* in Deer could be taken as an attempt to spell either of these, but in view of its entirely isolated character, little stress should be laid on it. In the case of the word *ele* from O. Ir. *aile*, I, 5 this had happened early in Irish, presumably because of its position in absolute initial, and *eile* is already familiar in, e.g., the Irish *Passions and Homilies*, about contemporary with Deer; so that this is on a different footing. *Malmori* in VII, 9 should probably also be included here. In early Irish the Virgin Mary is *Maire*, giving with rounding *Moire*, and becoming *Muire* in the M. Ir. period. It is often spelt *Muire* in Sc. G., but this appears to be due to Irish literary influence, and the normal pronunciation is $/mɤr'ə/$, which means what would naturally be – and in fact often is – spelt *Moire*; which is probably meant in *Malmori*.

In monosyllables, the M. Ir. spelling is *ai* when short and *ái* when long, since to omit the *i* would imply that the following consonant is not palatalised, there being no front-vowel after the consonant to indicate the contrary. The only example of any form in Deer is *Marr*, III, 7, where *Mairr*, genitive of *Marr*, is clearly needed. Here the influence of Latin documents is possible, or pure carelessness. It is not unthinkable, however, that since palatalised fortis *r* ('double-*r*') was depalatalised in all Common Gaelic (but whether so early is uncertain), this might be a pronunciation-spelling. But it is not quite established that this place was really *Marr* not *Már* (see Notes); if the second, this explanation would not apply.

(2) $/-o-/$. M. Ir. *o* when short (*ó* when long), and so always in Deer, except in *choir*, II, 15, for *chor*; this would seem to be simply a mistake.

(3) $/-o^1/$. M. Ir. *oi* when short, *ói* when long; but as with nos. (1), (4), and (7), the *i* may sometimes be left out in non-final syllables, for the same reason. In Deer in *non-final syllables*,

[1] Cf. also *Ériu*, XVI, 90.

Orthography and language

o is universal, cf. nos. (1), (4). So *Comgeall*, II, 1; *Chomded*, II, 22; *Comgell*, V, 3, 5; *cosecrad*, III, 2; *gorthe*, V, 7; *cotchenn*, VI, 5; *Gille-Comded*, VII, 10. Long, *Broccin*, VI, 6 (see Notes); *Brocin*, VII, 11.

In monosyllables, the expected *oi* is seen; *Cloic*, I, 11, and *Chloic, ibid.*; but in *Rosabard*, II, 11, the *o* is probably for *oi* (see Notes).

(4) /-u¹/ when short, /-u:¹/ when long. M. Ir. respectively *ui* and *úi*; but as with nos. (1) and (3), the *i* may sometimes be omitted in non-final syllables, for the same reason. As in (3), Deer seems almost never to write the *i* in *non-final syllables*. So, when short, *cruthnec*, I, 2; *Mulenn*, II, 6; *Culeon*, II, 8; *hule*, II, 13, 20; *huli*, VI, 3, 8; *hulib*, III, 3, VI, 4; *a hule*, II, 14; *Muredig*, III, 10; *Dubni*, III, 10. But with *ui*, *cuitid*, II, 15. When long, *Duni*, III, 4. The spelling *Moridac* for *Mu(i)redach* in II, 2 is isolated and presumably a mere error. In monosyllables, there is *ui*, in *cuit*, II, 4, 5, 10; VI, 4. Long, *Puir*, IV, 2.

(5) /¹e-/ when short, /¹e:-/ when long. Spelt in M. Ir. respectively *e* and *é*, but pronounced with on-glide to the following velarised or non-palatalised consonant, [eᵃ] and [e:ᵃ]. The on-glide is occasionally shown in both, as *ea* and *éa*, in M. Ir. spelling. The former 'broke' in Irish to [ʲa], already to some degree by the early thirteenth century,[1] and the development would seem to have begun earlier. In Scotland the same thing has taken place in dialect, but much less universally, and therefore probably later. In Deer, *e* is always written when short (contrast unstressed syllables), both in *non-final syllables* and in *monosyllables*, with one exception. So *rosbenact*, I, 14; *Malpetir*, III, 8; *Feradac*, IV, 3; etc. The exception is *ardmandaidib* in VI, 5, evidently for *ardmendaidib*; see the Notes. This is hardly to be taken as an instance of breaking, considering the lateness (and, in Scotland, the incompleteness) of the development, and the fact that this is unique in Deer. It is more likely due to scribal carelessness, perhaps under the influence of the flanking *a*'s. In *monosyllables*, e.g. *bec*, I, 9; *fer*, III, 9; etc.

[1] Cf. O'Rahilly in *Hermathena*, XX, 162.

Orthography and language

The long [eːᵃ] is spelt regularly *é* in M. Ir., though the on-glide later came to be written, as *éa*, already appearing on occasion in M. Ir.[1] In Deer it is *e* or *ea*. Examples: with *e*, in *non-final syllables, Eua*, VI, 1; *in a monosyllable, Der*, VII, 2. With *ea*, in *non-final syllables, deara*, I, 15; *in a monosyllable, Dear*, I, 16.

(6) /-eᴸ/. On this see no. (1).

(7) /ᴸeᴸ/ when short, /ᴸeːᴸ/ when long. The regular M. Ir. spellings are respectively *ei* and *éi*, but in non-final syllables quite often *e* and *é*. In Deer there is almost always *e* in non-final syllables and in monosyllables, whether short or long. So, short in non-final syllables: *Pette*, I, 11; *Uethe*, II, 17; *derad*, II, 21; *Brecini*, III, 6; *Pet*, IV, 1; *Cennedig* (first *e*), V, 5; *Merlec* (first *e*), V, 5; *cetri*, VI, 4. In monosyllables, *sen*, I, 9, 13; *mec*, V, 1; quasi-stressed in names, *Mec-*, III, 2, V, 1. Long in non-final syllables: *glerec* (first *e*), I, 8, 9, 11, 7; *brether* (first *e*), I, 14; *leginn*, III, 9; *Malechi*, V, 3; and in monosyllables: *es*, V, 10. The digraph *æ* in *Malæchin*, VI, 7, means simply (long) *e*, not a diphthong, and is not to be confused with no. (17).

But with *ei* written rarely: short, quasi-stressed in names, *Meic-*, II, 13, 17; long, *eis*, II, 23.

(8) /ᴸi-/ short. Normally written *i* in M. Ir. This is seen in *a ginn*, I, 3, and *i gginn*, V, 7. No examples of the corresponding long vowel.

(9) /ᴸiᴸ/ short. M. Ir. *i*, and so everywhere in Deer. Long, M. Ir. *í*, and normally *i* in Deer; but note *ii* in *Culii*, II, 5 and *riig*, II, 10.

Unstressed vowels

(10) [-ə(-)]; for the Irish spellings see p. 125. In Deer, normally *a*, e.g. *tangator* (second *a*), I, 1, 5; *buadacc*, I, 15; *Cathal*, II, 7; *ocmad*, III, 4; etc. The second *o* in *Domongart*, III, 9 is probably caused by the labial consonant, as also the *u* in *Colum* (numerous, see Glossarial Index); the second being

---

[1] The subsequent 'breaking' in certain circumstances, both in Ir. and Sc. G., may be ignored here as being too late to be relevant.

due also to historical reasons. But the *o* in *tangator* twice, above, is unexplained (see section (36), below), as is the *u* in *Morgunn*, VI, 6, cf. no. (12) below, near the end; and also the second *e* in *blienec*, I, 15. In the case of *testus*, V, 4, the *u* is no doubt due to traditional spelling. (On *Coluim* for *Colum* see (12).) In absolute final, this accounts also for the *-u* in *nesu*, V, 8, contrast the *-a* in *chetna*, II, 15, also from *-u*; and probably the *-e* in *Malsnecte*, II, 12, from O. Ir. *-ai*. The *-e* in *ere*, I, 8, can hardly be explained so, since the O. Ir was *éra*. In proclitics, *a*, 'his, her, their', see Glossarial Index.

(11) [ᴸə(-)]; for the Irish spellings, see above, p. 125. Non-final: as in Irish, the regular spelling is *e*; so in an internal syllable *Muredig*, III, 10; and in final syllables, *cruthnec*, I, 2; *glerec*, I, 8, 9, II, 7; *tosec(h)*, I, 4, II, 23; *taesec*, V, 6; *thesech*, II, 21; *Cainnec(h)*, II, 16, 19; *Chomded*, II, 22; *Gillecomded*, VII, 10; *Comgell*, V, 3, 5. There are two instances of *ea*, in *Comgeall*, II, 1, and *thesseach*, V, 9. The *a* in *derad*, II, 21 obscures the palatalised character of the *r* and is doubtless a slip; and the *i* in *Moridac*, II, 2, is not the only careless spelling in what should have been written *Muiredach*.

In absolute final, see the Irish spellings, p. 125; *-e* and *-i* are completely interchangeable in M. Ir. In Deer, *-e* is commoner. From O. Ir. *-e*, e.g. *ernacde* and *slante*, I, 10, 12; *Cille*, II, 2; *Clande*, V, 6. From O. Ir. *-i*, e.g. *saere*, I, 4, II, 21; *ele*, I, 5; *gonice*, I, 11 etc.; *hule*, II, 13, 20; *Gillecalline*, IV, 2. From O. Ir. *-iu*, *athle*, I, 5. However *-i* is also found, though Hand A prefers not to use it. So, from O. Ir. *-e*, e.g. *laithi*, II, 21 (Hand C); *eclasi*, III, 2; *rigi*, III, 5; *Cilli*, IV, 2, VI, 3; *Clenni*, VI, 2; *cetri*, VI, 4. From O. Ir. *-i*, *Finguni*, V, 3; *saeri*, V, 9; *huli*, VI, 3, 8.

(12) [-ɪᴸ]; for the Irish spellings see p. 125. In Deer as in M. Ir., *ai* is normal, though the *i* may be omitted in non-final syllables. E.g. *gathraig*, I, 4; *foracaib*, I, 14; *uactair*, II, 11; *Cormaic*, III, 8; *Gillecolaim* and *Malcolaim*, III, 10; *Morgainn*, VI, 2; *Donnchaid*, VI, 7. With *i* omitted, *tabart*, II, 14. In non-final syllables, *iaidnaisse* (second *ai*), VI, 8; *dolaidib*, VI, 4; *mandaidib*, VI, 5; but with *i* omitted, *ernacde*, I, 10, 12; *Etdanin*,

II, 19; *eclasi*, III, 2; *ienasi*, V, 4. The isolated *ae* of *dendaes*, I, 10 is similar to those of *Caerill*[1] and *Caennaig* where stressed, see no. (1) above.

There is also sometimes *oi* (rarely without the *i* in non-final syllables): *Abbordoboir*, I, 2; *rolaboir*, I, 16; *Gobroig*, II, 10; *Luloig*, II, 12; *abstoil*, III, 2. Without the *i*, *Nolloce*, II, 16; *dolodib* (the second *o*), III, 3. It is doubtless significant that in three of these the vowel is preceded in the same syllable by a labial consonant. In the unique *dorodloeg*, I, 6, the *e* is to be explained in the same way as that in *dendaes*.

The *ui* in *Malcoluim*, V, 4, and *Coluim* in V, 2 and 7,[2] and the *u* in an internal syllable in *Finguni*, V, 3, are accounted for on historical grounds; and in the first cases also the influence of the labial, see no. (10) above.

There is sometimes only *i*, the non-palatalised nature of the preceding consonant not being indicated; but this is purely graphic. E.g. *Cobrig*, III, 2 (beside *Gobroig* above); *Petir*, III, 2, 8; *bliadin*, III, 5; *Muredig*, III, 10; *Colim*, IV, 2; *Donnchid*, VI, 7 (beside *Donnchaid* in the same line). A couple of instances of *e*, in I and II only (i.e. Hand A) are further cases of the use of this instead of *i*, particularly favoured by Hand A; cf. section (13) below. *Cosgreg*, I, 1; *dabeg*, II, 11.

There are some cases in final syllables where the palatal nature of the following consonant is obscured by not writing the *i*, there being no front vowel after it which would show this; consequently making the word appear a nominative instead of an oblique case. Compare *Marr* in no. (1) above. These are *Buchan*, genitive, in I, 3, VI, 1, 8; *Morcunn*, genitive, II, 2 and *Morcunt*, 7; *thabart*, II, 14; *Madchor*, V, 1. In *Malcolum*, II, 8, 11 (the peculiar *Malcoloum* in II, 9, must be a slip for the same *Malcolum*) the failure to write the *-i-* might conceivably be due to the beginnings of the depalatalisation of labials which is characteristic of Sc. G. There would be no reason to treat this differently from the others just quoted if it were not that *Coluim*

---

[1] Hand A, which also wrote *dendaes* and *dorodloeg*.
[2] If these two last are being treated here as fem. *ā*-stems; see (31).

for *Colum* in v, 2 and 7, and this spelt *Colim* in IV, 2, look rather like hypercorrections, due to scribal uncertainty arising from, at any rate, a weakening in the palatalisation of labials. But little weight can be laid on this, and a different explanation for these is offered in (31) below.

(13) [*ɨᴸ*]; spelt *i* in M. Ir. In Deer, *i* is normal; e.g. *thoisig*, II, 15. But Hand A has the same fondness for *e* already observed in combinations with other vowels above: *roalseg*, I, 2; *doraten*, I, 5; *brether* (second *e*), I, 14; *toiseg*, II, 5; *Mulenn*, II, 6; also *Cannech*, III, I. Note also in a proclitic, *esse*, I, 3, for *issé*. The *ai* in *Caennaig*, v, 6, is evidently a slip.

Diphthongs

(14) /ᴸ(iʁ:)-/, spelt *ia* in M. Ir.; Deer *sliab*, v, 8. But note also *ie* in *blienec*, I, 15, and *ienasi*, v, 4; and *iai* in *iaidnaisse*, VI, 8. These are no doubt mistakes.

(15) /-(uʁ:)-/, spelt *ua* in M. Ir. No examples of [-(uʁ:)-], since *Turbrud* for *Turbruad in VII, 11 is probably to be taken as a bad spelling on the part of the Latin scribe. Of /-(uʁ:)ᴸ/, probably [-(uɛ:)-], normally M. Ir. *uai*, note *ua* in *Ruadri*, II, 8 and III, 7; and in an unstressed syllable *Turbruad*, III, 9, but the expected *Turbruaid* in VI, 6. The *ui* in *do-chuid*, I, 9, is not the diphthong but is disyllabic *uï*; Sc. G. *chaïdh*.

(16) /ᴸ(eo:)ᴸ/ (but probably already 'broken' to /ᴸjo:ᴸ/), spelt *éoi* in M. Ir.; in an unstressed syllable, *eo* in *Culeon*, II, 8. (No instances of /ᴸ(eo:)-/, spelt *éo* in M. Ir.)

(17) The early O. Ir. diphthongs written *aí* or *ae* and *oí* or *oe*, which were probably respectively /-(ai:)ᴸ/ and /-(oi:)ᴸ/, and had allophones [-(aɪ:)-] and [-(oɪ:)-] before non-palatalised or velarised consonants, fell together later in monophthongs, apparently including the complete early unrounding of the *o* in Irish. The resulting sounds differ greatly in the various dialects of the Gaelic world. In M. Ir. the spellings *ae*, *oe*, *aí*, *oí*, are used without distinction; but in Modern Irish *aoi* when final or before palatalised consonants and *ao* before non-palatalised consonants; the modern Sc. G. spelling is the same. In Scotland the

situation is most easily explained if we suppose that instead of *oí* (*oe*) being unrounded and falling together with *aí* (*ae*), the falling-together took the form, rather, of including a concurrent partial unrounding of the first and slight rounding of the second, producing one single monophthongal sound which was a slightly rounded [ʏ:], later wholly unrounded in most dialects, becoming advanced in some and raised in others. This explanation best suits the modern dialect situation when taken in conjunction with the evidence of the Book of Deer.

The Latin alphabet has no means of spelling such sounds, and they have always been a difficulty, in the sense that no exact representation can be found; for instance, the modern *ao* does not mean anything remotely approaching /*a-o*/ or /(*ao*)/ in any dialect. It was natural that at the date of Deer it was a considerable embarrassment, and the scribes struggled with a variety of spellings, namely *ae*, *e*, *æ*, *a* (probably for *aí*, cf. *a* for *ái*), and *oe*, *œ*, *o* (probably for *oí*, cf. *o* for *ói*). Cases where early O. Ir. had *aí*, *ae*, may appear with one of the *o*-spellings, and cases where early O. Ir. had *oí*, *oe* may appear with one of the *a*-spellings. It is the first of these which suggests that the falling-together had included a slight rounding of the unround sound under the influence of the partly unrounded round one. In the case of the word normalised here as *toísech*, it should be noted that though the direct descendant of this, *taoiseach*, appears in Sc. G. dictionaries, the normal thing is *tòiseach*, which is from the by-form known in early Irish as *tóisech*. In these circumstances it might seem wrong-headed to normalise the Deer instances as *toísech* rather than *tóisech*; but the fact is that the very varying spellings in Deer can only be explained if we assume that we are dealing with *oí* and not with *ói*.

The distribution of the spellings in Deer is as follows:

(*a*) From original stressed [(*ai*:)], with *a*, *Batin*, II, 5, if this is really = Irish *Baíthín*, see Notes.

(*b*) From original stressed [(*aɪ*:)], with *e* or its equivalent *æ*; *Eda*, II, 1; *Æd*, VII, 10; Irish *Aed*(*a*). With *o*; perhaps *Molini*, V, 4; see Notes.

Orthography and language

(*c*) From original unstressed [(*ai*:)], with *oi*; *mormoir* (genitive), II, 4; quasi-stressed, *Moilbrigte* (genitive), II, 11.

(*d*) From original unstressed [(*aɪ*:)], with *ae*; *mormaer*, I, 4. With *ai*, *mormair*, II, 3. With *e* or its equivalent *æ*; *mormer*, VI, 1; *mormær*, I, 3, 7.

(*e*) With reduction of original unstressed [(*aɪ*:)] to [*a*]; possibly *Cinatha* (first *a*), II, 10 and *mormar*, II, 23, III, 7, though these could be instances of *a* written for *aí*. See Note, II, 10. The same when quasi-stressed, the numerous names in *Mal-* (see Glossarial Index); but note the possibility that *Male-* in *Maledomni*, III, 6, is for *Mael-*, see Notes.

(*f*) From original stressed [(*oi*:)], with *oi*; *toiseg*, II, 5; *thoisig*, II, 15. With *œ*; *tœsech*, VI, 2. With *o*; *tosec*, I, 4; *tosech*, II, 23; *sore*, V, 2. With *ae*; *saere*, I, 4; *ssaere*, II, 21; *taesec*, V, 6; *ssaeri*, V, 9. With *e*; *thesech*, II, 21; *thesseach*, V, 9.

(*g*) From original stressed [(*oɪ*:)], with *e*; (*h*)*en*, V, 10 (2); *Engus*, VII, 10; *ser*, III, 3, unless this is to be taken as acc. sg. fem. in agreement with *Pet* in l. 2, in which case it belongs under (*f*).

No examples of original [(*oi*:)] or [(*oɪ*:)] unstressed.

Epenthetic vowels

(18) The development of these in certain consonant groups, found in all dialects of the Gaelic world, is difficult to date, as it has never been admitted in literary spelling. It seems not improbable that its rise goes back to the end of the M. Ir. period,[1] so that the following doubtful instances might just possibly be traces of its faint beginnings in Deer: for *marb*, *mareb*, I, 8, written with the punctum delens both above and below the *e*, as if the scribe wrote by ear and then realised this was 'incorrect' spelling; *anim*, I, 16, for *ainm*, but this could be a scribal error involving the wrong joining of the first three minims; *Brecini*, III, 6, perhaps for *Brecni*, see Note; and *Donnachac*, VI, 2, if for *Donnchad*, see Note.

[1] See my Rhys Lecture, 'Common Gaelic', *PBA*, xxxvii, 84.

Orthography and language

Consonants

(19) The voiceless stops, /p, t, k/, spelt p, t, c in M. Ir., but quite often doubled internally and finally. The same is the case in Deer; note with doubling, *dattac*, I, 9; *Pette*, I, 11; *Pett*, II, 2, 6, 10, 12; but *Pet*, III, 2, IV, 1; *Broccin*, VI, 6, but *Brocin*, VII, 11. In contact with *s* the voiceless stops were lenes, which explains the *b* in *abstoil* III, 2, beside *apstal*, VI, 4. The loss of *p* in *escob* from older *epscob*, III, 4, 5, is a genuine phonological development, a simplification of the consonant group, well known in M. Ir. That of *t* in *Garnait*, I, 12, II, 3, VI, 1, beside *Gartnait* (the older form of the name) in III, 1 and IV, 1, is no doubt of the same origin; and so perhaps is that of *t* in *ocmad*, III, 4, for *ochtmad* (see Note to III, 4). For *llt*, see the Note on *Aldin Alenn*, V, 8. In *slante*, I, 10 and 12, the *nt* is preserved, but in modern Sc. G. *t* is voiced in this group in some dialects. In the case of *Morcunn*, II, 2, *Morgainn*, VI, 2, and *Morgunn*, VI, 6, beside *Morcunt*, II, 7, it is uncertain whether we have Cumbric (or Pictish) -*nt* borrowed into Gaelic as -*nd* (spelt -*nt* in II, 7), as in Welsh *plant* borrowed as *cland*, and then regularly giving -*nn* as noted in (20); or whether the development of -*nt* to -*nn* had already happened in Cumbric (or Pictish) before it was borrowed, a feature which can be traced in Welsh to the ninth century (*LHEB*, § 103.)

(20) The voiced stops, /b, d, g/, spelt b, d, g, initially in M. Ir., but commonly p, t, c internally and finally though sometimes b, d, g. In Deer initial b, d, g are invariable. Internal and final p, t, c are common; e.g. *Tiprat*, I, 11; *tangator*, I, 1, 5; *tharat*, I, 7; *cuit*, II, 4, 5; *Malbrigte*, II, 6; *doratsator*, II, 17; *Petir*, III, 2; *Leot*, III, 6; *etar*, V, 8; *Petar*, VI, 3; *dorat* passim; *foracaib*, I, 14; (*go*)*nic*(*e*), I, 2, 11, II, 1, 18; *tanic*, I, 12; *Dubbacin*, II, 13; *eclasi*, III, 2; *sacart*, IV, 3; *Morcunn*, II, 2, *Morcunt*, II, 7. There are a few cases of internal and final b, d, g, however:[1] *edbarta* (the *b*), II, 14, 20, VI, 3; *ab*, III, 6; *escob*, III, 4, 5; *edar*, II, 18, beside *etar* above; *Cennedig* (the *d*),

---

[1] As to *dendaes*, I, 10, note that nearly 25% of the 3rd pl. -*t*(*a*)*is* verbal endings in the *Saltair na Rann* as analysed by Strachan in *TPhS*, 1895, have -*d*-.

Orthography and language

V, 5; *mandaidib* (second *d*), VI, 5; *tangator*, I, 1, 5; *gonige*, V, 5, 7, in Hand B, beside *c* in this word in Hand A above; *Morgunn*, VI, 6, *Morgainn*, VI, 2, in Hand C, beside *c* in this name in Hand A, above. There is *bb* in *Abbordoboir*, I, 2; *Abberdeon*, III, 6, VII, 5, 12; and *abb*, VI, 6, beside *ab* above; and *td* in *Etdanin*, II, 19. The *Gg-* of *Ggillebrite* in VII, 10 seems a freak, and the scribe, who went on to write *Ggillecomded*, corrected himself in the second case with the punctum delens over the first *g*.

In proclitics, original initial *c*, which must have been lenis, had become /g/ by or in the M. Ir. period, though in M. Ir. the recognition of this in spelling was rare. In Deer, however, *g-* is common; so *go*, I, 4, 7, 9, 10; II, 21, V, 8; *gebe*, I, 14; and the examples of *gonice* mentioned above. But there is *c-* in *co*, III, 4; and in *cu*, II, 21, V, 9, 10 (all three Hand C), and VI, 5. In the word *cech* or *cach*, spellings with *g-* do not appear at all; with *c-*, II, 15, 16 and 22, 23; V, 9, 10.

In the O. Ir. groups /dl/, /dn/, /ld/, and /nd/ the voiced stop became assimilated to the liquid or nasal in the O. Ir. period, apparently in the ninth century; but the dental stop continued to be written often for centuries (in some words, to the present day) by orthographical conservatism; and particularly in the case of *nd* this came to be felt in M. Ir. as merely an alternative way of writing *nn*; so that original *nn* and original *nd*, both already /nn/, may both be written quite indifferently *nd* or *nn* in M. Ir. In Deer, for original *dl* note *Nolloce*, II, 16 for M. Ir. *Notlaice* (but traditional *Athotla*, VII, 9); for original *ld*, *mallact*, V, 10, and *Callenn*, III, 4, beside more traditional *Callden*, VII, 7 (see *SHR*, XXXIII, 14–16); for original *dn*, *chetna* in II, 15 is traditional; for original *nd*, *bennact*, II, 22, spelt by a slip *benact*, I, 14; *proinn*, II, 15; *leginn*, III, 9; *Clenni*, VI, 2, but spelt more traditionally *Clande* in V, 6.

(21) The voiceless spirants, /f, θ, χ/, spelt normally respectively *f* (or, when the lenition of *p-*, spelt *ph-* or *p-*), *th*, and *ch* in M. Ir. In Deer, the situation is as follows: Original *f* is written *f*, e.g. *foracaib*, I, 14; *fer leginn*, III, 9. But for lenited *p-* note *f-* in *fris*, V, 8, and probably in *Furene*, II, 1; but *ph-* in

Orthography and language

phusta, VI, 2, and *p*- probably in *Puir*, IV, 2. Where *f*- is lenited it became nil, and is therefore sometimes omitted in Irish MSS. As might be expected, Deer uses pronunciation-spelling here, and omits it in all cases; so *ro alseg*, I, 2; *inna ienasi*, V, 4; *na iaidnaisse*, VI, 8; *Malechi*[*n*], V, 3; *Malæchin*, VI, 7.

For *th* Deer usually has *th*, e.g. *cruthnec*, I, 2; *gathraig*, I, 4; *braith*, I, 4; *gorthe*, V, 7; *o thesseach*, V, 9; *Sithig*, VI, 2. There is however sometimes *d*, which may also be found in M. Ir.; it appears to be relatively commoner in Deer than in M. Ir. So *dorodloeg*, I, 6 (second *d*); *chadraig*, I, 13; *Bidbin*, II, 9, 10; *brad*, V, 2. Note *t* in *cetri*, VI, 4; and perhaps in *Batin*, II, 5, if this is for *Baíthín* (see Notes). On the *h* in *hule*, II, 14, and the nil in *Mecbead*, III, 7, V, 1, see the Notes.

For *ch*, Deer is notably aberrant: much the commonest spelling is *c*, particularly in I (though VI has *ch* throughout). So *cruthnec* (second *c*), I, 2; *thosec*, I, 4, II, 4; *glerec*, I, 8, II, 7; *attac*, I, 9; *ua Cloic* (both), I, 11; *Chloic*, I, 11; *blienec*, I, 15; *Moridac*, II, 2; *a cuitid*, II, 15; *cec*, II, 15, 16, 22, 23 (second *c* in all cases); *Cainnec*, II, 19 (second *c*); *do Colum Cille*, III, 3 (both); *Brecini*, III, 6; *Gillemicael*, IV, 1; *Feradac*, IV, 3; *taesec*, V, 6; *Ferdomnac*, VII, 11. Instead of *c* there is *cc* twice in I; *buadacc* (beside *blienec*), 15, and *imacc*, 17. However, *ch* is not uncommon; e.g. *Buchan*, I, 3; *chadraig*, I, 13; *Toche*, II, 3; *choir chétna*, II, 15; *Cainnech*, II, 16; *Donchad*, V, 1; *Choluim*, V, 2, 7; *achad*, V, 9; *chomallfas*, V, 10. There is *cch* in *Acchad*, V, 1. In *cht*, note *ct* in *benact*, I, 14; *uactair*, II, 11; *bennact*, II, 22; *Nectan*, III, 5; *mallact*, V, 10; but *cht* in *bennacht*, V, 9, beside *mallact*. Note also *c* for *cht* in *ocmad*, III, 4, on which see the Note. There is no linguistic significance in this fondness for *c*; it is purely a question of scribal practice.[1] *C*, *cc*, and *cch* all occur in Irish MSS, beside the (there) very much commoner *ch*.

(22) The voiced spirants /v, ð, γ/ (the last /γ'/ or /j/ when palatalised). These are normally written *b*, *d*, *g* in M. Ir., and this is also the case in Deer.

---

[1] Possibly a specially Scottish one; the Andersons note that the B. MSS of Adamnán's *Life of Columba* frequently write *c* for *ch* in Gaelic names (*VC*, p. 126).

Orthography and language

For *b*, e.g. *doib* and *Abbordoboir*, I, 2; *ro baith*, II, 13; *dolodib*, III, 3; *sliab*, V, 8; *dabach*, VI, 4; *Fib*, VII, 9. The *u* in *Uethe*, II, 17 (beside *b* in *in beith* in the next line) is a not very rare spelling of /*v*/ in M. Ir., see Notes. However *bb* in *Meic dubbacin*, II, 13, is abnormal.

For *d*, e.g. *tisad*, I, 14; *dabeg*, II, 11; *cuitid*, II, 15; *nascad*, III, 4; *bliadin*, III, 5; *Dubuci*, V, 8; *dolaidib* (second *d*), VI, 4; *Doncado* (second *d*), VII, 9. There is *th* in *Cinatha*, II, 10, and *ro baith* in II, 13, 14, 19 (beside *ro baid* in VI, 1); compare the hesitation between *th* and *d* in spelling /θ/, above. In the group /ðn/ the dental spirant became assimilated, giving /nn/, both in M. Ir. and in Sc. G., and this had evidently happened by the time of Deer. So beside *iaidnaisse* (for *fiadnaisse*), VI, 8, which is a traditional spelling, we have *ienasi* in V, 4; and *blienec* for *bliadnach* in I, 15 (cf. *bliadin*, III, 5).

For *g*, e.g. *ro gab*, I, 7; *Malbrigte*, II, 6; *ingen*, III, 1; *rigi*, III, 5; *Domongart*, III, 9; *Finguni*, V, 3; *Comgell*, V, 5. In *ernacde*, I, 10 and 12 it is spelt, very irregularly, *c*; which may well be simply a mistake, a confusion arising from the regular use of *c* for /*g*/ and *g* for /γ'/; though *cd* might perhaps mean *chth* with unvoicing. Final palatalised /γ'/ or /*j*/ is ordinarily spelt -*g* in Deer, as in M. Ir. So *gathraig*, I, 4; *rüig*, II, 10; *Mec gobroig*, II, 10; *thoisig*, II, 15; *Muredig*, III, 10; *Caennaig*, V, 6; *Sithig*, VI, 2. The same is true where -*e*- is written for -*ai*- or -*i*- before it; see (12) and (13) above; so *Cosgreg*, *ro alseg*, *dorodloeg*, *dabeg*, *toiseg*; see the references there. There is one case of -*ch*, in *Cannech* for *Cainnig*, III, 1. It is just possible that this might represent the beginning of what became later the normal development in Scotland of Common Gaelic -/γ'/, namely -/χ'/; but on the other hand it could well be a 'wrong spelling' for -*g*; or the whole might conceivably be the 'ungrammatical' use of nominative for genitive, on which see the discussion of the noun, (31) below. In the case of *ro thidnaig*, I, 3, it is hardly possible to say whether -*g* means the original -/γ'/, or whether it is a spelling for the -/k'/ which replaced it in this verb in M. Ir. and Sc. G. The former seems much more probable, however. On *Male-*

139

domni = *Maeldomnig* in III, 6, see the Notes; it seems likely that here -/*ij*/ is written simply -*i*. Note that in *Ggillebrite* for *Gille-Brigte* in VII, 10, the scribe, who was writing Latin not Gaelic, spelt as he pronounced; -/*ijd′*/- had evidently already become -/*i*:*d′*/-.

(23) There are two cases of writing of *ll* for *l*, in *Collum*, I, 13 and 16, which must be errors. Various groups with *n* have been discussed in (19), (20), and (22). There appear to be only two cases of old *nn* written *nd*, namely *ind* in *ind Elerc*, II, 12, for O. Ir. and M. Ir. *in n-*; and *mandaidib*, VI, 5, for *mennaitib*. Otherwise, note *Donchad*, V, 1; *Donnachac*, VI, 2; *Donnchid*, VI, 7; *Doncado*, VII, 9. In *Callenn*, III, 4, the double -*nn* is unhistorical but is the modern form. In *inna*, V, 3, for *ina* the double *n* is a slip; contrast *na* in VI, 8.

(24) In early Irish, /*h*/ was either the lenited form of initial *s*-, in which case it was written *sh*-, or it was prefixed to initial vowels by certain proclitics, by the initial mutation called 'gemination', on which see (29) below. The only example of the first in Deer is *o hunn*, I, 17, for *o shunn*, where the *h*- is a pronunciation-spelling. An otiose *h*- is sometimes prefixed to words beginning with vowels, where it had no etymological justification and was doubtless not pronounced but was purely scribal; see *Gr. O. Ir.*, § 25. Examples in Deer are *cach hen*, V, 9; *Hidid*, V, 1; *mathe Buchan huli*, VI, 8; and *i nHelain* (for *i n-Elain*), VI, 9.

(25) Sandhi. In the spoken Gaelic languages at the present day, various accommodations of an assimilative character may take place when two words come together in a close speech-group, particularly if rapidly or carelessly spoken. These are ignored in writing, as the same sort of thing is in English. In Deer, however, with its fumbling and ill-educated scribes, examples might be looked for. There are two. First *be Dear*, I, 16, for *bed Déar*, where the two dentals are assimilated to one (at any rate in spelling); and second, *Mec cobrig*, III, 2, which is probably for *Mec-Gobrig* (see Note to II, 10), where -/*kg*/- has become -/*kk*/- by assimilation.

Orthography and language

(26) In concluding the analysis of the spelling, it may be useful to have a list of the probable scribal mistakes, as distinct from merely rather abnormal things like *ae* for *ai*, with references to the paragraph-numbers or Notes. Fairly certain errors are *braith* (1); *choir* (2); *Moridac* (4), (11); *ardmandaidib* (5); *blienec* (10); *ere* (10); *derad* (11); *Buchan* (12); *Morcunn* and *Morcunt* (12); *Malcolum* and *Malcoloum* (12); *thabart* (12); *Madchor* (12); *Caennaig* (13); *blienec* (14); *ienasi* (14); *iaidnaisse* (14); *Turbrud* and *Turbruad* (15); *Culeon* (16); *Maledomni* (17e); *benact* (20); *hule* (21); *Collum* (23); *iar* (Notes I, 6); *benact* (Notes I, 14). Probable ones are *Ggillebrite* (20); *ernacde* (22); omission of the contraction-marks for *n* (Notes II, 15, IV, 1, V, 3). Possible, *Marr* (1); *Cannech* (22).

2. THE LANGUAGE OF THE NOTES

N.B. The spellings in sections (27) to the end are those of the edited texts.

(27) The initial mutation of *lenition* appears in the Deer documents in the following cases, though it is often omitted where it should have been shown:

(*a*) In the noun after the definite article: sg. fem. (nom. for acc.), *in chadraig*, I, 13; gen. sg. masc., *in Chomded*, II, 22; *in fris*, V, 7; dat. sg. masc., *air a[n] choir*, II, 15.

(*b*) In the adjective after the noun: nom. sg. fem., *ben phústa*, VI, 1; dat. sg. masc., *a[n] choir chétna*, II, 15.

(*c*) In the qualifying genitive after the noun: sg. fem. (nom. for acc.), *proinn chét*, II, 15, and *cuitid thoísig, ibid.*

(*d*) Fixed lenition of a masc. genitive proper name: *mac Chathail*, II, 6.

(*e*) In the noun after the 3rd sg. masc. possessive *a: a [t]hule*, II, 14, see Notes; *i nn-a [f]ienasi*, V, 3, *'n-a [f]iaidnaisse*, VI, 8, see (21). On *a cuitid* see (21).

(*f*) In the noun after prepositions: *ar thabart*, II, 14; *ar chuit*, VI, 4. *Do Choluim Cille*, V, 2, 7. *O [s]hunn*, I, 17; *o thosach*, II, 21; *o thésech*, II, 21; *o thésseach*, V, 9. In *gonice Chloic*,

I, II, and *'nice Fúréne*, II, I, the lenition is strictly speaking post-verbal.

(*g*) In the second element of a nominal compound: *ardchellaib*, VI, 5 (contrast, e.g., *Dobarcon*, II, 17).

(*h*) In the predicate of the copula: *robo thosec*, II, 4.

(*i*) In the verb after preverbs: *ro thidnaig* (or this could belong under (*k*)), I, 3; *ní tharat*, I, 7.

(*j*) In the compound verb after prepositions: *do-chuid*, I, 9.

(*k*) Lenition of the verb in a relative clause: *chomallfas*, II, 23, V, 10; *thíssad*, VI, 4 (but e.g. *ticfa*, V, 11).

(28) The initial mutation of nasalisation is of special interest in Deer. Caused by proclitic or quasi-proclitic words originally ending in -*n* in Primitive Irish, the effect in M. Ir. is that the following changes appear at the beginning of the next word: *n*- is prefixed to vowels; *p*-, *t*-, *c*- become /b, d, g/ but the spelling is normally unchanged (or sometimes written double, specially *c*-); *b*-, *d*-, *g*- become /m, n, ŋ/, written *mb*-, *nd*-, *ng*-; *f*- becomes /v/, written *f*-, sometimes with a punctum delens above it; *m*-, *n*-, *l*-, *r*-, and *s*- may be written double. This is also the regular practice in the Deer documents, apart from the fact that some pronunciation-spellings like *g*- or *gg*- for the M. Ir. *c*- = /g/ may be even more indicative than the Irish treatment. In modern spoken Scottish Gaelic, however, the old system of nasalisation has been replaced, apart from a handful of vestigial survivals in fixed phrases, by a new one, whereby certain proclitics (not quasi-proclitics) *now* ending in nasals voice the initial occlusives, both the voiceless fortis *p*-, *t*-, *c*- and the voiceless lenis *b*-, *d*-, *g*-, the first series usually remaining aspirate,[1] but affect no other consonants;[2] and, the old consonant *n* remaining before vowels, it has attached itself permanently to the proclitic as a consonant instead of as a mere potentiality of nasalisation. Thus, M. Ir. *i* (*n*)-, 'in', is treated as *an* in Sc. G., with the result that M. Ir. *i s*(*s*)*aíre* 'in freedom'

---

[1] There are some variations in dialect, notably the true nasalisation of occlusives found in the far north-west; but this is a secondary development.

[2] Except for dialectal voicing of *f*- and *s*- in certain regions, an analogical development.

is Sc. G. *an saoire*. Apart from this last, the effects of the new nasalisation are not recognised in spelling, or by traditional Sc. G. grammars. Such evidence as is available on the date of the rise of this new system in Scotland suggests that it was late, probably distinctly later than the time of the notes in Deer.[1]

The following are the instances where the Irish type of nasalisation is clearly shown in Deer by the spelling: After the acc. sg. of the def. article, *in gathraig*, I, 3; *in n-ernacde*, I, 12; *i[n] mbréther*, I, 14; *ind Elerc*, II, 12 (spelling for *in n-Elerc*, see (23)); *in n-ocmad*, III, 4; *in gorthe*, V, 7. After the gen. pl. of the art., *na glérec*, I, 8, 9, II, 7. After the 3rd pl. possessive, *ar a ginn*, I, 3. After prepositions: *iar n-ére*, I, 8; *i ssaere*, II, 21; *co n-a*, III, 4; *i ssaeri*, V, 9; *i gginn*, V, 7. In *i Pet* in IV, 1 we must see the Irish type, since the nasal would be preserved in the Scottish as in *in Pett* below. Some further instances are ambiguous, because the spelling does not decide either way: *in cathraig* (def. art.), I, 5 (but this could also represent *in chathraig*, analogous to *in chadraig*, see (27a); *in beith* (def. art.), II, 18 instead of *in mbeith*, is probably another such case); *da n-éis* (possessive 3rd pl.), II, 23; after prepositions, *i n-edbairt*, I, 11; *i n-Alteri*, II, 5; after conjunctions, *go-ndas*, I, 7; *go ndéndaes*, I, 9; *go ndísad*, 10.[2] The curious *i bBidbin*, 'in Biffie', II, 10, cannot be explained on either Irish or Sc. G. lines; it is probably a mistake.

Leaving all these aside, there are four cases where the spelling is such as to suit the later, Sc. G., treatment of nasalisation. These are *da'n síl* (3rd pl. possessive), II, 23; *in Pett*, II, 10; *in testus*, V, 4; and *in sore*, V, 2 (compare the note above, p. 142); the last three after the preposition. The absence of nasalisation of *d-* after a quasi-proclitic in *cetri dabach*, VI, 4, could be another, but it may be a mere slip; see, however, below. In view of the probability mentioned above that the new, Sc. G., type of nasalisation appears to be clearly later than the twelfth century, these few examples can hardly have much weight against the

---

[1] See *Ériu*, XVI, 94f.; *PBA*, XXXVII, 90, 95.
[2] This last need not be a Sc. G. type of case (contrast *Ériu*, XVI, 94f.), since the new *dísad* could still be nasalised as *ndísad*.

more numerous ones which prove the Irish type or prove neither. They are probably merely analogical spellings under the influence of cases like *iar n-ére*, from which analogies indeed the Sc. G. type itself arose.[1] However, the possibility that the new development was just faintly beginning, in the northeast, should perhaps not be totally excluded. In the case of *cetri dabach*, loss of eclipsis after quasi-proclitics is the rule in Manx also, and is therefore likely to have happened earlier than the other,[2] and may thus be an instance.

(29) The initial mutation of 'gemination' may be explained as follows. In Primitive Irish the final consonant of certain proclitics and quasi-proclitics was assimilated to the initial consonant of the next word, doubling it; or when that word began with a vowel, survived as an *h-* prefixed to it, and has so survived to the present day in Irish and to a less extent in Sc. G. E.g. in both, *na h-innse* 'of the island', from late Pr. Ir. **indah inissjah*. The gemination of consonants was vestigial already in early O. Ir., but the custom of sometimes writing certain initial consonants double in these cases continued for a long time.[3] There is one instance of this orthographic gemination in Deer, after the preterite of the copula: *fa llán*, I, 6. Prefixing of *h-* is seen after the article in *na h-ule*, II, 13, 20; *na h-uli*, VI, 2; *ó na h-ulib*, III, 3; VI, 4; after the possessive 3rd sg. fem. in *ar [a] h-ardchellaib*, VI, 5; after the preposition *a* 'out of' in *a hí*, I, 1; and after the preterite of the copula in *ba h-é*, II, 3.

(30) Apart from the fem. sg. gen. *na*, the definite article in Deer is *in* in all cases of the singular (except the later form *a[n]* once) and *na* in all of the plural. This agrees well with contemporary M. Ir., except that on that analogy *an* might have been looked for rather more often. Examples: masc. sg., nom. *in morm(a)er*, I, 9, VI, 1; acc. *in mac*, I, 10; *in gorthe*, V, 7; gen.

---

[1] Cf. O'Rahilly, *Irish Dialects Past and Present*, p. 155.

[2] Cf. O'Rahilly, *op. cit.*, pp. 150f.

[3] It will be seen that I am not any more persuaded by Greene's arguments about gemination in Irish in *Celtica*, III, 284ff. than I am by those about it in Brittonic, *ibid.* and revised – not for the better – in *Celtica*, VII, 116ff. I hope to discuss this elsewhere.

Orthography and language

in Típrat, I, 11; *in Mulenn,* II, 6; *in Chomded,* II, 22; *i[n] Púir,* IV, 1;[1] *in fris,* V, 7; dat. *in mormær,* I, 6; *a[n] choir,* II, 15 (see the Note). Pl., gen. *na glérec,* I, 8, 9; II, 7; dat. *na h-ulib,* III, 3; VI, 4. Fem. sg. nom. (for acc.) *in chadraig,* I, 13; acc., *in gathraig,* I, 3 (*in cathraig,* I, 5, ambiguous but probably acc.); *in n-ernacde,* I, 12; *ind Elerc* (for *in nElerc*), II, 12; *in n-ocmad,* III, 4. Pl. acc. *na h-ule (-i),* II, 13, 20, VI, 2.

(31) The noun is declined exactly the same as in contemporary M. Ir., but there are a number of examples, almost all in *o*-stems and almost all in proper names, which look at first sight as if the nominative is being used for the genitive. These are *Buchan,* I, 3, VI, 1; *Morcunn,* II, 2; *Morcunt,* II, 7; *toíseg,* II, 5; *in Mulenn,* II, 6; *Cannech,* III, 1; *Marr,* III, 7; *Turbruad,* III, 9 (but the correct *Turbruaid,* VI, 6); and *Madchor,* V, 1. On genitive *Drostán* see Note to I, 15. In the names *Mael-Colaim* and *Gille-Colaim,* 'Servant of St Columba', we have the genitive correctly given as *-Coluim* or *-Colaim* in III, 10 and V, 4; but *-Colum,* II, 8 and 11 and *-Coloum,* 9 appear at first sight to be nominative for genitive. It is probable, however, that they are a slip on the part of the scribe, repeated three times close together. *Æd,* VII, 10 and *Ferdomnac,* VII, 11, can hardly be quoted here, as the document is a Latin one, and the proper cases of Gaelic names are often ignored in such things. The breakdown of the case-system, and the consequent use of the nominative as an all-purpose case, is a familiar feature in some modern Sc. G. dialects, above all in the eastern parts of the mainland; and its beginnings may be traced to the end of the fourteenth century if the place-name *Lurgyndaspok,* 'The Bischapis Leg', in Aberdeenshire in 1391 (*CPNS,* p. 412) is reliable, since this would represent *in t-Easpog,* nominative, for *in Easpuig,* genitive. But the examples of *-e-* for *-i-,* at least, are explained differently in (13) above, and a wholesale breakdown of the case-system as early as the twelfth century is neither probable nor supported by the rest of the Deer examples. These things are probably instances of the carelessness of the scribes of Deer.

---

[1] On the [n] see the Note on II, 15.

Orthography and language

The accusative case, however, as the object of verbs was in process of falling together with the nominative already in early M. Ir., though it survived, side by side with the nominative, much later, at any rate in verse. In Deer, in those relatively few instances where its form in any event distinguishes it from the nominative, the accusative is always used; but it is notable that though *in gathraig*, I, 3 and *in chadraig*, I, 13, have the correct acc. sg. form (nom. *caithir*), the lenition in the second case shows that the article is treated as nom.; *in cathraig*, I, 5, being ambiguous. See (30).

o-stem nouns are frequent, of course, and apart from the above apparent confusions of nom. and gen. they call for no comment, except to note that in the name *Colum Cille*, otherwise correctly declined, the dative appears three times as if it were an *ā*-stem (*Coluim*, V, 2, 7, and spelt *Colim*, IV, 2; side by side with the proper *Colum* in II, 1 and III, 3). On this see (12).

ā-stems. The acc. sg., note *gonice Chloic*, I, 11; gen. sg., *eclasi* (probably to be included here), III, 2; dat. sg. *i n-edbairt*, I, 11; acc. dual, *dá dabeg*, II, 11; acc. pl., *na hule (-i) edbarta*, II, 13, 20, VI, 2; dat. pl. *-chellaib*, VI, 5.

jā-stems. Acc. sg., *ernacde*, I, 10, 12.

u-stems. Gen. sg. *Éda*, II, 1; *brátha*, II, 22.

Consonant stems: t-stems, gen. sg. *in Chomded*, II, 22; *Mec-Bead*, III, 7, V, 1; *Gille-Comded*, VII, 10; *nt-stem*, gen. sg. *in Tiprat*, I, 11; *k-stem*, acc. sg. *in gathraig*, I, 3; *in cathraig*, 5; *in chadraig*, 13; *g-stem*, gen. sg. *ríig*, II, 10; *n-stems*, acc. sg. *Bibdin*, II, 9; *Alterin*, II, 17; *Etdanin*, II, 19; gen. sg. *Meic-Dobarcon*, II, 17; *Canan*, V, 6; *Alban*, VI, 5; dat. sg. *Bidbin*, II, 10; 'short' dat. sg. *Alteri*, II, 5; acc. dual, *dá Alterin*, II, 18.

(32) Adjectives hardly occur. There are masc. nom. pl. *huli*, VI, 8; dat. *na h-ulib*, III, 3, VI, 4 (N.B. dat. pl. in *-ib*, see p. 151); fem. acc. pl. *na h-ule*, II, 13, 20; *na h-uli*, VI, 2. Apart from these, masc. acc. sg. *mór*, V, 7; fem. gen. pl. *cetri*, VI, 4 (N.B. not *cetheora*, which would not be expected at this late date). There is one comparative, *nesu*, V, 8 (N.B. comparative for superlative, as is natural at this late date).

Orthography and language

(33) There are only two independent personal pronouns, both nominative; masc. sg. *ba h-é*, II, 3, and fem. sg. *do-raten...sí*, I, 5. The indefinite pronoun *ge* occurs in *ge bé* 'whoever it be', I, 14. There are two infixed object pronouns, both fem. sg., and both in I; -*das*-, 7, and -*s*-, 14. Apart from I, the texts do not lend themselves to the appearance of personal pronouns, and with so small a specimen (two infixed, no independent objective) no conclusions about date can be drawn, not even in the case of I. Prepositional pronouns: the only ones are *dó* 'to him' five times; *doib* 'to them', I, 2, 3, 11; and *ris* 'against it' I, 14, V, 11. *Doib* is *doïb* rather than *dóib*, since the hiatus *o-i* remained until late in Sc. G. Demonstratives: -*sain*, I, 4; *sen*, I, 9, 13; -*sen*, I, 5, 13; *don-í*, VI, 4. Possessives: masc.3rd sg., *a*, I, 1, 5, II, 14, 15, V, 3, 9, 10, VI, 1, 8; fem., *a*, III, 4, VI, 5; masc. 3rd pl., *a*, I, 3; in *da'n*, *da n*-, II, 23.

(34) Prepositions are naturally not rare. There are (1) *a* 'from', I, 1. (2) *ar* 'before', etc. (see Glossarial Index, and note that there are six cases of *ar* for *for*, and none of *for*); I, 3, 15, II, 14, 15, VI, 4, 5 (twice). (3) *co* 'with', III, 4. (4) *co* 'up to', spelt *cu*, II, 21, V, 9, 10, VI, 5, and *go*, I, 4, II, 21, V, 2, 8. (5) *do* 'to', twenty-five times (elided in *d'*, I, 9, V, 8); and in *da* 'to their', II, 23 (twice). (6) *do* for *de*, 'from', I, 6. (7) *etar, edar* 'between', II, 18, V, 8. (8) *fri* 'towards', etc. (see Glossarial Index), I, 15; *ri*, II, 20 (twice), III, 2, VI, 3 (thrice); *ria, ibid.*; *ro* (see Notes), II, 14. (9) *gonice*, etc., 'as far as' (really a verbal phrase; for the various forms see Glossarial Index), I, 2, II, II, 1, 18, V, 5, 7. (10) *i* or *in* 'in' twelve times, and with possessive (*i*)*n* (*n*)*a*, V, 3, VI, 8. (11) *iar* 'after', I, 8, 9, 13. (12) *le* 'with', with def. art. *lesin*, I, 10. (13) *ó, ua* 'from', I, 4 (twice), II, 17, II, 1, 21 three times, III, 3, V, 8, 9, VI, 4.

(35) Conjunctions: 'and' is always written with the 7-contraction, except once, where it is *ac3*, that is, *acus*; V, 2. There are also *act* 'but', I, 8; *air* 'because', written by a slip *iar*, I, 6; *go* 'that', I, 7, 9, 10; and *mar* 'as', I, 2.

(36) Verbs are rare, apart from the narrative passage I; this is the consequence of the character of the contents of II–VI, in which such few verbs as occur chiefly mean 'gave'. There are no

habitual presents, imperfects, or conditionals at all; and outside the verb 'to be', there are no presents indicative or subjunctive, no imperatives, and no old preterites. The old perfect has become wholly preterite in sense; and no constructions expressing the idea of the perfect occur. The only tenses which do occur, apart from 'to be', are a couple of futures and past subjunctives, and a number of old perfects expressing the preterite.

Future: 3rd sg. (in relative clause) *ticfa* 'shall come', V, 11; relative form, *chomallfas* 'who shall fulfil', II, 23, V, 10.

Past subjunctive: 3rd sg. *tabrad* 'might give', I, 7; *thíssad* (in relative clause) 'might come', VI, 4; 3rd pl. *déndaes* (spelling for *déntais*) 'they might make', I, 10.

Old perfects functioning as preterites: 3rd sg. independent, *do-chuid* 'went', I, 9; *do-rat* (seventeen cases), 'gave', I, II, IV, V; *do-raten* 'pleased', I, 5; *do-rodloeg* 'begged', I, 6; *fo-rácaib* 'left', I, 14; *ro alseg* 'revealed', I, 2; *ro báid*, VI, I, *ro báith*, II, 13, 14, 19 'he quenched'; *ro gab* 'took', I, 7; *ro-s benact* 'blessed it', I, 14; *ro laboir* 'said', I, 16; *ro thidnaig* 'bestowed', I, 3; *tánic* 'came', I, 12. Dependent, *-tarat* 'gave', I, 7. 3rd pl. independent, *do-ratsat* 'they gave', II, 9, III, 1; *do-ratsator, id.*, II, 17; *do-rónsat* 'they made', I, 12; *tángator* 'they came' I, 1, 5, 15 (the ending is twice written out as *-or* and once contracted; the second is also true of *do-ratsator*. I have expanded both contractions as *-or*, since the scribe is the same in all instances, but *-ar* would be normal; see (10) above).

The verb 'to be' occurs as follows: substantive verb, 3rd sg. pres. subj. *ge bé* 'whoever it be', I, 14. Copula (3rd sg. in all cases), pres. indic. *is*, 'it is', V, 8 (relative), *ess* (in *ess é* 'it is he'), I, 3; pres. subj. *mad* 'if it be', I, 8; past subj. negative *ná bad* 'that he might not be', I, 14; preterite *ba*, II, 3, *fa*, I, 6, *robo* 'was', I, 3, 8, II, 3, 4; imperat. *be[d]* 'let it be', I, 16.

(37) There is little to say about syntax, since apart from I, the sentences are of a very simple nature and virtually nothing about it is in the least unusual. On the construction *Colbán in mormer Buchan* see the Notes to VI, 1. As regards the question of *X do-rat Y*, 'X gave Y', and *X ro báid Y*, 'X "quenched" Y', this

is of course a special type of word-order. The normal order is *do-rat* (or *ro báid*) *X Y*, with verb first, subject second, and object third, not with the subject preceding the verb; the *X do-rat* order is however normal when the subject is emphasised, though it would be more usual to prefix the copula, '*it is* X who gave', etc. There are fifteen cases of *X do-rat* (or *do-ratsat, do-ratsator*) namely II, 1, 2, 4, 5, 6, 7, 9, 10, 12 (twice), 17, III, 1 and V, 1, 5, and 6, and one of *X ro báith*, II, 13; but to set against these there are three of *do-rat X*, I, 13, II, 18, and IV, 1, and three of *ro báith X*, II, 14, 19 and VI, 1. What is unusual about all this is not the occurrence of the emphatic word-order but its frequency;[1] but we must remember the special circumstances. Here is a long list of gifts named in short main-clauses, in which the important point distinguishing each from the others is not that someone *gave* certain lands but that they were given by certain *persons* – the emphasis is on the donors' names, not on the fact of the lands being given. It is notable that the same thing is found in the almost contemporary Irish land-grants in the Book of Kells (see p. 86), in *muinter Cennansa...ro edpair*, 'the community of Kells granted', in no. 1, side by side with *ro edpair rí Temhrach*, 'the king of Tara granted', in no. 11.[2]

Summing up the above analysis of the language of the entries in the Book of Deer, we may say that in all essentials it is identical with the Irish of Ireland of the first half and middle of the twelfth century, and that no clear linguistic differences between any of the individual entries can be demonstrated, apart of course from those dictated by the fact that 1 is telling a connected story, and the rest are short details about numerous separate benefactions.[3] The chief ways in which the Gaelic of

---

[1] There is however no need to follow Fraser (Sc. G. St., v, 59) in regarding this as due to Latin influence.　　[2] Nos. IX and II in *NLC*.

[3] Compare Strachan, *TGSI*, XIX, 17 and 15: 'The Gaelic of the Book of Deer is practically identical with Middle Irish', and 'shows the practical identity of Scotch with Irish Gaelic at the time when it was written'. Also Fraser, *Sc. G. St.*, v, 52, 'It has been assumed...that the language...shows characteristic[s] of Scottish Gaelic. There appear to be no good reasons for supposing that to be the case.'

Orthography and language

Deer differs from normal late Middle Irish are as follows: First, the numerous incorrect, and occasionally fantastic, spellings. But these are due to the carelessness and ignorance of the scribes of this remote monastery, and not to a genuine linguistic differentiation already occurring as between Scotland and Ireland. On this see particularly pp. 125f. Secondly, there are a few cases where phonetic and morphological developments peculiar to Scottish Gaelic[1] have been at least mooted above; these being *nt* and *lt* becoming *nd* and *ld* (19); final γ' yielding χ' (22); the appearance of the peculiarly Sc. G. type of nasalisation (28), and the use of nominative for genitive found in some modern Sc. G. dialects (31). But all these, on examination, prove to be more or less highly improbable, and on balance one must say that the conclusion of the question whether the notes in the Book of Deer are in any sense what we mean by Scottish Gaelic – other than that they are Gaelic and Scottish – is negative. Quite certainly, at any rate, if such traces exist at all they are very few and slight; in these texts we are dealing with the Common Gaelic language used and understood at this period by the clergy who wrote them, the nobles for whom they were written, and doubtless by and large by the common people who were their tenants and followers. Whether the speech of the wholly non-literary classes had evolved far beyond this in the twelfth century is a point on which we have, of course, no information. It is likely that it had not, since signs of anything of the sort are so doubtful in the Deer notes. If the scribes had been in very close touch with the standards of the Irish bardic schools, they would write a high-class literary Common Gaelic in which traces of significant evolved colloquial local Gaelic would not be expected; but as we have seen, it is obvious that they were not, but were writing much as they

[1] Others, such as the apparent development of the *ai* and *oi* diphthongs to a weakly round centralised back vowel (17; this should not have been included in *Ériu*, XVI, 96, ll. 32–6), or the faint possibility of depalatalisation of labials (12), are shared with N. Irish and therefore not relevant here; while others, like the suspicion that svarabhakti was beginning (18), or the matter of *th* giving *h* (21), are common to Gaelic as a whole.

spoke; and the absence of such clear and evident traces must be taken to mean that this colloquial evolution had not yet manifestly begun. This is in agreement with what may be inferred from other sources about the probable date of the rise of a real distinction between 'Western Gaelic' (Irish) and 'Eastern Gaelic' (Sc. G. and Manx), on which see the writer's 'Common Gaelic'.[1] As to the question whether any spoken Pictish still survived in this part of the old Pictland so late as this, see *Ériu*, XVI, 93f., where it is answered in the negative.

Finally, what of the *date* of the language of these entries? It is unquestionably Middle Irish, or better, Middle Common Gaelic; that is, it belongs to the period between about the middle of the tenth century and the very end of the twelfth, and is certainly neither earlier nor later. Features which could be as old as (or of course later than) the tenth century, chiefly the later part of it, but not older, are masc. *dá* (II, 11) and *cetri* (VI, 4) for fem. *dí* and *ceitheora*; infixed 3rd pl. pronoun *-das-* (I, 7) for *-s-*; demonstrative *sen* (I, 9, 13) for *sin*; the total confusion of preterite and perfect (see (36) above); and the verbal forms *do-rónsat* (I, 12), *-tabrad* (I, 7) and *-tíssad* (VI, 4), respectively for *do-rigénsat*, *-taibred*, and *-tísed*. Of these, some, such as the complete absence of preterite forms outside the copula, though possible in the tenth century, are more likely to be later, and of course any of them are even more probable later still. Indeed, *ar* (I, 15, II, 15, 22, 23, VI, 5 twice,) for *for* is late rather than early M. Ir.; *fa* (I, 6) for *ba* is apparently not older than the twelfth century. There is nothing at all to show that any of the notes are modernised copies of older documents, and this is relevant particularly to I, which might in theory be copied from some very old source, going back to the early days of the monastery. But if so, the 'modernisation' is complete, and there is no trace of the 'archaic' exemplar. As regards the terminus ante quem, the survival of dat. pl. *-ib* in the adjective *ulib* (III, 3, VI, 4), and of the accusative case of nouns distinct from the nominative (see (31) above), is not probable in texts

[1] *PBA*, xxxvii, 71ff.

of this sort, as distinct from traditionalising literary prose or verse, much after the middle of the twelfth century.

There is therefore nothing here to conflict with the date already arrived at on historical grounds – not long before the middle of the twelfth century – and in fact the evidence quoted positively suggests the earlier part of the twelfth century as the most likely date on linguistic grounds.

GLOSSARIAL INDEX

The forms are those of the 'edited' texts, and the roman-plus-arabic-figure reference-numbers are to these; but arabic-figure references in brackets are to the numbered sections of the discussion on orthography and language, pp. 127ff. A lemma given in italics instead of Clarendon type does not occur in that form in the text, but only in the Clarendon form or forms which follow.

1. **a**, possessive; 3rd sg. masc. 'his, its' (causes lenition, see (27e)); I, 1, 5, II, 14, 15, V, 3, 9, 10 (twice), VI, 1, 8; 3rd sg. fem. 'her, its' (prefixes *h*- to vowels, see (29)); III, 4, VI, 5; 3rd pl. 'their' (on the mutation see (28)); I, 3, and in *da* 'to their', II, 23 twice.

2. **a**, preposition, with dat., 'out of, from' (prefixes *h*- to vowels, see (29)); I, 1. See **as**.

ab, abb, noun, masc., 'abbot'; III, 6, VI, 6.

abstoil, see **apstal**.

achad, noun, masc., 'field, pasture'; acc. sg. II, 3, 7 (in place-name), V, 1 (in place-name), 9.

act (spelling for *acht*), conjunction, 'but'; **act mad bec**, I, 8, 'almost'; lit. 'but if it be a little'.

acus, conjunction, 'and', occurs semi-abbreviated as *ac₃*, in V, 2; otherwise always the full contraction 7.

air, conjunction, 'because', see 2. **iar**.

all, noun, fem., 'cliff'; gen. sg. **alla** probably in **Alla Uethe**, II, 17; see Notes.

a[n], see 1. **in**.

anim, noun, masc., 'name'; I, 16. Either a mere mis-spelling for *ainm* or possibly an instance of epenthetic vowel written; see (18).

apstal, noun, masc., 'apostle'; acc. sg. *id.*, VI, 4; gen. sg. **abstoil** (see (19)), III, 2.

ar, preposition, with acc. and dat., leniting. (1) 'Before, in front of', I, 3. (2) With verbs of asking, 'of, from'; I, 6. (3) 'In exchange for'; II, 14; VI, 4. (4) 'On', II, 15, 22, 23, VI, 5 twice (see *tic*-). (5) 'At, on the occasion of'; I, 15 (see Notes). The meanings (4) and (5) are instances of the confusion of original *for* with *ar*.

ard, adjective, 'high; chief'. As first element of a compound, VI, 5 twice.

as, preposition, with dat. (form of 2. **a**, *q.v.*), 'out of, from', in the phrase **as a athle** (see **athle**).

athle, noun, 'remainder'; dat. sg. in the phrase *as a aithle*, 'after it', I, 5; lit. 'out of its remainder'.

attac, verbal noun, masc., 'beseeching'; dat. sg., I, 9.

ba, bad, see **ess**.

báid-, 'to submerge, quench, drown', but on the meaning in Deer see pp. 120ff. 3rd sg. pret. **ro báid**, VI, 1; spelt **ro báith**, II, 13, 14, 19.

ball, noun, masc., 'spot, place', in **Ball Domin**, IV, 1, see Index of Place-Names.

bé, 3rd sg. pres. subj. of substantive verb 'to be', in **ge bé**, 'whoever it be (who)', I, 14.

bec, adjective, 'little'; nom. sg. masc., I, 9.

bed, see **ess**.

Index

cruthnec, noun, masc., 'a Pict'; nom. sg., I, 2.

cu, see I. **go**.

cuit, noun, fem., 'share' (on the technical sense, see p. 119); acc. sg. *id.*, II, 4, 5, 10; dat. sg. *id.*, VI, 4.

cuitid, noun, fem., same as *cuit*; acc. sg. II, 15.

d', da, see **do**.

dá, numeral adjective, 'two'; nom. masc. VI, 8; acc. fem. *id.*, II, 11; acc. with place-name, II, 18.

dabach, noun, fem., 'a *davoch*', see pp. 116f.; acc. dual **dabeg**, II, 11; gen. pl. **dabach**, VI, 4.

dalta, noun, masc., 'foster-son'; here, 'disciple'; I, 1.

da'n, see **do**.

das, infixed object pronoun 3rd sg. fem., 'her, it' (cf. **s**); **go-ndas tabrad**, 'that he should give it', I, 7.

déndaes, see *do-gni*.

dér, noun, fem., 'tear'; nom. pl. **déara**, I, 15.

dered, noun, masc., 'end'; acc. **derad** (spelling for *dered*, (11)), II, 21.

dísad, see *tic-*.

do, d', preposition with dative, leniting. (1) 'to'; I, 9 (**d'**), 13, II, 1, 2, 7, 8, 9 (twice), 13, 16 (twice), 19 (twice), III, 3 (twice), 4, IV, 2 (three times), V, 2 (three times), 6 (twice), 7, 8 (**d'**). Prepositional pronoun, 3rd sg. masc. **dó** 'to him', I, 7, 8 (**mac dó**, 'a son of his'), 10, 12, II, 14; 3rd pl. **doib** (see (33)), 'to them', I, 2, 3, 11. With 3rd pl. possessive, **da'n, da n-**, 'to their', II, 23. (2) 'from, of' (for *de*), I, 6. With definite article, **don**, VI, 4.

dó, see **do**.

do-beir-, 'to give'. 3rd sg. past subj. dependent **-tabrad**, 'should give', I, 7 (cf. p. 151). 3rd sg. pret. inde-

pendent, **do-rat**, I, 10, 13, II, 1, 2, 4, 5, 6, 7, 10, 12 (twice), 15, 18, IV, 1, V, 1, 5, 6; dependent, **-tarat**, I, 7. 3rd pl. pret. independent **do-ratsat**, II, 9, III, 1; **do-ratsator**, II, 17.

do-chuid (M. Ir. *do-chuaid*, Sc. G. *chaidh*, see (15)), 3rd sg. pret., 'went' (3rd sg. pres. *téit*), I, 9.

do-gni-, 'does, makes' (Sc. G. *nì*). 3rd pl. past subj. **déndaes** (M. Ir. *déntais*; on the spelling see (12, 20)); I, 10. 3rd pl. pret. **do-rónsat**, I, 12.

doib, see **do**.

dolaid, noun, masc., 'impost, burden'; dat. pl. **dolaidib**, VI, 4; **dolodib**, III, 3, is a spelling for this.

domin, adjective, 'deep', in **Ball Domin**, IV, 1; see Index of Place-Names.

do-rat, do-ratsat(or), see *do-beir-*.

do-raten (M. Ir. *do-raitne, ro thaitin*; Sc. G. *thaitinn*), 3rd sg. pret., 'pleased' (3rd sg. pres. *do-aitne*; *do-raten* is pret. *do-aitin* with the *ro* perfective particle infixed), I, 5.

do-rodloeg (M. Ir. *do-rothlaig, ro thothlaig*), 3rd sg. pret., 'begged' (3rd sg. pres. *do-thluich*; *do-rodloeg* is pret. *do-thluich* with the *ro* perfective particle infixed; on the spelling see (12, 21, 22)), I, 6. Takes the preposition *ar*.

dún, noun, masc., 'fort'; gen. sg. **Dúni** in place-name, III, 4; in Latin context (ablative), **Dún**, VII, 7; see Index of Place-Names.

é, personal pronoun, 3rd sg. masc., 'he'; I, 3, II, 3.

eclais, noun, fem., 'church'; gen. sg. **eclasi**, III, 2.

edar, etar, preposition, with accusative, 'between', II, 18; **etar...acus** 'both...and...', V, 8.

155

Index

edbart, noun and verbal noun, fem., 'offering; presentation (for religious purposes); grant (of land)'; dat. sg. **edbairt**, I, 11; acc. pl. **edbarta**, II, 14, 20, VI, 3.

éis, noun, fem., 'trace, track'; dat. sg. in the phrases **da n-éis** 'after them', II, 23, and **ar a és** 'after him, afterwards', V, 10.

ele, adjective, 'other'; acc. sg. fem., I, 5.

én, numeral adjective, 'one'; as noun, 'person' (spelling for *oen*, see (17g)); dat. sg. **cach (h)én** 'everyone', V, 9, 10.

ére, verbal-noun, fem., 'refusing, refusal' (spelling for *éra*, see (10)); dat. sg. *id.*, I, 8.

ernacde, verbal-noun (of *ernaigid*, O. Ir. *ar-neget*), fem., 'praying, prayer'; acc. sg. *id.*, I, 10, 12.

escob, noun, masc., 'bishop'; nom. sg., III, 5; dat. sg. *id.*, III, 4.

ess (spelling for *is*, see (13)), 3rd sg. pres. of the copula, 'is', in **ess é** 'it is he', I, 3; the same in a relative sentence, **is**, V, 8. 3rd sg. pres. subj. with *ma*, 'if', **mad** 'if it be', I, 8 (see *s.v.* **act**). 3rd sg. past subj., dependent, **-bad**, 'might be', I, 15. 3rd sg. imperat., **be[d]**, 'let it be', I, 16 (see (25)). 3rd sg. pret. **fa** or **ba**, 'was', geminating (see (29)), I, 6, II, 3; **robo** *id.* (originally perfect), I, 3, 8, II, 3, 4.

etar, see **edar**.

faillsig-, 'to reveal'; with *do*, to guide'. 3rd sg. pret. **ro [f]alseg doib**, 'guided them' (M. Ir. *ro fhaillsig*, Sc. G. *fhoillsich*; spelling, see (13, 21)), I, 2.

fer léginn, noun, masc., 'lector, head of a monastic school'; see Notes (*fer*, 'man', and *léginn*, gen. sg. of *légenn*, 'reading, studying, learning'); III, 9.

fiadnaise, noun, fem., 'testimony'; dat. sg. **i nn-a [f]ienasi**, V, 3;

'n-a [f]iaidnaisse, VI, 8; 'in witness of it'. On the spellings see (14, 21, 22).

fo-rácaib, 3rd sg. pret., 'left' (3rd sg. pres. *fo-ácaib*, old pret. *id.*; *forácaib* is old perfect with *ro* perfective particle infixed); I, 14.

fri, see **ri**.

fris, see *pres*.

ro gab, 3rd sg. pret., 'took' (3rd sg. pres. *gabaid*), I, 7.

galar, noun, masc., 'sickness'; acc. sg. *id.*, I, 8.

ge, indefinite pronoun, 'whoever', in **ge bé** 'whoever it be (who)', I, 14.

ginn, see **cenn**.

glérec, see *clérech*.

1. **go** (Hands A and B), **cu** (Hand C), preposition with accusative, 'to, up to, as far as'; **go**, I, 4, II, 21, V, 2, 8; **cu**, II, 21, V, 9, 10; with an adjective forming adverb, **cu cotchenn** 'in general', VI, 5.

2. **go**, conjunction, nasalising, 'until, so that, that', I, 7, 9, 10; also in **gonice**, *q.v.*

gonice, **gonige**, preposition with accusative, leniting, 'as far as, to'; I, 11, II, 18, V, 5, 7; with elision, **gonic'**, I, 2; with aphesis, **'nice**, II, 1. Originally a verbal form, *co n-icci*, 'till you come to'.

gorthe, see **corthe**.

hule, in **a hule**, II, 14, see *tol*; in **na hule** etc., see **ule**.

hunn, see **sunn**.

í, demonstrative particle with def. article and relative verb, 'that which'; dat. sg. **don-í**, VI, 4.

i, **in**, preposition, nasalising (see (28)); 'in, as'; I, 4, 11, II, 5, 10 (twice), 21, IV, 1, V, 2, 4, 7, 9, VI, 9; with possessive 3rd sg. masc., **i nn-a**, V, 3; **'n-a**, VI, 8.

1. **iar**, preposition with dative, nasalising, 'after'; I, 8, 9, 13.

156

Index

pett, noun, fem., in place-names only; on the meaning see pp. 114ff. Acc. sg. **pett**, II, 2, 6, 12; **pet**, III, 2; gen. sg. **pette**, I, 11; dat. sg. **pett**, II, 10, **pet**, IV, 1 (both spellings for *peit(t)*).

pres, noun, masc., 'thicket'; gen. sg., with lenition, **fris** (for *phris*, see (21)), V, 8; see Notes.

proinn, noun, fem., 'meal, dinner'; acc. sg. *id.*, in **proinn chét**, II, 15, see Notes.

púr, noun, apparently masc., seems to mean 'pasture'; gen. sg. **púir** in place-name, IV, 2; see Notes.

pústa, past participle passive, 'married'; nom. sg. fem., VI, 2; see Notes.

rath, noun, masc., 'grace'; dat. sg., I, 6.

ri, preposition, with accusative, 'to, towards; against; with'. I, 5, II, 20 (twice), III, 2, VI, 3 (three times); **ria**, *id.*, *ibid.*; the older form **fri**, *id.*, I, 15; the rare form **ro** (see Notes), II, 14. Prepositional pronoun, 3rd sg. masc., **ris**, 'against it', I, 14, V, 11.

rí, noun, masc., 'king'; gen. sg. **ríig** (spelling for *ríg*, see (9)), II, 10.

ríge, noun, fem., 'kingship, reign'; gen. sg. **rígi**, III, 5.

ris, see **ri**.

1. **ro**, see **ri**.

2. **ro**, perfective particle, originally changing a preterite tense to a perfect, but the whole form functioning by this time as a preterite. See **do-rat, do-raten, do-rodloeg, robo** (sv. **ess**), **ro-s benact, ro thidnaig**, etc.

robo, see **ess**.

s, infixed object pronoun 3rd sg. fem., 'her, it' (cf. **das**); **ro-s benact** 'blessed it', I, 14.

sacart, noun, masc., 'priest'; nom. sg., IV, 3.

saer, adjective, 'free', acc. sg. fem. **sér** (see (17g)), III, 3.

saíre, noun, fem., 'freedom'; dat. sg. **saere**, I, 4, II, 21; **saeri**, V, 9; **sore**, V, 2 (on the spellings see (17f)).

scarthain, verbal-noun, 'parting'; dat. sg. *id.*, I, 15.

sen, demonstrative pronoun, 'that, the aforesaid'; I, 9, 13. Demonstrative adjective, **-sen**, I, 5, 13; **-sain**, I, 4.

sí, personal pronoun, 3rd sg. fem., 'she, it', I, 6.

síl, noun, masc., 'seed; descendants'; dat. sg. *id.*, II, 23.

slánte, noun, fem., 'health'; nom. sg. I, 10, 12.

sliab, noun, masc., 'moor' (here, rough-grazing); acc. sg. *id.*, V, 8.

sore, see **saíre**.

sunn, demonstrative, 'this'; dat. sg. **ó hunn imacc** (spelling for *shunn*, see (24)), 'from this [time] on'; I, 17.

tabairt, verbal-noun (of *do-beir-*, *q.v.*), fem., 'giving'; dat. sg. **tabart** (spelling for *tabairt*, see (12)), II, 14.

tabrad, see *do-beir-*.

tánic, tángator, see *tic-*.

tarat, see *do-beir-*.

teste (Latin), '[the following] being witness', IV, 2, VII, 6, 7, 8 (twice); **testibus his**, 'these being the witnesses', VI, 6; **testibus istis**, *id.*, III, 5.

testus, noun, masc., 'witness, evidence'; dat. sg. **in testus** 'as evidence', V, 4.

ro thidnaig, 3rd sg. pret., 'granted, bestowed' (M. Ir. *ro thidnaic*, Sc. G. *thiodhlaic*), I, 3. On the *-g* see (22).

tic-, 'comes'; *tic- ri*, 'comes against, breaks [a condition laid down], violates [a grant]'; *tic- ar*, 'de-

INDEX OF PERSONAL
AND FAMILY NAMES

See the introductory note to the Glossarial Index, and in all cases also consult the Notes.

Ádam, man's name; nom., VII, 11.

Aed, man's name; gen. **Éda**, II, 1 (on the spelling see (17*b*)); **Æd** in a Latin context (nom. for gen.), VII, 10.

Algune, man's name; nom., III, 7; see Notes.

Andreas, man's name; in Latin context, ablative **Andrea**, VII, 7.

Arcill, man's name; gen., III, 7.

Batín, man's name; gen. *id.*, II, 5; probably for *Baíthín*, see Notes.

Bede, man's name (Pictish); nom., I, 2, 7.

Bróc(c)ín, man's name; nom., VI, 6; in Latin context, ablative, VII, 11.

Caerell, man's name; gen. **Caerill**, II, 4 (on the spelling see (1)).

Cainnec(h), man's name; nom., II, 16, 19; gen. **Cannech**, III, 1 (on the spelling see (13, 22)); **Caennaig**, V, 6 (on the spelling see (1, 13, 22)).

Cathal, man's name; nom., II, 7, 14, 17, 19, 20; gen. **Cathail**, II, 6.

Cennédig, man's name; gen. *id.*, V, 5.

Cinaed, man's name; gen. **Cinatha** (on the spelling, see (17*e*)); II, 10.

Clann Chanann, family name, 'the Descendants of Cano'; gen. **Clande Canan**, V, 6.

Clann Morgainn, family name, 'the Descendants of Morgann'; gen. **Clenni Morgainn**, VI, 2.

Colbán, man's name; nom., VI, 1.

Colum Cille, man's name, St Columba; see Note to I, 1. Nom. I, 1, 16; **Collum Cille**, I, 13; acc. **Colum Cille**, I, 5; **Collum Cille**, I, 16; **Colum Cilli**, VI, 3; dat. **Colum Cille**, II, 1, III, 3; **Colim Cilli**, IV, 2; **Coluim Cille**, V, 2, 7. On the various spellings of what should be throughout *Colum Cille* (dat. *Chille*), see (10, 11, 12, 23, 31).

Comgell, man's name; nom., II, 1 (spelt **Comgeall**, see (11)), V, 3, 5.

Cormac, man's name; nom., V, 4, VI, 6; gen. **Cormaic**, III, 8; dat. **Cormac**, III, 4; in Latin context, ablative **Cormac**, VII, 11.

Coscrach, man's name; gen. **Cosgreg** (see (12)), I, 1.

Críst; gen., III, 2; dat., V, 2, 6.

Culén, man's name; gen. **Culéon** (spelling for *Culéoin*, see (16)), II, 8.

Cú Líi, man's name (spelling for *Lí*, see (9)); nom., II, 5.

Dauíd, man's name; nom., VII, 1; gen. III, 5.

Dia, God; nom. *id.*, I, 2; acc. *id.*, II, 20, VI, 3; gen. **Dé**, I, 6; dat. **Dia**, II, 9, 16, 19.

Domnall, man's name; nom., II, 5, 8, 13, 18, 20; gen. **Domnaill**, III, 9.

Domongart, man's name; nom., III, 9.

Donnachac, man's name; nom., VI, 2 (see Notes).

Index

161

Index

Mal-Girc, man's name; nom., IV, 3.

Mal-Mori, man's name; ablative in Latin context, VII, 9.

Mal-Petir, man's name; nom., III, 8.

Mal-Snecte, man's name (spelling for *Mal-Snechta*, see (10)); nom., II, 12.

Matadín, man's name; nom., III, 8.

Matain, man's name; nom., II, 4.

Matne, man's name; gen. **Matni**, VI, 8, VII, 12. On the question whether this is the genitive of **Matain**, see Note on II, 4.

Molíni, man's name, perhaps for *Moíline*, see Notes; gen., V, 4.

Morcunn, **Morgunn**, man's name; nom. **Morgunn**, VI, 6; gen. **Morgainn**, VI, 2, **Morcunn**, II, 2, **Morcunt**, II, 7; on the spelling of the last two see (12).

Muiredach, man's name; nom. **Moridac** (on the spelling see (4, 11, 21)), II, 2; gen. **Muredig**, III, 10.

Nectan, man's name; nom., III, 5.

Petar, man's name, St Peter; acc. *id.*, VI, 3; gen. **Petir**, III, 2.

Ruadrí, man's name; nom., III, 7; gen. *id.*, II, 8.

Samson, man's name (Latin); Latin ablative **Samsone**, VII, 8.

Síthech, man's name; gen. **Síthig**, VI, 2.

Trálín, man's name; gen. *id.*, IV, 4.

INDEX OF PLACE-
AND REGIONAL-NAMES

See the introductory note to the Glossarial Index, and in all cases also
consult the Notes.

Abberdeon, Aberdeen; gen. *id.*, III,
6; accusative in Latin context, *id.*,
VII, 5, 12.
Abbordoboir, Aberdour; acc., I,
2.
Acchad Madchor, Auchmachar;
acc., V, 1.
Achad na Glérec, unidentified; acc.,
II, 7.
All Uethe na Camsse, unidentified;
II, 17; see Notes.
Alba, Scotland; gen. **Alban,** VI, 5.
Aldín Alenn, unidentified; dat.,
V, 8.
Altere, Altrie; acc. **Alterin,** II, 17;
'short' dat. **Alteri,** II, 5; acc. dual
Alterin, II, 18.
Athótla, Atholl; dat., VII, 9.

Ball Domin, unidentified; acc., IV,
1.
Banb, Banff; accusative in Latin
context, VII, 4.
Bidbe, Biffie; acc. **Bidbin,** II, 9; dat.
id., II, 10.
Brechin, Brechin; gen. **Brecini,** III,
6; ablative in Latin context,
Brechin, VII, 8.
Buchan, Buchan; gen., I, 3, VI, 1, 8.

Camsse, II, 18; see Notes.
Catenes, Caithness; ablative in
Latin context, VII, 8.
Cloch in Tiprat, unidentified; dat.
Cloic in Tiprat, I, 11.
Cloch Pette Mec-Garnait, unidenti-
fied; acc. **Cloic Pette Mec-Gar-
nait,** I, 11.

Dér, Déar, Deer; nom., I, 16;
ablative in Latin context, VII, 2.
Dubuci, unidentified; dat., V, 8.
Dún Caillen, Dunkeld; gen. **Dúni
Callenn,** III, 4; ablative in Latin
context, **Dún Callden,** VII, 7.

Elan, Ellon; dat. **Helain,** VI, 9 (on
the *H-* see (24)).
Elerc, Elrick; acc., II, 12.
Éngus, Angus; dative in Gaelic
context, VII, 10.
Etdane, Ednie; acc. **Etdanin,** II'
19.

Fíb, Fife; ablative in Latin context,
VII, 9.
Fúréne, see *Púréne.*

Helain, see *Elan.*

Í, Iona; dat., **Í,** I, 1.

Lurchari, unidentified; acc., V, 8.

Marr, Mar; gen., III, 7 (see (1)).

Orti, unidentified; dat., II, 1.

Pet i[n] Púir, Pitfour; dat., IV, 1.
Pett in Mulenn, unidentified; acc.,
II, 6 (spelling, see (13)).
Pett Malduib, unidentified; II, 12.
Pett Mec-Garnait, unidentified;
acc. *id.*, II, 2; gen. **Pette Mec-
Garnait,** I, 11.
Pett Mec-Gobroig, unidentified;
acc. (spelt **-Cobrig,** see Notes),

163

Index

Pett (*cont.*)
III, 2; dat. **Pett Mec-Gobroig**, II, 10.
Púréne, unidentified; acc., with lenition (see (27*f*)), **Fúréne**, II, 1.

Ros abard, unidentified; gen., II, 11.

Scáli Merlec, Skillymarno; acc., v, 5.

Toche Temni, unidentified; gen., II, 3.

Turbruad, Turriff; gen. **Turbruad**, III, 9; **Turbruaid**, VI, 6; ablative in Latin context, **Turbrud**, VII, 11. On these spellings see (15).

Made in the USA
Middletown, DE
03 February 2019